Colli

OCR GATEWAY

SCIENCE

FOR OCR GCSE
SCIENCE B

Chris Sherry SERIES EDITOR
Colin Bell
Louise Smiles
Ann Daniels
Phil Hills
Dave Berrington
Edmund Walsh

William Collins' dream of knowledge for all began with the publication of his first book in 1819. A self-educated mill worker, he not only enriched millions of lives, but also founded a flourishing publishing house. Today, staying true to this spirit, Collins books are packed with inspiration, innovation and a practical expertise. They place you at the centre of a world of possibility and give you exactly what you need to explore it.

Collins. Freedom to teach.

Published by Collins
An imprint of HarperCollinsPublishers
77–85 Fulham Palace Road
Hammersmith
London
W6 8JB

Browse the complete Collins catalogue at
www.collinseducation.com

10 9 8 7 6 5 4

ISBN-13 978-0-00-721447-1
ISBN-10 0-00-721447-2

British Library Cataloguing in Publication Data. A Catalogue record for this publication is available from the British Library

Commissioned by Kate Haywood and Cassandra Birmingham

Publishing Manager Michael Cotter

Project managed by Nicola Tidman

Exam questions written by Dr Martin Barker, Lesley Owen and Karen Nicola Thomas

Glossary written by Gareth Price

Edited by Camilla Behrens and Anita Clark

Proofread by Margaret Shepherd and Anita Clark

Internal design by JPD

Page make-up by IFADesign Ltd

Picture research by Caroline Thompson

Illustrations by IFADesign Ltd and Bob Lea

Cover artwork by Bob Lea

Cover design by John Fordham

Production by Natasha Buckland

Printed and bound in Great Britain by Butler and Tanner, Frome

Acknowledgements

The Publishers gratefully acknowledge the following for permission to reproduce copyright material. Whilst every effort has been made to trace the copyright holders, in cases where this has been unsuccessful or if any have inadvertently been overlooked, the Publishers will be pleased to make the necessary arrangements at the first opportunity.

W. L. Gore & Associates, Inc. for permission to use their trademark, GORE-TEX®; MGM Ltd, for permission to reproduce lines from 'Goldfinger'; Guardian Newspapers Limited 2002, for permission to reproduce copyright material; The Telegraph Ltd, for permission to reproduce copyright material.

The publishers would like to thank the following for permission to reproduce photographs (T = Top, B = Bottom, C = Centre, L= Left, R = Right):

Action Plus/Neil Tingle, p26B;
Arcaid.co.uk/Richard Bryant, p116R;
Ardea.com/John Daniels, p60R, Francois Gohier, p86C;
Audi AG, pp150/151;
Colin Bell, p22TR, p42B;
Neill Bruce's Automobile Photo Library, p155;
Martyn Chillmaid, p10TL, p16, p19R, p36C, p56, p94BCL, p116L, p120T, p122, p129, p137, p148BR, p174T, p218T&BR;
Corbis, p202R/Jose Luis Pelaez, Inc, p6BR, p44, Bettmann, p20T, Michael Prince, p54R, Royalty-Free, p58CR&BCL, Lester V. Bergman, p59CR, Sally A.Morgan/Ecoscene, p59BR, Julie Meech/Ecoscene, p64L, James L. Amos, p75CR, Stephen Hird/Reuters, p76TL, Peter Schouten/National Geographic Society/Reuters, p76TR, Jonathan Blair, p76B, Layne Kennedy, p77C, Frank Lane Picture Agency, p78T, Larry Lee Photography, p80CL, Anders Ryman, p80CR, James Leynse, p80R, Shoot/zefa, p82T, Herbert Kehrer/zefa, p82CL, H. Spichtinger/zefa, p84CL, Academy of Natural Sciences of Philadelphia, p85T, Brian A. Vikander, p86R, Michael S. Yamashita, p139, Roger Ressmeyer, p144, Louie Psihoyos, p149L, Elizabeth Whiting & Associates, p181, Morton Beebe, p182L, Jay Syverson, p184T, Larry Williams, p188, Peter M Fisher, p196, David Pu'u, p201, Punit Paranjpe/Reuters, p204T, Jim Craigmyle, p242B;
Tina Cork, p222T;
© Crown Copyright/MOD. Reproduced with the permission of the Controller of Her Majesty's Stationery Office, p10BR, p202L;
Getty Images/Time Life Pictures, p18T, p79R, Dorling Kindersley, p60C, The Image Bank, p178T, p180, p186C, FoodPix, p186B, p187, Brand X Pictures, p194;
The book contains copyrighted material reproduced with the permission of W L Gore & Associates. Copyright © 2006 W L Gore & Associates, p111, p117R;
Hearing Dogs for the Deaf/Tim Rose, p26T;
Holt Studios/Nigel Cattlin, p55R, Rosemary Mayer, p64R;
iStockphoto, p3C, p8TL,BL&BR, p9TL, p11BL, p58CL, p94C&BCR, p95L, p96T,CL&BCR, p98, p100, p101C, p102, p108, p112L&C, 117L, p118T&BR, p120CR, p123L, p124, p125, p127, p128, p134C, p138R,TL,CL,C,BL&BC, p141, p147L&C, p148C&R, p156B, p168T&B, p207T, p217T, p218C, p226B, p229T, p232C, p248T;
© 2006 JupiterImages Corporation, p7, p9TR,BL&BR, p11TR, p20L, p28, p32C, p43TL&C, p48C, p54L, p58TR,TCL&R, p58TC,BCR&BR, p61L&C, p63C, p67R, p69R, p72T&C, p73R, p75T, p82C, p83C&R, p84TR&CR, p85C, p88, p96CR&BC, p106, p109B, p112R, p113, p116C, p118BL&C, p120C, p138TC, p178B, p182T&R, p219T, p220, p239C;
The Kobal Collection/ Warner Bros/DC Comics, p58TL, Danjaq/Eon/UA, p200T;
Mary Evans Picture Library, p84TL, p94T;
Andy Murdock, 2002 - Moorea Digital Flora Project, 40BR;
NASA Jet Propulsion Laboratory (NASA-JPL), p241;
NASA, p18R;
Natural Visions/Heather Angel, p58C, p62, p70BL,BC&BR, Francesco Tomasinelli, p58R;
NHPA/Ann & Steve Toon, p67CR;
www.nought.de/james.php#birne, p186T;
Oxford Scientific, p69L, p75BR/photolibrary, p6TL, TR&BL, p72B, p79C, p83L, p175L, p252L, Lon E Lauber, p60CL, Alain Christof, p63T, Ben Osborne, p66T, David Tipling, p66R, John Downer, p67T, Michael Fogden, p67C, Stan Osolinski, p68, Paul Kay, p70T&C, Iain Sarjeant, p71, Daniel Cox, p74, Doug Allan, p78B, David Fox, p79T;
© ONE WORLD IMAGES /Alamy, p3CT, p61CR;
Rex Features, p32B/Novastock, p36T, Peter MacDiarmid, p101T, Heikki Saukkomaa, p153, Sipa Press, p156T, Paul France, p160R, Mark Bacon, p214R, Glenn Harvey, p216B, Charles M Ommanney, p226T;
Marc van Roosmalen, p59CL;
Science Photo Library, p47C, p107, p198, p238T/Tony McConnell, p3CB, p175R, p208, Pekka Parviainen, p3B, p232T, Alexis Rosenfeld, p3T, p20R, Alfred Pasieka, pp8/9, Andrew Lambert Photography, p8TR, p115, p152C, p165, p174R, p176, Joe Tucciarone, pp10/11, p247T, John Mead, p11TL, p184B, p217CR, Robin Scagell, p11BR, p236C, John Bavosi, pp12/13, NASA, p14, p48T, p207BR, p214L, p234T, p235C, p238C, p239T, p246R, Coneyl Jay, p15, Sam Ogden, p17, Andy Crump/TDR/WHO, p19C, Martin/Custom Medical Stock Photo, p21, Steve Gschmeissner, p22C, Russell Kightley, p22CR, Martin Dohrn, p23TC, p228R, Eye of Science, p23C, James M Hogle/Harvard Medical School, p31, Charles D Winters, p32T, p193, Oscar Burriel, p33TL, Adam Hart-Davis, p33TC, p158L, p189L, Garry Watson, p33CL, Victor Habbick Visions, p33CR, p240T, BSIP/Estiot, p33B, Dr Arthur Tucker, p36B, A. Barrington Brown, p40T, Dr Bernard Lunaud, p40R, Biophoto Associates, p42T, p45, Jack K. Clark/Agstock, p43TR, Peter Scoones, p55L, Antarctic Survey, p55C, Astrid & Hanns-Frieder Michler, p57, National Museum, Denmark/Munoz-Yague, p77T, Dr Morley Read, p89, Peter Menzel, pp92/93, p204C, Dr Tim Evans, p95T, Dr Jeremy Burgess, p97, Jerry Mason, p104L, Robert Brook, p120BR, p223, Tony Craddock, p123R, Pascal Goetgheluck, p134T, Jesse, p136, Martin Bond, p140, p159, p169, p189T&C, p215L, p222CR, p224L, James King-Holmes, p142, P.G. Adam, Publiphoto Diffusion, p146T, Novosti, p146CR, Maxmillian Stock Ltd, p146BR, Thomas Hollyman, p147T, Mark Thomas, p148L, Ton Kinsbergen, p152T, p168C, Cordelia Molloy, p154T, Jeremy Walker, p154B, Simon Fraser, p158C, Peter Bowater, p160L, Martyn F Chillmaid, p164, Carlos Dominguez, p189BC, David M Martin, M.D., p192, Gusto, p200C, Sheila Terry, p202T, p252R, Andrew Syred, p203, CNRI, p206R, Custom Medical Stock Photo, p206L, Detlev van Ravensswaay, pp212/213, p234BL, p240CL, p246C, p248B, David Parker, p214T, Alex Bartel, p215R, David Nunuk, p216T, BSIP Ducloux, p224C, US Department of Energy, p224B, p225, Steve Allen, p228L, ISM, p229C, Ted Kinsman, p233, PLI, p234R, Mark Garlick, p235T, p240BR, David A Hardy, p236T, Jerry Lodriguss, p242T, NOAO, p244, Take 27 Ltd, p246TL, Jeff Hester & Paul Scowen, Arizona State University, p247T, Annabella Bluesky, p252L, George Ranalli, p260B, p262B, p264B, p266B;
Silhouette, p149R;
Still Pictures/Danilo Balducci, p109T;
© Stock Connection/Alamy, p61R;
Tony Waltham/Geophotos, p73L;
Wisconsin Fast Plants Program, University of Wisconsin – Madison, USA, p47B.

The publishers would also like to thank the Copper Association, for their advice on the content of pages 146-147.

Contents

Keeping teeth healthy

Creating hybrid animals

Chemistry for breakfast

Hot property

Watch the sky

PAGE 30

PAGE 61

PAGE 94

PAGE 175

PAGE 232

Welcome to Collins GCSE Science!

This book has been written by teachers who are also experienced examiners. We hope you will find it gives you an insight into the fascinating world of Science. We have tried to make things relevant for you and your life in today's world. Science opens many gateways to exciting careers and further studies.

USING THIS BOOK

What you should know

Can you remember back to Key Stage 3? Well, the science you studied then is still important. During your GCSE course, your teachers will develop this work and explain things in more detail.

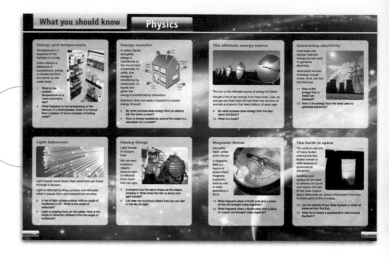

Module opener

This is designed to get you thinking about one or two of the important aspects of the module.

Main content

The main content is presented in three, coloured columns. Students entering foundation tier should understand the work in the green and blue columns. Higher tier students should concentrate on the blue and purple columns. Throughout the book, watch out for some fascinating facts that you might be able to include in your answers to examination questions, or in any coursework you do. There are also examples of common misunderstandings that examiners often find on examination papers.

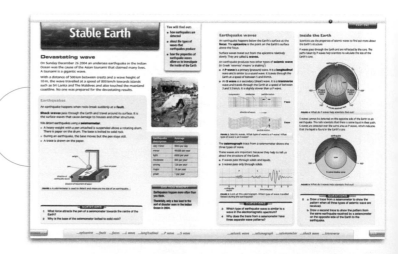

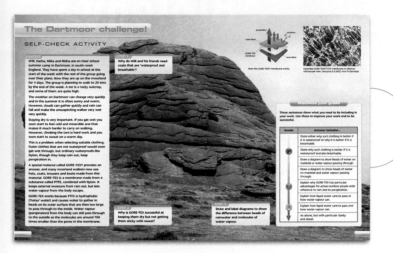

Mid-module assessment

These activities give you an opportunity to find out how you are progressing through each module. You may be asked to work through this assessment for homework, or discuss and work with another student in the class who may assess you.

Module summary

At the end of each module, the key facts are summarised. There is also a quiz and an activity, to test your understanding. You could use these as a revision aid. Make sure that as you look at the key facts, you recall the content of the chapters in each module.

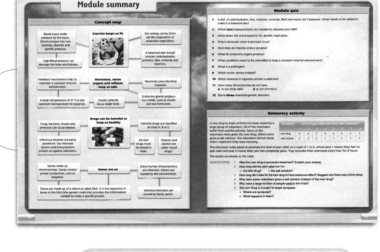

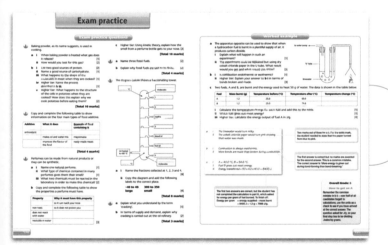

Exam practice

You may sit examinations at regular intervals during your course, or at the end of your course. One of the best ways to prepare for your examination is to practise answering examination questions. Learn from the example answers and mark schemes provided. In particular, be careful about the use of scientific language.

Skills assessment

In your examination papers, you will have to plot graphs, interpret data and understand scientific writings. Similar skills will be needed if you are to achieve high marks with coursework. Look at the examples of coursework you may be asked to do and make sure you understand how to gain the best marks you can.

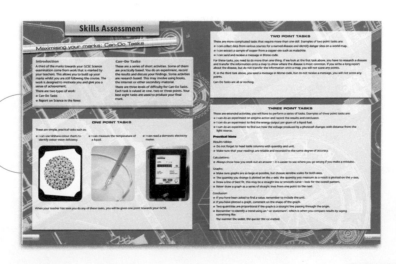

Cells

Cells are the building blocks of plants and animals. This is an animal cell. It contains many specialised structures, such as a nucleus.

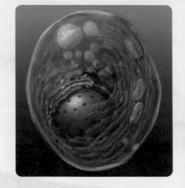

Many plants and animals have only one cell. Larger and more complex plants and animals have more cells. These are organised and coordinated.

In animals, similar cells are found in tissues, such as nervous tissue. Different types of tissues form organs, such as the brain.

1 Name **two** specialised structures inside a cell.
2 How is an organ different from a tissue?

Cell functions and life processes

Many plants and animals have only one cell. So a single cell has to do all the things necessary for life. It respires, reproduces, repairs itself, reacts, feeds, excretes and grows.

Larger and more complicated plants and animals need specialised cells, such as blood cells and nerve cells in animals. These have special jobs and are adapted to do them. For example, red blood cells carry oxygen to cells so they can respire.

3 What is meant by a 'specialised cell'?
4 Name **two** specialised animal cells, other than the red blood cell or nerve cell.

Fertilisation

All plants and animals reproduce to make sure that their species will continue and produce the next generation.

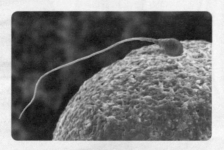

Sexual reproduction needs a male and a female. The male organism produces sperm and the female organism produces eggs.

Only one sperm is needed to fuse with an egg and fertilise it. Information about what the new individual will be is carried in the fertilised egg.

5 Why do plants and animals reproduce?
6 In sexual reproduction, what do the male and female sex organs produce?

Variation

All buttercups may look like buttercups and all cod fish may look alike. A closer examination, however, shows that there are many small differences in individuals. This is called variation.

Human beings are also different from one another. Some differences, such as scars or muscle development, are due to the environment. Other differences, such as eye colour, are due to your parents. These differences are inherited.

7 What are the small differences between individuals called?
8 What type of differences are inherited? Can you think of an example?

Classification

Living things can be classified into different groups. The toucan is a bird because it has feathers. Birds belong to a much larger group called vertebrates. Fish, amphibians, reptiles, and mammals are also vertebrates because they all have backbones.

Animals without backbones are grouped together as invertebrates.

9 Write down the names of **five** different mammals.

10 Explain why snails are invertebrates.

Plants

Bamboo is the world's tallest grass. It can grow as tall as 4 m. To grow this tall, bamboo, like all plants, must carry out photosynthesis.

Photosynthesis is a chemical reaction that takes place in plant cells. The plants use light energy to turn carbon dioxide and water into glucose and oxygen.

11 Name the raw materials used in photosynthesis.

12 Name the **two** products of photosynthesis.

Adaptation

Animals and plants are adapted to survive in their habitats. Dolphins are streamlined and have flippers to help them swim.

Many living things have to adapt to yearly changes. Some hibernate from the cold, others migrate to warmer areas.

13 Describe **two** ways in which the dolphin is adapted to swim.

14 Suggest **one** reason why swallows fly south in the winter.

Populations and survival

The population of a species can rise or fall.

- If the environment changes and the species cannot adapt, the population could fall.

- Living things compete with other species for food. The strongest will survive and reproduce to increase their population.

- The population of prey will increase when there are fewer predators around. The population of predators can increase if there is more prey to eat.

15 Suggest **two** things that animals might compete for.

16 Write down an example of a predator and its prey.

Chemistry

Food and cooking

All materials are made through chemical reactions, including those in living systems.

Fruit ripening and cooking food are both chemical reactions.

When a chemical reaction takes place, new products are made. Protein in meat and eggs, and carbohydrate in potatoes and flour change when heated. The changes are irreversible.

1   How does food cook in a microwave?
2   How do we stop apples from going brown?

Using crude oil

Lots of useful materials can be made from crude oil. Crude oil is a mixture of different substances, which are not combined. Each

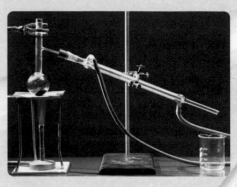

substance has a different melting point, boiling point and density.

We can separate crude oil using distillation. Chromatography is another method that can be used to separate some mixtures.

3   Why does crude oil separate into different fractions during distillation?
4   How can different coloured dyes be separated?

Polymers

Man-made materials, such as plastic, are very important to the way we live.

These materials are all made by chemical reactions. They would not exist without chemists finding new ways to join chemicals together.

5   If lots of ethene molecules are joined together what polymer is made?
6   What material is used to make waterproof jackets that are also breathable?

Fuels and energy

Energy is released during chemical reactions. When a fuel burns, energy is released in the form of heat.

We use the energy released when a fuel burns for heating, cooking, transport and fireworks!

Burning fossil fuels produces acid rain, carbon dioxide and solid particles. These affect the environment and need to be minimised.

7   Why are petrol and diesel the best fuels for a car?
8   How does burning fossil fuels affect the environment?

Rocks

Rocks are formed over a very long time by different processes.

Igneous rocks are formed when magma cools.

Sedimentary rocks can be formed from fragments of eroded rock that are deposited. Sometimes dead organisms can form layers of sedimentary rock.

Metamorphic rocks are made by the action of heat and pressure on existing rocks.

11 How are rocks eroded?

12 Where does magma come from?

Using rocks

Limestone, marble and granite are all rocks used for building.

We can even make artificial rock, called concrete.

Rocks are used to make a wide range of substances, including paint.

9 What **three** components make up paint?

10 What is the chemical name for limestone?

Metals and non-metals

Elements are very different from one another, in their appearance and state, at room temperature. Some are magnetic, some conduct heat and some conduct electricity. These properties can be used to classify elements as metals or non-metals.

Metals often react with oxygen, water and acids to make different products. There is often a pattern in chemical reactions, such as the action of acids on metals.

13 Why is copper used for electric wiring?

14 Which metals react with cold water?

Solids, liquids and gases

The behaviour of solids, liquids and gases can be explained by the particle theory. Particles are close together in solids, but are moving rapidly and randomly in gases.

This is why a perfume reaches our nose. The particles of the perfume move through the air. This is called diffusion.

15 How are the particles in a liquid arranged?

16 Why does hot acid react faster with marble than cold acid? Include ideas about particles in your answer.

Energy and temperature

Temperature is a measure of the hotness of a body.

When there is a difference in temperature, energy is transferred from the hotter to the cooler body.

1   What is the outside temperature on a warm summer's day?

2   What happens to the temperature of the mercury in a thermometer when it is moved from a beaker of ice to a beaker of boiling water?

Energy transfer

In solids, liquids and gases, energy is transferred by the movement of particles. In solids, the energy is transferred by conduction. In liquids and gases the energy is transferred by convection.

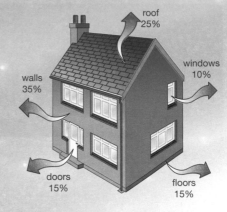

Radiation does not need a material to transfer energy through.

3   By what process does energy from an electric bar fire warm a room?

4   How is energy transferred around the water in a saucepan on a cooker?

Light behaviour

Light travels much faster than sound and can travel through a vacuum.

Light is reflected by shiny surfaces and refracted when it passes from one material into another.

5   A ray of light strikes a mirror with an angle of incidence of 30°. What is the angle of reflection?

6   Light is passing from air into glass. How is the angle of refraction different from the angle of incidence?

Seeing things

Light travels in straight lines.

We see non-luminous objects because light is reflected from them into our eyes.

7   A shadow has the same shape as the object causing it. What does this tell us about how light travels?

8   List **one** non-luminous object that you can see in the sky at night.

The ultimate energy source

The Sun is the ultimate source of energy for Earth.

We get a lot of our energy from fossil fuels. Coal, oil and gas are fossil fuels formed from the remains of animals and plants that lived millions of years ago.

9   By what process does energy from the Sun reach the Earth?

10 What is a fossil?

Generating electricity

Fossil fuels and nuclear fuels are energy sources used to generate electricity.

Alternative sources of energy include water, wind, the Sun and biomass.

11 How is the energy from a fossil fuel released?

12 How is the energy from the wind used to generate electricity?

Magnetic forces

Like poles repel. Unlike poles attract.

A magnetic field is a region of space where magnetic materials, such as iron or steel, experience a force.

13 What happens when a North pole and a piece of iron are brought close together?

14 What happens when a South pole and a piece of copper are brought close together?

The Earth in space

The Earth is only one of many bodies orbiting the Sun. Bodies remain in orbit because of gravitational attraction.

Satellites and spacecraft are used to observe the Earth and explore the rest of the Solar System. Space telescopes can obtain information from the furthest parts of the Universe.

15 List the planets of our Solar System in order of distance from the Sun.

16 What force keeps a spacecraft in orbit around the Earth?

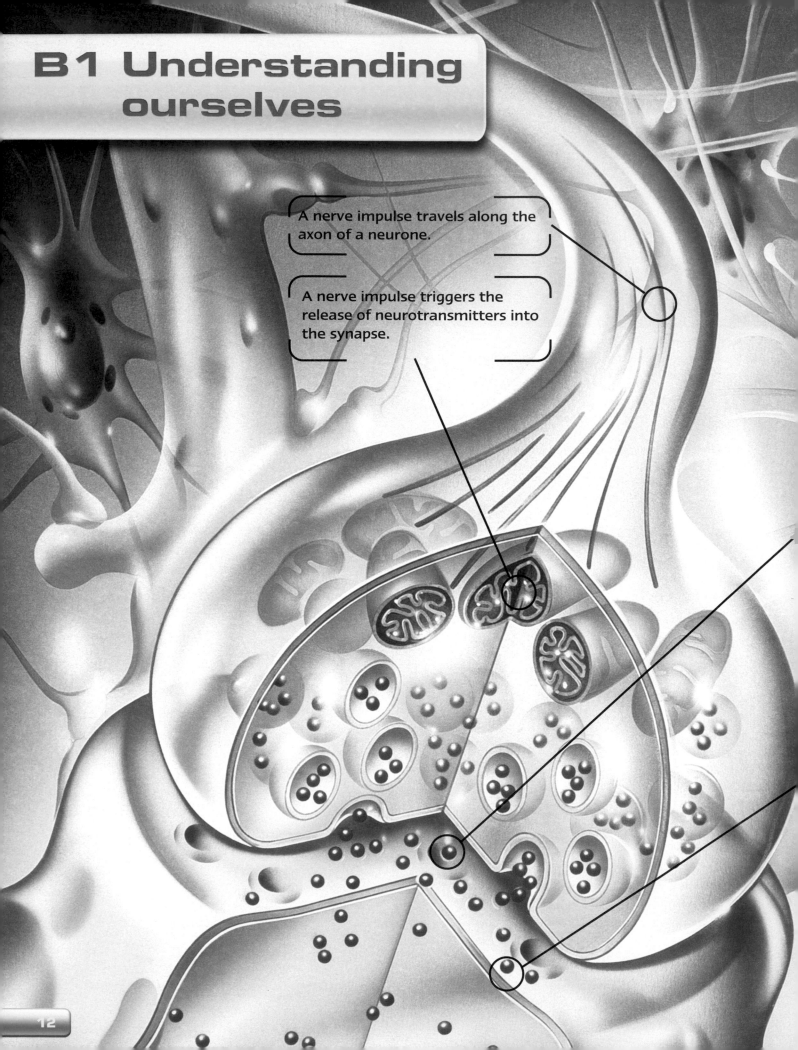

A nerve impulse travels along the axon of a neurone.

A nerve impulse triggers the release of neurotransmitters into the synapse.

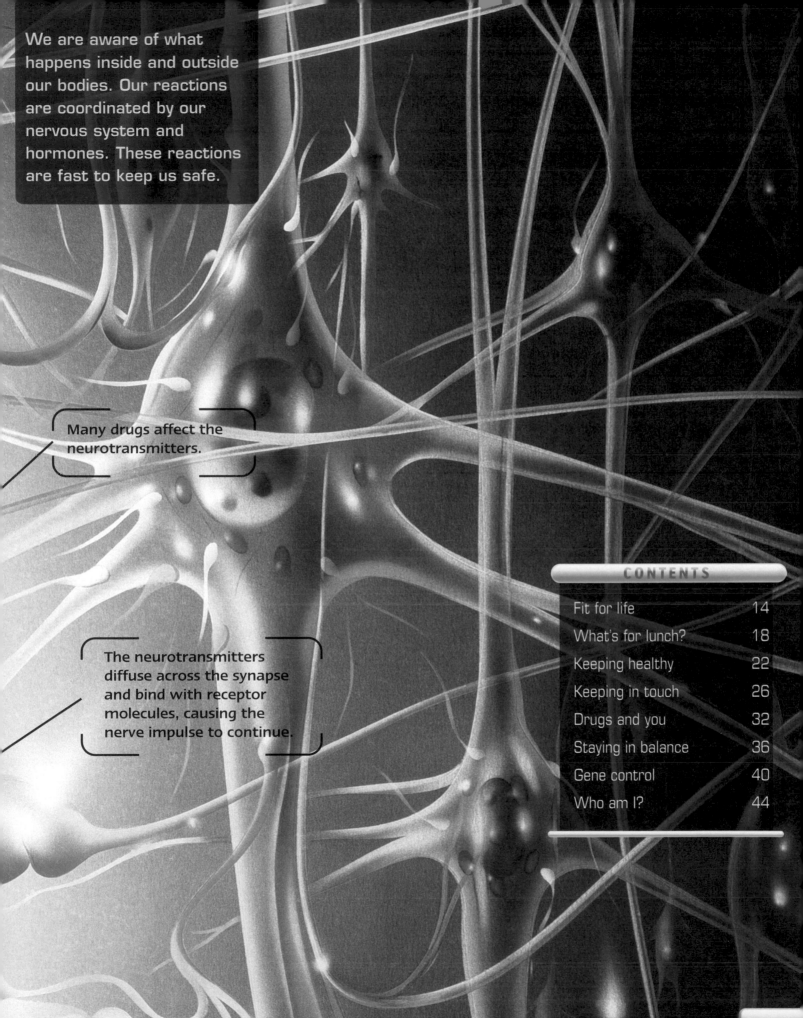

We are aware of what happens inside and outside our bodies. Our reactions are coordinated by our nervous system and hormones. These reactions are fast to keep us safe.

Many drugs affect the neurotransmitters.

The neurotransmitters diffuse across the synapse and bind with receptor molecules, causing the nerve impulse to continue.

CONTENTS

Fit for life

You will find out:

- why you get tired after exercise
- how energy is released
- why exercise changes breathing and pulse rate
- about the difference between aerobic respiration and anaerobic respiration

Football in space!

Do you enjoy a game of football?

Even the astronaut John Blaka trained on board the space shuttle Discovery.

A footballer runs about 11 kilometres (7 miles) in a game of football. However, the fitness programme of a professional footballer is not just running round the pitch a few times a day!

Footballers need special training programmes. They must develop their:

- stamina
- flexibility
- agility
- explosive speed.

WOW FACTOR!

Each day you:

- breathe about 25 000 times
- breathe about 6 litres of air every minute!

Joe uses a lot of energy

It has been a long, hard game of football. Joe feels tired.

His muscle cells have done a lot of work. They have used oxygen to release **energy** from **glucose**. This process is called **respiration**.

When the cells in Joe's body do more work, they need more oxygen and glucose. His **breathing rate** and **pulse rate** increase.

This also helps to get rid of the waste carbon dioxide produced by his cells as quickly as possible. Carbon dioxide is breathed out of Joe's lungs.

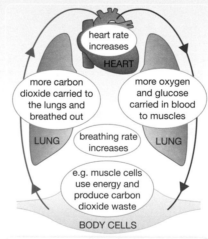

heart rate increases

HEART

more carbon dioxide carried to the lungs and breathed out

more oxygen and glucose carried in blood to muscles

LUNG

breathing rate increases

LUNG

e.g. muscle cells use energy and produce carbon dioxide waste

BODY CELLS

FIGURE 1: How does Joe get rid of carbon dioxide from his body?

Watch Out Breathing is simply getting air into and out of the body.

Respiration is the release of energy from glucose.

QUESTIONS

1   Which gas is used in respiration?
2   Which gas is produced during respiration?
3   What happens to Joe's breathing rate and pulse rate when he plays football?

...aerobic respiration   ...anaerobic respiration   ...breathing rate   ...energy

Joe's respiration

Joe goes to training sessions to get fit.

FIGURE 2: Joe's cells are getting enough oxygen.

FIGURE 3: Joe has increased his exercise rate and his cells are now not getting enough oxygen.

He uses **aerobic respiration** to release energy from food:

glucose + oxygen ⟶ carbon dioxide + water + energy

He uses **anaerobic respiration** to release energy from food:

glucose ⟶ **lactic acid** + energy

Anaerobic respiration releases much less energy than aerobic respiration.

The training coach tells Joe that after hard exercise lactic acid collects in his muscles. Lactic acid damages the muscles temporarily. This explains why Joe's muscles hurt after a game of football.

Fitness

After a lot of training sessions Joe thinks he is very fit. His sister challenges him to a tennis match. After two sets he is exhausted and she beats him! Tennis uses different muscles than football does and more twisting and turning are needed to return the tennis ball.

Joe decides to go to his local sports centre to increase his general fitness.

He can measure his general fitness by timing how long his heart rate and breathing rate take to return to normal.

Fitness and health

Joe catches a cold. He is surprised because he is very fit.

His coach explains that being fit does not stop bacteria and viruses entering his body and causing infections.

What is an oxygen debt?

When Joe is walking his body uses aerobic respiration.

$C_6H_{12}O_6 + 6O_2 \longrightarrow 6CO_2 + 6H_2O + energy$

When Joe sprints, his muscles cannot get oxygen quickly enough. He has an **oxygen debt.** His cells use anaerobic respiration to release some energy.

The energy released during anaerobic respiration is less than that from aerobic respiration because glucose is only partly broken down.

At the end of the sprint:

- Joe breathes heavily for a few minutes to replace the oxygen
- Joe's heart continues to beat faster than normal so his blood can carry lactic acid away from his muscles to be broken down in his liver.

QUESTIONS

4 What type of respiration does Joe use when he sprints?
5 What chemical is produced during anaerobic respiration?
6 Why do Joe's muscles hurt after a hard game of football?
7 What is the difference between fitness and health?

QUESTIONS

8 Explain the difference between aerobic and anaerobic respiration.
9 How does Joe's body recover from hard exercise?

Measuring Joe's blood pressure

Joe checks his **blood pressure** at the sports centre.

FIGURE 4: Why does Joe want to know what his blood pressure is?

He knows his **heart muscles** contract to make his heart beat. This squeezes the blood through blood vessels called **arteries**. The blood in arteries is under pressure.

Blood can reach all parts of the body because it is under pressure. This is important because the blood carries food and oxygen to cells all around the body.

Blood pressure measurements check the health of the heart. Joe's father has his blood pressure measured by his doctor every month.

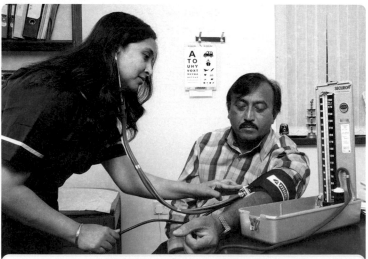

FIGURE 5: Suggest why older people have their blood pressure checked regularly.

You will find out:

- why blood in arteries is under pressure
- about measuring blood pressure
- about the dangers of high and low blood pressure

EXAM HINTS AND TIPS

Blood vessels going away from the heart are called arteries.

Blood vessels returning to the heart are called veins.

WOW FACTOR!

Many dinosaurs had problems with their blood pressure!

This dinosaur's head was 8 m above its heart.

Enormous blood pressure was needed to pump blood around its body.

QUESTIONS

10 What type of blood vessel carries blood under pressure?

11 What puts blood under pressure?

12 Why is it important for blood to reach all parts of the body?

...artery ...blood pressure ...cardio-vascular efficiency ...diastolic pressure ...heart muscle

Joe's blood pressure

Joe finds out that blood pressure is measured in millimetres of mercury. This is written as **mmHg**.

Blood pressure has two measurements:

- **systolic pressure** is the maximum pressure the heart produces
- **diastolic pressure** is the blood pressure between heart beats.

The systolic pressure is written first and then the diastolic pressure.

Joe finds out how blood pressure changes with age.

Average readings		
	Systolic pressure in mmHg	Diastolic pressure in mmHg
child	80–100	60
teenager	90–110	60
adult	110–125	60–70
middle-aged	130–150	80–90

Joe's father visits his doctor every month. He is worried about his **high blood pressure**. He fills in a questionnaire about his lifestyle.

Blood pressure questionnaire

Questions	Notes	Answers Yes	No
1 Do you take regular exercise?	Strong heart muscles will lower blood pressure		✓
2 Do you eat a healthy balanced diet?	Reducing salt intake will lower blood pressure		✓
3 Are you overweight?	Being overweight by 5 kg raises blood pressure by 5 units	✓	
4 Do you regularly drink alcohol?	A high alcohol intake will damage liver and kidneys	✓	
5 Are you under stress?	Relaxation will lower blood pressure	✓	

FIGURE 6: What changes could Joe's father make to lead a more healthy lifestyle?

QUESTIONS

13 What does mmHg mean?

14 What happens to the average blood pressure as a person gets older?

15 Why does regular exercise help to lower blood pressure?

The importance of measuring blood pressure

Joe's father has high blood pressure. He must have it measured regularly so that he can be treated. If his blood pressure was left untreated, he would be at increased risk of small blood vessels bursting, due to the high pressure exerted on the blood vessel walls.

- If a small blood vessel bursts in the brain it is called a stroke. Brain damage from a stroke can result in some paralysis and loss of speech.
- If a small blood vessel bursts in a kidney, the kidney can fail.

He also knows that **low blood pressure** can cause problems such as poor circulation, dizziness and fainting.

He decides to go to the sports centre with Joe.

At the centre the instructor measures Joe's father's:

- heart rate
- breathing rate
- blood pressure
- **cardio-vascular efficiency**.

FIGURE 7: Why is it important to keep fit?

There are other ways of measuring fitness:

- strength
- flexibility
- stamina
- agility
- speed.

DID YOU KNOW?

- There are about 4000 sports centres in the UK.
- About 30 million people do some sort of physical activity every month.
- About £10 billion is spent on sports in the UK each year.

QUESTIONS

16 What are the possible consequences of high blood pressure?

17 Explain how low blood pressure can cause poor blood circulation.

18 What are the different ways of measuring fitness. Suggest how you could measure each.

...high blood pressure   ...low blood pressure   ...mmHg   ...systolic pressure

What's for lunch?

You will find out:

- why we eat food
- about the importance of a balanced diet
- how to calculate your Body Mass Index
- how to calculate your recommended average protein intake
- about people having different diets

War rations

During the Second World War (1939–45), Britain introduced food rationing. This was to make sure that any available food was shared out. Even sweets were rationed!

Queues like this were common. A 'national loaf' of brown bread was the only available bread. Most people ate less meat, fat and sugar.

Because their diet was better, the health of children improved. They were taller and heavier than before the war.

FIGURE 1: Do you have any relatives who remember rationing during the war?

Chardonnay goes shopping

Chardonnay sees a lot of information on the packets of food in the supermarket.

Chardonnay knows that the food she eats is called her **diet**. To get a **balanced diet** she must eat all the foods and nutrients listed on the right.

Chardonnay is 15 years old. She needs a high protein diet because she is growing fast. Proteins are needed to make new cells such as muscle cells. In some countries in the world there is a shortage of protein.

Chardonnay eats carbohydrates and fats to give her **energy**. If she eats too many and does not exercise enough she could become very overweight **(obese)**.

If she is obese she will have a higher risk of suffering from arthritis, heart disease, diabetes and breast cancer.

- Vitamins (such as vitamin C, which prevents scurvy); minerals (such as iron, used to make haemoglobin in red blood cells) and fibre (which prevents constipation) are called nutrients.

- Carbohydrates, fats and proteins are called foods and provide energy.
- Proteins are also used by the body for growth and repair.

FIGURE 2: Shopping for a balanced diet.

DID YOU KNOW?

Even astronauts have to eat, despite being upside down! A typical meal would be shrimp cocktail, chicken, vegetables and butterscotch pudding.

Their meals provide about 12 kJ (**kilojoules**) of energy each day.

Watch Out Carbohydrates, fats and proteins provide energy. Minerals, vitamins and fibre do not provide energy.

▪ QUESTIONS ▪

1. Why did children's health improve during the Second World War?
2. Why do we eat carbohydrates and fats?
3. Why does Chardonnay need a high protein diet?

...amino acid   ...balanced diet   ...diet   ...energy   ...first class proteins

How much food do you need?

A person's balanced diet will depend on their age, gender and how active they are.

Chardonnay knows that:

- she will need more energy than her parents because she is more active
- her brother will need more energy than her because he is much bigger
- they will both need a high protein diet because they are growing fast.

Chardonnay finds out that 66 per cent of men and 53 per cent of women are overweight.

She calculates her Body Mass Index (BMI) by using the formula:

$$BMI = \frac{\text{mass (in kilograms, kg)}}{\text{height (in metres, m)}^2}$$

She uses the BMI chart to find out if she is underweight, normal, overweight, or obese.

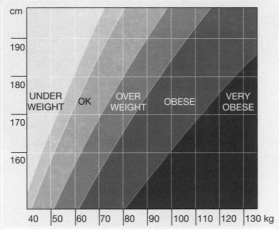

FIGURE 3: This chart shows the bands of BMI. Look up your height and weight to see where you come.

How much protein do you need?

If you eat too much fat and carbohydrate, they are stored in your body. Proteins are different. They cannot be stored. Proteins from meat and fish are called **first class proteins**. They contain **amino acids**, which cannot be made by your body.

In countries where famines are common because of crop failures and overcrowding, starvation can affect many thousands of people. A sign of starving in children is when their bellies are very swollen. This means they are desperately short of protein. With very little protein in their blood, their bodies cannot absorb excess water from body tissues and the abdomen swells up with the water. They have **kwashiorkor**.

Chardonnay finds out that there is a recommended daily amount (**RDA**) of protein that she should eat. She calculates her RDA using the formula:

RDA (in grams, g) = 0.75 × body mass (in kilograms, kg)

FIGURE 4: a What causes this child's abdomen to be swollen?
b This map of Africa shows countries with famines.

Special diets

Chardonnay knows that she must ensure that she eats a sensible diet. She also knows that most people do not have a perfect body shape and that she must be careful not to be influenced by the 'perfect' images that she sees in magazines and on the television. She has a positive self-image.

Chardonnay is a **vegetarian**. She does not eat meat or fish. She thinks it is wrong to kill and eat animals.

FIGURE 5: What sort of diet is shown here?

Vegans do not eat any foods of animal origin, including milk, cheese and eggs. They get their protein from cereals, beans, peas and nuts.

Vegetarians and vegans must make sure they get enough vitamins, especially B1. B1 is mainly found in animal products.

Some of Chardonnay's friends have special diets.

- Shabeen is a Muslim. She eats halal meat.
- Gina is a Jew and does not eat pork.
- Sue has a nut allergy and must not eat nuts.

QUESTIONS

4 Which **two** measurements does Chardonnay need to calculate her BMI?

5 What type of food contains first class proteins?

6 What causes kwashiorkor?

7 Chardonnay has a mass of 60 kg. What is her RDA of protein?

QUESTIONS

8 Explain why some people have special diets.

9 How can poor self-image lead to a poor diet?

What can you see, doctor?

In 1700, Alexis St Martin, a Canadian hunter, was shot. The wound did not heal. His doctor was able to see into his stomach!

Pieces of meat were tied together by a thread and then placed into Alexis's stomach. After a few hours the meat had broken down into smaller pieces.

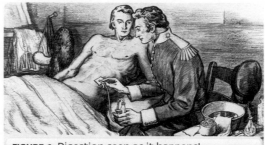

FIGURE 6: Digestion seen as it happens!

You will find out:

- about the main parts of the digestive system
- about the jobs of the main parts of the digestive system
- how food is broken down physically and by enzymes
- how food is absorbed by the body

What happens to Chardonnay's food?

Chardonnay takes care of her teeth. They give her an attractive smile. Her teeth are used to cut and grind food into smaller pieces. This is an example of **physical digestion**.

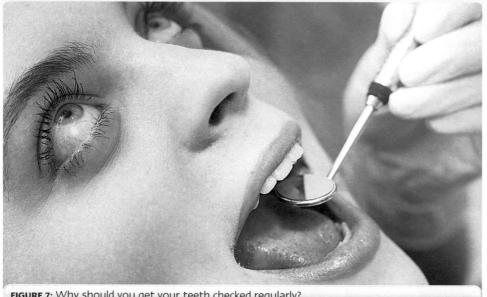

FIGURE 7: Why should you get your teeth checked regularly?

WOW FACTOR!

Sharks have teeth all over their skin as well as in their jaws.

So don't stroke a shark!

WOW FACTOR!

Your digestive system is about 9 m long, nearly the length of a bus!

This gives time for food to be digested.

The food can then easily pass down her **digestive system**.

Muscles in the wall of the stomach help to digest food by squeezing it. Muscles in other parts of the digestive system also squeeze the food. This keeps it moving.

Chardonnay thinks this is like squeezing toothpaste out of its tube. Now she knows how astronauts can eat when floating upside down in space!

QUESTIONS

10 What process breaks food down into smaller pieces?

11 Which system digests food?

12 How long is our digestive system?

...carbohydrase ...diffuse ...digestive system ...emulsify ...enzyme ...lipase

Chemical breakdown of food

Chardonnay knows that her food gets into her blood so that it can be carried to all the cells in her body.

She is puzzled because when she cuts her finger, she doesn't see lumps of potato and carrots in her blood!

Parts of the digestive system produce digestive **enzymes**. Different enzymes break down carbohydrates, proteins and fats into smaller and soluble molecules. These molecules **diffuse** through the walls of the small intestine and into the blood plasma (carbohydrates and proteins) or lymph (fats) and are carried to the cells.

Chardonnay does not see lumps of food in her blood because the food has been digested and has dissolved in the blood.

Enzymes are **specific** in their action.

- **Carbohydrases** break carbohydrates down into simple sugars, such as glucose.
- **Proteases** break proteins down into simpler amino acids.
- **Lipases** break fats down into simpler fatty acids and glycerol.

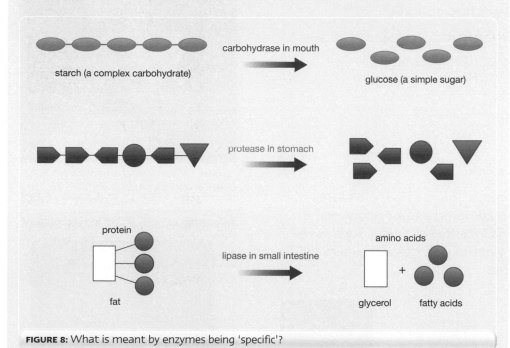

FIGURE 8: What is meant by enzymes being 'specific'?

Chardonnay finds out that parts of the digestive system produce:

- enzymes
- acid or alkali conditions so the enzymes can work, for example the stomach makes hydrochloric acid so that the protease enzyme called pepsin can work.

Fat digestion

Fats are difficult to digest and absorb because they are not soluble in water.

To help with fat digestion, the gall bladder produces bile. This **emulsifies** fats, which increases their **surface area** for enzymes to act on. Glucose and amino acids diffuse into the blood capillaries. Fatty acids pass into the lacteals, which are part of the **lymphatic system**.

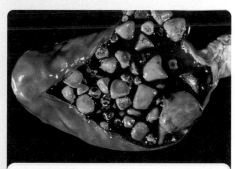

FIGURE 9: What are gall stones made of?

Gall stones can form in the gall bladder and may block the bile duct. They are made from bile pigments, cholesterol and calcium salts. Laser surgery is often used to break them down.

Keeping healthy

You will find out:

- what causes diseases
- why some diseases are infectious
- how your body defends itself against diseases
- how vectors spread disease

Tishoo, tishoo – we all fall down!

This nursery rhyme is believed to describe conditions in London in 1665 during the Great Plague.

The plague killed 60 000 people in London.

Sneezing was one symptom of the disease, now known to be Bubonic Plague.

People carried posies (bunches) of flowers to hide the smell of dead bodies.

Amanda's baby

Amanda knows she must sterilise baby Ben's feeding bottles.

She wants to protect Ben from **microorganisms**, which spread disease. These are called **pathogens**.

There are different types of pathogen:

- fungi that can cause athlete's foot
- bacteria that can cause cholera
- viruses that can cause flu (influenza)
- protozoa that can cause dysentery.

These pathogens cause **infectious diseases**. This means the diseases spread to other people. If the disease spreads directly from person to person it is called **contagious**. Cancer and inherited disorders, such as red-green colour deficiency, are not caused by pathogens. Diseases which are not caused by pathogens are not infectious.

skin stops entry of pathogens

hydrochloric acid in stomach kills pathogens

sticky mucus lines mucous membranes in breathing system trapping pathogens

blood clots to seal wounds

FIGURE 2: In what ways does the body protect itself from pathogens?

FIGURE 1: What special care must Amanda take to protect Ben from infections?

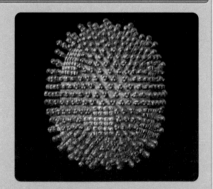
WOW FACTOR!

This is the virus that causes flu. It has been magnified (made bigger) under a microscope.

In 1918, a flu pandemic swept the world, killing millions of people.

In Australia, it killed half the population. In India, it killed one person in 20. In England it killed one person in 200.

■ QUESTIONS ■

1 Why does Amanda sterilise Ben's feeding bottles?
2 What type of pathogen causes flu?
3 How does your skin protect you from pathogens?
4 If your school had 1200 students, how many would have died of flu in 1918?

...benign ...contagious ...host ...infectious disease ...insecticide ...life cycle

How do vectors spread disease?

Amanda makes sure that there are no house flies in her house.

Some animals, such as the house fly and mosquito, carry microorganisms that cause disease while not suffering from the disease themselves. These animals are called **vectors**.

Amanda knows that mosquitoes are vectors for malaria. The weather in the UK is not warm enough for mosquitoes to be a problem.

Malaria is caused by a **protozoan** called *Plasmodium falciparum*, which is carried by female mosquitoes. *Plasmodium* is a **parasite** since it gets its food from its living **host**, humans and animals.

Mosquitoes feed on human blood using sharp mouthparts to pierce the skin. Some of the *Plasmodium* parasites are left in the host's blood. Here they feed on red blood cells, causing fever in the host which is often fatal.

Every year about 2000 people in the UK get malaria on holiday abroad. In 2003, 16 people from the UK died from malaria.

How to help the body fight disease

Amanda finds out that Ben could suffer from other disorders. She makes sure that:

- Ben's diet includes vitamin C to avoid scurvy
- Ben's diet includes iron to avoid anaemia
- Ben has a healthy lifestyle and a balanced diet so there is less risk of him developing diabetes and some cancers.

Amanda hopes that Ben's genes don't contain information to cause inherited disorders, such as red-green colour blindness.

Watch Out Flies and mosquitoes do not carry diseases; they carry the pathogens that cause diseases.

FIGURE 3: How does a mosquito infect a human?

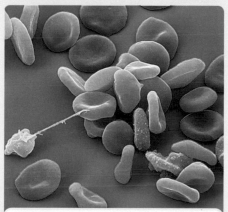

FIGURE 4: Plasmodium attacking a red blood cell. Magnified under a microscope.

Targeting vectors

Knowledge of a vector's **life cycle** is useful in finding ways to control it and prevent the spread of disease.

The mosquito has a complicated life cycle.

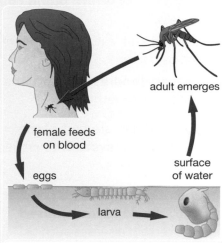

female feeds on blood

adult emerges

surface of water

eggs

larva

FIGURE 5: The mosquito's life cycle.

The mosquito larva (young stage) lives in water. Mosquitoes can therefore be controlled by draining stagnant water, or putting oil on the water surface to prevent the larvae from breathing.

The adult can be killed by spraying **insecticide**. Some drugs, such as Larium, can be taken by people to kill the protozoan in their blood.

Types of cancer

Cancer is a result of cells dividing out of control. The new cells may be odd shapes and form tumours.

Benign tumour cells, such as in warts, are slow to divide and are harmless. **Malignant** tumours are cancerous. The cells divide out of control and spread throughout the body.

QUESTIONS

5   Why are house flies and mosquitoes called vectors?

6   What type of microorganism is carried by mosquitoes?

7   Why is *Plasmodium* called a parasite?

QUESTIONS

8   Explain how understanding the mosquito's life cycle helps us to control malaria.

...malignant ...microorganism ...parasite ...pathogen ...protozoan ...vector

Amanda's baby is poorly

Ben feels hot. Amanda takes his temperature. The temperature should be about 37 °C. It is higher than this. Ben has an infection.

Many pathogens that enter the body are destroyed by **white blood cells**. These cells:

- surround and 'eat up' pathogens such as bacteria
- make **antibodies** that stick the pathogens together.

White blood cells are part of the body's **immune system** to protect against pathogens.

Amanda's doctor reminds her that her baby should be **immunised** against certain diseases such as measles, mumps and rubella.

Amanda asks the doctor if any new drug could help Ben. She knows that a new drug must be thoroughly tested before it can be used.

In many parts of the world some diseases are a serious problem. This is often due to a lack of drugs, doctors and hospitals.

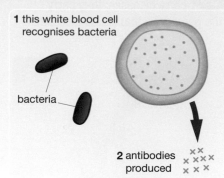

1 this white blood cell recognises bacteria

bacteria

2 antibodies produced

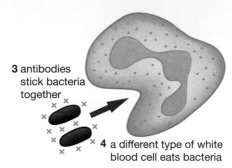

3 antibodies stick bacteria together

4 a different type of white blood cell eats bacteria

FIGURE 6: How do these white blood cells work?

WOW FACTOR!

You sneeze when the lining of your nose is irritated. Your diaphragm contracts violently. It sends out air, dust and bacteria at about 100 mph, spreading almost 10 million bacteria per sneeze!

A mumps epidemic?

In 2005 Britain faced a sudden increase in the number of people with mumps. There were 3504 cases in January, compared with 248 the previous year.

Some doctors think that the sudden rise was due to parents refusing to let their child have the MMR (measles, mumps and rubella) vaccine.

Mumps is a disease caused by a virus. It only affects humans.

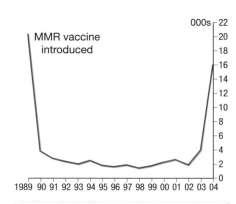

MMR vaccine introduced

000s

1989 90 91 92 93 94 95 96 97 98 99 00 01 02 03 04

FIGURE 7: Number of reported mumps cases.

▐ QUESTIONS ▐

9   What does a high body temperature show?

10 What type of blood cell destroys pathogens such as bacteria?

11 What do white blood cells make to stick pathogens together?

12 Why should Amanda's baby be immunised?

...active immunity ...antibiotic ...antibody ...antigen ...blind trial ...immune system

Protecting Ben

As Ben has a fever, the doctor gives him an **antibiotic**. Antibiotics are drugs that attack bacteria. They cannot be used against viruses.

Ben's fever is a symptom of an infection. His body reacts to:

- **antigens** on the surface of a 'foreign invader'
- the poisonous chemicals, called **toxins**, which are produced
- damage to his cells caused by the pathogen.

Immunity

If the same type of pathogen invades Ben's body again, his white blood cells recognise it and quickly make lots of antibodies. These lock on to the antigens. The pathogen is quickly destroyed so Ben is immune to that disease.

This sort of immunity is called **active immunity** because Ben's white blood cells make their own antibodies.

When Ben is vaccinated with the MMR vaccine, he will have active immunity against the diseases measles, mumps and rubella. Active immunity has a lasting effect but can take a few weeks to be effective.

Some vaccinations, such as those protecting against a snakebite, give **passive immunity**. An animal such as the rabbit provides the antibodies. Passive immunity is fast acting but only lasts a short time.

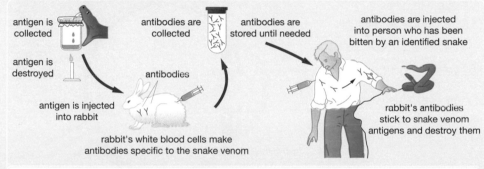

antigen is collected

antigen is destroyed

antigen is injected into rabbit

rabbit's white blood cells make antibodies specific to the snake venom

antibodies are collected

antibodies

antibodies are stored until needed

antibodies are injected into person who has been bitten by an identified snake

rabbit's antibodies stick to snake venom antigens and destroy them

FIGURE 8: A vaccination against snake venom being prepared.

Testing drugs

Amanda knows that drugs, such as antibiotics, are tested in various ways. The drug must not only work, but also must not cause any further damage to the body.

Drugs can be tested on animals, specially grown human tissue or by using computer models.

Some of Amanda's friends are not happy with the idea of using animals in such tests.

QUESTIONS

13 Which types of pathogens can be controlled by antibiotics?

14 Which type of immunity is needed in an outbreak of disease?

15 Suggest why people may object to testing drugs on animals.

Is vaccination the complete answer?

Each pathogen has its own set of antigens. This means that specific antibodies are needed to protect against different diseases.

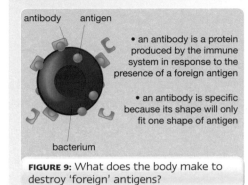

antibody   antigen

- an antibody is a protein produced by the immune system in response to the presence of a foreign antigen
- an antibody is specific because its shape will only fit one shape of antigen

bacterium

FIGURE 9: What does the body make to destroy 'foreign' antigens?

A vaccination against tetanus gives long term protection. A flu vaccination does not. This is because bacteria and viruses can change by mutation and the antibodies don't fit the new shapes (see 'Who am I?' on pages 44–47).

Immunisation, like any medical treatment, carries a small risk to the individual, such as an adverse side effect. However, once the majority of the population has been immunised against an infection, there is little chance of the disease spreading.

Doctors are worried that some antibiotics no longer work. Excessive use of antibiotics has meant that resistant forms of bacteria are more common than the non-resistant forms. With less competition, these new strains thrive. An example is the 'superbug' MRSA (methicillin resistant *Staphylococcus aureus*).

In testing a new drug, doctors use groups of volunteers. Some take the drug and some a harmless pill called a **placebo**. In some trials the volunteers do not know which treatment they are receiving (**blind trial**). In other trials the doctors do not know which treatment is used either (double blind trial). The information is kept by other doctors.

QUESTIONS

16 Explain why MRSA has thrived.

17 Discuss the advantages and disadvantages of immunisation.

Keeping in touch

You will find out:
- about the body's sense organs
- how the eye works
- about problems with your vision
- about your range of vision

Guide dogs

Guide Dogs for The Blind was set up in 1931 to help blind and partially sighted people. Now there are about 5000 working guide dogs in the UK.

Hearing Dogs for Deaf People trains dogs to alert people to sounds such as an alarm clock, smoke alarm, telephone or baby crying.

Rashid has an accident

Rashid thinks he has some pieces of grit in his eye. He goes to hospital. A doctor removes the grit and puts a bandage over his damaged eye.

Rashid sees a chart showing the inside of his eye.

He realises that he can now only see out of one eye. This is called **monocular** vision. He is told not to ride his bike at home because he will not be able to judge distances. He will not see in three dimensions (3-D).

When he can use both eyes again he will have **binocular** vision and be able to ride his bike safely. Since humans have only a small **range** of vision, he has learnt to turn his head or use mirrors on the handlebars.

His sight is later checked at hospital to see if he has any problems such as **long-sight**, **short-sight** or red-green colour blindness.

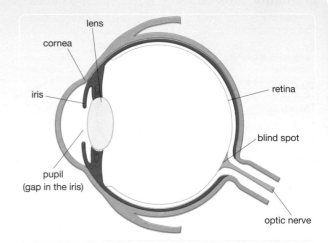

FIGURE 1: What is the coloured part of your eye called?

Senses

Sense organs (**receptors**) keep us informed of what is happening.

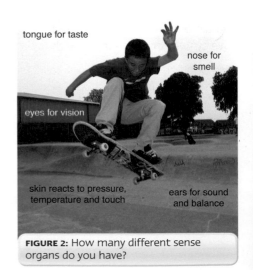

FIGURE 2: How many different sense organs do you have?

■■ QUESTIONS ■■

1. What is monocular vision?
2. Why is it dangerous to ride a bike with one eye covered up?
3. Which sense organ reacts to a change in temperature?
4. Which sense organ reacts to the body changing position?

...accommodate ...binocular ...concave ...convex ...long sight

How do Rashid's eyes work?

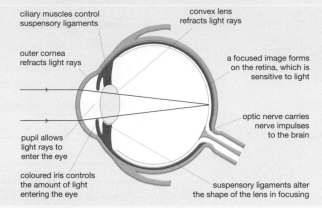

ciliary muscles control suspensory ligaments

convex lens refracts light rays

outer cornea refracts light rays

a focused image forms on the retina, which is sensitive to light

optic nerve carries nerve impulses to the brain

pupil allows light rays to enter the eye

coloured iris controls the amount of light entering the eye

suspensory ligaments alter the shape of the lens in focusing

FIGURE 3: What do the cornea and lens do to light rays as they enter the eye?

Rashid finds out that light rays are **refracted** (bent) as they go through his cornea and lens. The lens can change shape to focus on different distances.

An image is formed on his retina. The retina has special light receptors which react to light. Nerve impulses are sent from the retina, through the optic nerve, to the brain.

The amount of light entering the eye is controlled by the iris (the coloured part of the eye).

Binocular vision

Rashid is glad when the bandages are removed from his eye. He can judge distances because the range of vision from his two eyes overlaps.

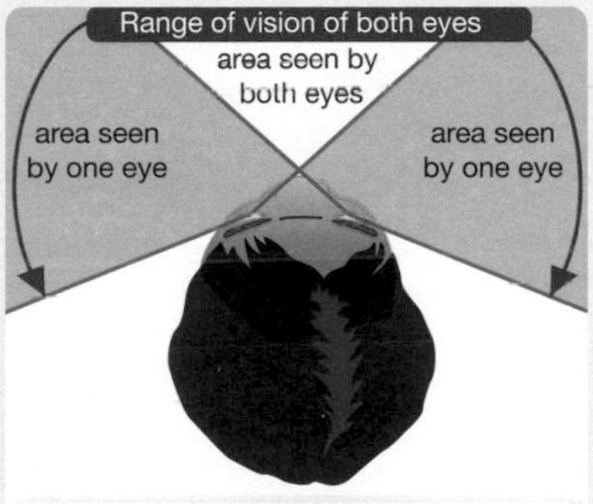

Range of vision of both eyes

area seen by both eyes

area seen by one eye

area seen by one eye

FIGURE 4: Binocular vision.

Vision problems

At the hospital, Rashid finds out he is slightly short-sighted. He cannot see distant things very well. His eyeballs or lens are the wrong shape. Long-sighted people also have eyeballs or lenses that are the wrong shape.

After looking at special charts Rashid knows his colour vision is normal. Some people lack specialised cells in their retinas. This causes red-green colour blindness, which is inherited (see 'Who am I?', page 46).

QUESTIONS

5 What could cause Rashid to be short-sighted?

6 Suggest why red-green colour blindness cannot be cured.

Elderly eyes

Rashid's grandad nearly stepped out in front of a bus! He had been looking in a shop window, then turned to cross the road. His eyes did not change focus (**accommodate**) fast enough so he did not see how near the bus was.

The ciliary muscles and suspensory ligaments in the eye act together to pull or push on the lens. The fatter the lens, the more the light is refracted. As we get older our muscles and ligaments become less flexible.

The muscles in the iris alter the size of the pupil. This controls how much light enters the eye.

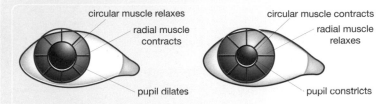

circular muscle relaxes

radial muscle contracts

circular muscle contracts

radial muscle relaxes

pupil dilates

pupil constricts

FIGURE 5: What happens to the muscles in the iris when the pupil dilates?

Correcting short- and long-sight problems

Rashid is short-sighted. His optician recommends glasses or contact lenses with **concave** (curving in) lenses. Long-sighted people need **convex** (bulging out) lenses.

The lenses are fitted into glasses or used as contact lenses.

Cornea surgery is now quite common. Lasers alter the curvature of the cornea to correct focusing problems.

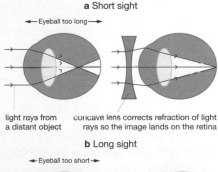

a Short sight

←Eyeball too long→

light rays from a distant object

concave lens corrects refraction of light rays so the image lands on the retina

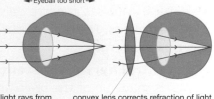

b Long sight

←Eyeball too short→

light rays from a distant object

convex lens corrects refraction of light rays so the image lands on the retina

FIGURE 6: How do concave and convex lenses correct short and long sight?

 Watch Out A concave lens curves inwards like a 'cave'.

A convex lens curves outwards.

QUESTIONS

7 Why may elderly people have problems with their vision?

8 Why do changes take place in the eye when a person goes from a dark room to daylight?

Becoming coordinated

Getting your muscles and nerves to work together takes time! It takes about a year for a baby to stack bricks on top of each other.

six months   eight months   one year

FIGURE 7: A baby's hand grasp improves as it gets older.

You will find out:

- about the parts of your nervous system
- how reflex actions work
- how to find out how fast your reactions are

Reflexes

Rashid looks into a friend's eyes.

He notices that the friend's irises are blue and his pupils are black. When a bright light goes on, he notices that the pupils immediately get smaller.

This is a **reflex** (not thought about) action. Other reflex actions are:

- knee jerk (tapping below the knee)
- taking a hand away from a hot plate.

Reflex actions protect us because they are fast and automatic.

Actions we think about first are **voluntary** actions.

Information is carried round the body as electrical impulses in nerve cells called **neurones**. These form our **nervous system**.

- The **central nervous system** (CNS) is made up of the brain and spinal cord.
- The **peripheral nervous system** is made up of nerves to and from the brain and spinal cord.

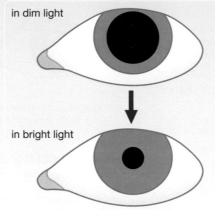

in dim light

in bright light

Reflex action of the pupil

FIGURE 8: Do the pupils get smaller or bigger when moving from daylight to a dark room?

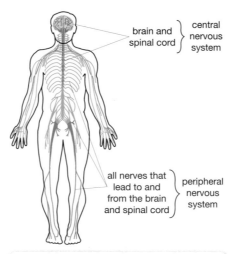

brain and spinal cord — central nervous system

all nerves that lead to and from the brain and spinal cord — peripheral nervous system

FIGURE 9: How is information carried in the nervous system?

DID YOU KNOW?

Sprinters are allowed 0.1 seconds to react. A faster time means they have 'jumped the gun' and the race has to restart. If they do this twice they are disqualified.

WANT TO KNOW MORE?

Test your reflexes at:

www.happyhub.com/network/reflex

QUESTIONS

9   What happens to your pupils in bright light?

10 Why do your pupils need to be able to change size?

11 Name **two** other reflex actions.

12 What do neurones carry?

...acetylcholine ...central nervous system ...nervous system ...neurone

Rashid tries to help

Rashid helps at lunchtime. Unfortunately he picks up a hot plate. By reflex he immediately drops it and then examines his fingers. The high temperature was the stimulus, dropping the plate was the response.

Dropping a hot plate is an example of a spinal reflex. The reaction takes place without the brain thinking about it.

Rashid's brain also receives nerve impulses from his fingers. This is why he examines his fingers to see if they are damaged.

The nerve impulse is carried in neurones.

- Sensory neurones carry impulses away from a sense organ.
- Motor neurones carry impulses to an effector (muscle or gland).

So when Rashid dropped the plate, impulses travelled through his neurones in a spinal reflex.

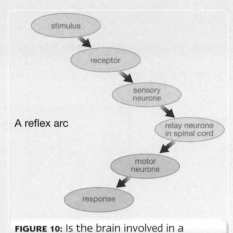

FIGURE 10: Is the brain involved in a spinal reflex?

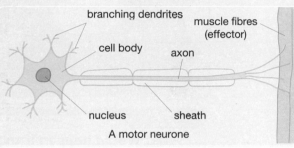

FIGURE 11: In which direction do impulses travel in motor neurones?

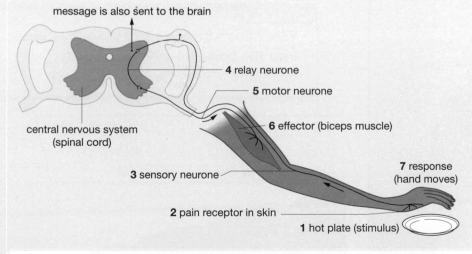

FIGURE 12: A relay neurone connects the sensory neurone to the motor neurone in the spinal cord.

QUESTIONS

13 Why are reflex actions very fast?

14 Which part of a neurone carries the nerve impulse?

15 Why is it important for the brain to be kept informed of a reflex action?

Neurones

Neurones are adapted to carry and pass on nerve impulses quickly.

Neurones:

- are long (nearly 2 m)
- have branched endings (dendrites) to pick up impulses
- are insulated by a fatty sheath, so that the electrical impulses do not cross over.

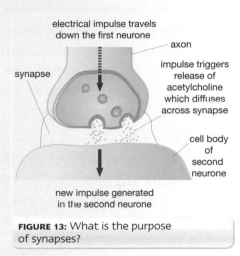

FIGURE 13: What is the purpose of synapses?

Signals have to pass from one neurone to another. There is a gap called the **synapse** between two neurones to allow some control of the impulses. An impulse triggers the release of transmitter substances, such as **acetylcholine**, which diffuse across the synapse.

Since the brain is kept informed during a reflex action, it is possible to modify or 'condition' some reflexes.

Watch Out Remember sensory neurones carry impulses away from a sense organ; motor neurones carry impulses to effectors, such as muscles so you move.

QUESTIONS

16 How are neurones adapted to their function?

17 Describe how an impulse travels from a receptor to an effector.

New polio vaccine to save thousands of lives worldwide

SELF-CHECK ACTIVITY

CONTEXT

Read the cartoon story. It tells the story of an American girl called Abi, being vaccinated against polio. Polio is a disease that can be prevented but not cured. Teams of scientists came up with vaccines in the 1950s and since then it has been virtually eradicated in North America and Europe.

The vaccination meant that it was then almost impossible for Abi to catch polio, even if the virus entered her body. Discuss in your group how the vaccination works.

STEP 1

What would happen if the polio virus got into Abi's body after she had been vaccinated?

STEP 2

Vaccination involves putting a 'live' virus into the body. How does the body recognise a virus?

THE **VACCINE** HAS REACHED THE **INTESTINES!** IT CONTAINS A **VIRUS** WHICH IS **MULTIPLYING** AND **ENTERING THE BLOODSTREAM!**

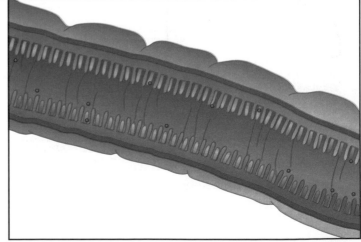

STEP 3

How does the body respond to a virus?

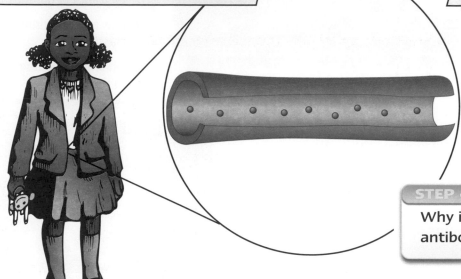

THE VIRUS ENTERS THE BLOODSTREAM! IT IS THE JOB OF THE WHITE BLOOD CELLS TO **KILL THE VIRUS**, BUT THEY ARE CAUGHT **UNPREPARED**! THEY HAVE NEVER COME ACROSS ANYTHING LIKE THIS BEFORE! ABI'S **ANTIBODIES** ARE **USELESS**!

THIS TYPE OF POLIO VIRUS **DOESN'T CAUSE** THE DISEASE THOUGH, AND SOON ABI'S WHITE BLOOD CELLS ARE BUSY **MAKING ANTIBODIES** TO DEAL WITH IT!

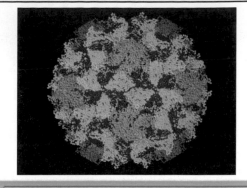

STEP 4

Why is the body unable to use its existing antibodies to deal with this virus?

NOW ABI'S BODY IS READY TO **FIGHT ANY DANGEROUS POLIO** VIRUS THAT ATTACKS HER – SHE HAS THE RIGHT TYPE OF ANTIBODIES **READY AND WAITING**!

STEP 5

How is the body now protected?

Maximise your grade

These sentences show what you need to be including in your work. Use these to improve your work and to be successful.

Grade	Answer includes...
F	Use the term immunisation.
	Recall that immunisation gives protection against certain pathogens.
	State that being given the polio vaccine means that the person is protected from the disease in the future.
	Describe how the body reacts to the polio virus by producing antibodies.
C	Describe how immunity to polio comes from prior infection.
	Explain how being infected by polio causes the production of specific antibodies.
A	Explain that polio has its own antigens and that specific antibodies are needed. Explain how immunisation works.
	As above, but with particular clarity and detail.

Drugs and you

You will find out:

- about how drugs can be useful or harmful
- how and why drugs are classified
- what harmful drugs do to the body

The wonder drug

In 1897 Felix Hoffman was trying to develop a drug to help his father who was suffering from arthritis. He succeeded and developed aspirin. Aspirin is a painkiller.

Today over 100 billion tablets of aspirin are made each year.

In recent years scientists have discovered other uses for aspirin. It reduces the risk of some cancers and helps to prevent heart attacks. It has earned the name 'wonder drug'!

Harmful and useful drugs

Useful drugs help the body. Insulin helps diabetics. Penicillin kills bacteria. You need a doctor's prescription to get many useful drugs.

Different types of drugs and their effects

Harmful drugs change how you behave and feel. They damage your health. Alcohol and cannabis are harmful drugs.

- **Depressants** slow down the workings of the brain.
- **Hallucinogens** change what a person sees and hears.
- **Painkillers** stop nerve impulses so no pain is felt.
- **Performance enhancers** develop muscles.
- **Stimulants** speed up the workings of the brain.

A person can become **addicted** to a drug, such as nicotine in tobacco. This means it is hard to give it up.

When a person has been taking a drug for a long time they find they need to take bigger doses of the drug to get the same effects. This is called **tolerance.**

When a person decides to try to give up a drug addiction they join a **rehabilitation** group that helps them to stop taking the drug.

The person suffers **withdrawal symptoms**, such as being bad tempered, if they do try to give the drug up.

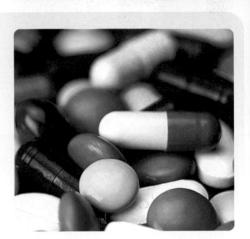

WANT TO KNOW MORE?

You can find out more about aspirin from:
www.aspirin-foundation.com

⬛ QUESTIONS ⬛

1. Name **three** things that harmful drugs do to you.
2. Penicillin is used to treat some diseases. What do you need before you can get this drug?
3. What type of drug would you take for a toothache?

...addiction   ...depressant   ...hallucinogen   ...painkiller   ...performance enhancer

Drug classification

Drugs are classified by law based on how dangerous they are.

CLASS A

7 years in prison* and a fine for possession

Life in prison for supplying

heroin, methadone, cocaine, ecstasy, LSD, magic mushrooms

CLASS B

5 years in prison* and a fine for possession

14 years in prison for supplying

amphetamines, barbiturates

CLASS C

2 years in prison* and a fine for possession

5 years in prison for supplying

anabolic steroids, Valium, temazepan, cannabis

*These are the maximum prison sentences.

Examples of drugs

FIGURE 1: Depressants such as alcohol, solvents and temazepan.

FIGURE 2: Hallucinogens such as cannabis and LSD.

FIGURE 3: Painkillers such as aspirin and heroin.

FIGURE 4: Performance enhancers such as anabolic steroids.

FIGURE 5: Stimulants such as nicotine, ecstasy and caffeine.

QUESTIONS

4   Which class of drug (A, B or C) is the most dangerous?
5   Aspirin and heroin are both painkillers. Why is heroin illegal?

More on drug classification

Different countries have different views on drugs. In Belgium, people over 18 years old can carry a small amount of cannabis for personal use.

In Indonesia, smuggling of drugs carries a death sentence.

Some people in the UK believe that the personal use of drugs such as cannabis should be allowed. They argue that prohibition of alcohol in America in the 1930s did not stop its use. It simply created organised crime.

Other people highlight scientific studies that show how dangerous and destructive these drugs can be.

Your school will have a policy on drug abuse. Read and discuss it in class.

Effect of drugs on the nervous system

Nicotine acts as a stimulant. It affects synapses (junction of two neurones). It stimulates the acetylcholine receptors allowing more impulses to pass. (To learn more about synapses see Keeping in touch, page 29.)

Alcohol is a depressant. It affects the brain, interfering with coordination and balance. It binds with acetylcholine receptors, blocking nerve impulses.

QUESTIONS

6   Why is it important to check Customs regulations when travelling abroad?
7   How does nicotine affect the nervous system?

What is in tobacco smoke?

The main chemicals in tobacco smoke are:

- carbon monoxide
- nicotine
- tar
- particulates.

When tobacco smoke gets into the lungs there is no way out.

Many lung diseases are linked to smoking.

Some chemicals get into the blood and can cause heart disease.

In February 2003 a ban was placed on advertising tobacco products in newspapers, magazines and posters.

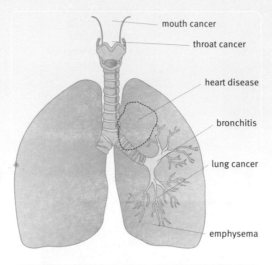

FIGURE 6: Diseases of the lungs and heart caused by tobacco smoke.

WOW FACTOR!

Hundreds of years ago Native Americans smoked tobacco in pipes. They used it for special occasions.

The explorer Christopher Columbus brought some tobacco leaves and seeds back from America.

Smoking did not become popular until the 16th Century.

Now smoking kills 120 000 people in the UK every year.

What are the effects of drinking alcohol?

Drinking alcohol has quick (short-term) effects. A person who has drunk alcohol may:

- do silly things
- easily lose their balance
- find it hard to talk clearly
- find it difficult to use their muscles
- die of alcohol poisoning if they have drunk too much.

No wonder there is a legal limit to the amount of alcohol car drivers can have in their bloodstream!

There are long-term effects too. A person may suffer from damage to the liver and brain.

People tend to smoke and drink alcohol in groups. Tobacco and alcohol are called 'social drugs'.

 Alcohol is a depressant NOT a stimulant.

QUESTIONS

8 Name **two** 'social drugs'.

9 Suggest why it is illegal to advertise tobacco products in magazines, newspapers and on posters.

10 Name the **four** main chemicals in tobacco smoke.

...carcinogen ...cilia ...cirrhosis

Tobacco smoke and its effects

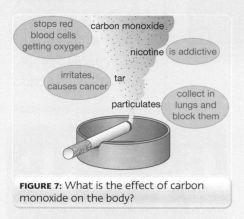

FIGURE 7: What is the effect of carbon monoxide on the body?

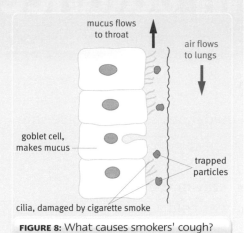

FIGURE 8: What causes smokers' cough?

Smoker's cough

Cells that line the trachea and bronchioles are called **epithelial cells**. Some cells have tiny hairs called **cilia** and others make sticky mucus.

Cigarette smoke stops the cilia from moving. Dust and particulates collect and irritate the cells. Smokers cough to move this mess upwards so it can be swallowed.

Data on the effects of smoking

The idea of smoking being a harmless habit changed about 50 years ago.

A report was published linking smoking with lung cancer and other diseases. It showed that in the UK nearly 140 men (who smoked only cigarettes) in every 100 000 died from lung cancer each year.

In 1970 about 50% of the population of the UK smoked cigarettes. It is now about 30%.

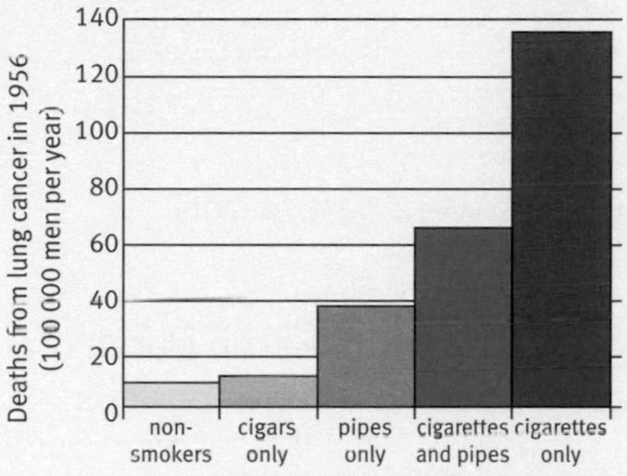

FIGURE 9: Does smoking a pipe or cigar present the same risk of death as smoking cigarettes?

The effect of alcohol on the liver

The liver breaks down toxic chemicals such as alcohol. The alcohol content of a drink is measured in **units** of alcohol.

The amount of alcohol in drinks varies. One unit of alcohol contains 10 ml of pure alcohol.

Half a pint (250 ml) of ordinary beer, one glass of wine and one pub measure of spirits all contain one unit of alcohol. Alcopop drinks contain about one and a half units of alcohol.

Alcohol kills liver cells and causes liver **cirrhosis**. Liver cirrhosis kills over 4000 people in the UK every year.

QUESTIONS

11 What chemical makes a person addicted to smoking?

12 Why are cilia in the trachea important?

13 What does alcohol do to liver cells?

14 Using the data in the bar chart, calculate the rate of all types of smoking-related deaths.

Dangerous smoke

Many manufacturers produce 'low tar' cigarettes. This is because tars in cigarettes are especially dangerous, collecting in air sacs and alveoli deep inside the lungs. They irritate the delicate lung tissue and are **carcinogens**.

The tiny particulates in smoke also collect in lung tissue. They block the exchange of gases and reduce the amount of oxygen available to the rest of the body.

Drunken drivers

The legal limit of alcohol when driving is 80 mg of alcohol per 100 ml of blood. A breathalyser is used as a roadside test to see if a more accurate blood test is required.

Data on alcohol-related vehicle accident deaths in the UK show a welcome reduction from 1550 to 480 in the last 20 years.

This could be due to the use of breathalysers or better car design.

The information on ambulance call-outs linked to alcohol-related injuries is also interesting.

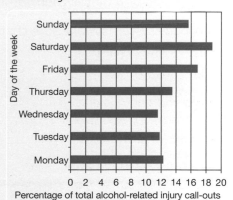

FIGURE 10: On which day do ambulance crews receive the least alcohol-related injury call-outs?

QUESTIONS

15 Suggest why alcohol-related injury call-outs vary during the week.

16 Suggest **one** feature of improved car design that has helped reduce fatalities.

Staying in balance

You will find out:
- how the insides of our bodies are kept in balance
- about homeostasis
- about the dangers of being too hot or cold

Weather warning!

In 2005 the government published guidelines to keep people safe in very hot weather.

People were advised to:
- avoid going out at midday
- take cool showers
- stay in the shade
- eat cold salads.

The heat wave in 2003 caused 27 000 deaths in Europe. In England, 2000 people died.

Keeping steady

Evie is taking part in the Duke of Edinburgh's Gold Medal Award. She is training for a 50-mile walk.

She could be in danger if she gets too hot or too cold.

Her normal body temperature is 37 °C. Body cells work best at this temperature.

Evie can check her body temperature using a heat-sensitive strip placed on her forehead or a clinical thermometer placed inside her mouth or anus.

Evie's body systems make sure that her water, oxygen and carbon dioxide levels are kept steady.

FIGURE 1: A heat-sensitive strip uses colour to show temperature.

Evie loses heat by:
- sweating
- more blood flow near to the surface of her skin.

Evie gains or keeps heat by:
- exercising
- shivering
- releasing energy from food
- less blood flow near to the surface of her skin.

DID YOU KNOW?

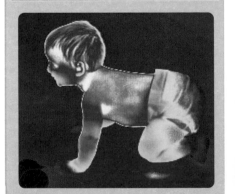

Hospitals use thermal imaging to show the temperature of parts of the body.

Hotter parts are shown in red, colder parts in blue.

QUESTIONS

1. How many people died in England as a result of the heat wave in 2003?
2. What is Evie's normal body temperature?
3. Write down **one** way in which Evie can lose heat.

...dehydration ...homeostasis ...hypothermia ...negative feedback

What is homeostasis?

Various body systems keep the levels of oxygen, water, carbon dioxide and temperature constant. Keeping a constant internal environment is called **homeostasis**.

Sweating

Evie knows she sweats all the time.

Sweat comes from **sweat glands** in her skin.

She wears anti-perspirant and showers after exercise. This stops bacteria from living on the sweat and causing smells.

When she steps out of the shower she feels very cold. The water has evaporated. It has used heat from her skin to change from a liquid to a gas. (See the chocolate experiment on page 174.)

The more Evie sweats the cooler she gets. This is one of the methods used by the body to cool down.

Dangers of high and low temperatures

Evie knows that she must wear the correct clothing and be well-equipped for her expedition to help her body keep a steady internal environment.

If she gets too hot on her walk she could suffer from:

- heat stroke, when her skin becomes cold and clammy and her pulse is rapid and weak
- **dehydration** because she has lost too much water.

If these conditions are left untreated she could die.

Evie must not get too cold on her walk. If her temperature falls too low she could suffer from **hypothermia**. Her pulse rate slows down and she shivers violently.

She could also die from this condition if it is untreated.

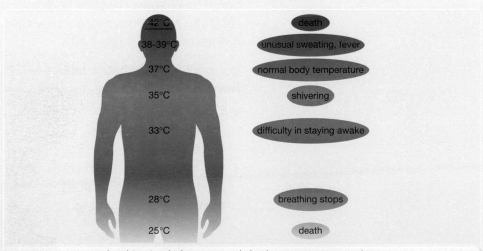

FIGURE 2: Suggest why shivering helps a person's body temperature to rise.

42°C	death
38-39°C	unusual sweating, fever
37°C	normal body temperature
35°C	shivering
33°C	difficulty in staying awake
28°C	breathing stops
25°C	death

QUESTIONS

4 Why does Evie feel cold when she steps out of the shower?

5 What are the symptoms of hypothermia?

6 At which **two** temperatures are people likely to die?

Feedback controls

Premature babies are put into an incubator. The temperature of an incubator is controlled by a feedback mechanism.

If the temperature is too low the heater is switched on. This is called a **negative feedback** since turning on the heater negates (cancels out) the decreasing temperature.

It is important to keep the body temperature at 37 °C. This is the **optimum temperature** for enzymes.

The hypothalamus

A small gland in the brain, called the hypothalamus, helps to keep the body in balance by detecting when the blood is too hot or cold.

The hypothalamus then triggers protective measures such as shivering or sweating, or changing the size of blood capillaries in the skin (**vasoconstriction** and **vasodilation**).

Vasoconstriction. When the body is too cold. blood capillaries in the skin constrict and so less blood flows through them, reducing heat loss

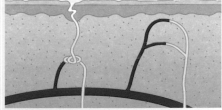

Vasodilation. When the body is too hot. blood capillaries in the skin dilate and so blood flow increases, bringing more blood to the surface where it loses heat

sweat evaporates from the skin surface, cooling it

FIGURE 3: Vasoconstriction and vasodilation.

QUESTIONS

7 Explain how the hypothalamus helps to maintain a constant body temperature.

Hormones

Evie has diabetes. Her **pancreas** does not produce enough **insulin**.

You will find out:
- where hormones are produced
- about sex hormones
- why a lack of insulin causes a problem

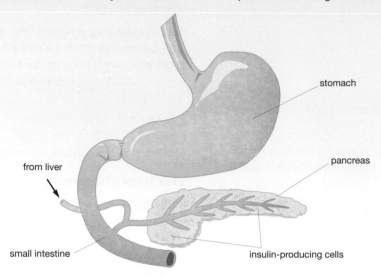

FIGURE 4: What hormone is produced in the pancreas?

stomach

from liver

pancreas

small intestine

insulin-producing cells

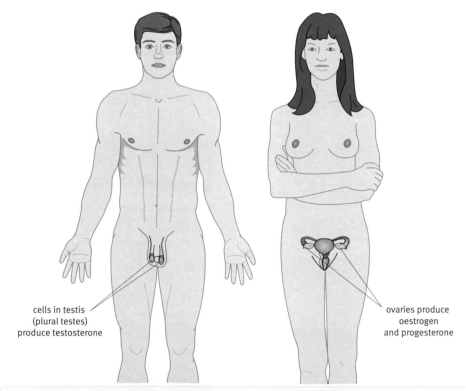

cells in testis
(plural testes)
produce testosterone

ovaries produce
oestrogen
and progesterone

FIGURE 5: What are the names of the organs that produce the male and female sex hormones?

Insulin is a **hormone**. Hormones are made in special **glands**. Hormones are carried in the blood to where they have an effect. The part of the body a hormone affects is called the **target organ**.

Blood takes time to travel around the body. This means that the body reacts to hormones more slowly than it does to nervous reactions.

Our bodies also produce **sex hormones**.

- Evie's ovaries produce hormones called **oestrogen** and **progesterone**.
- Evie has an older brother. His testes produce a hormone called **testosterone**.

QUESTIONS

8 How do hormones get around the body?

9 Where are hormones taken to?

10 Write down the name of **one** female sex hormone and **one** male sex hormone.

...diabetes ...gland ...hormone ...insulin ...menstrual cycle ...oestrogen ...ovulation

Evie and insulin

Evie's pancreas does not make enough insulin. This condition is called **diabetes**.

Sometimes diabetes can be controlled by eating a diet low in sugar. Other diabetics have to inject insulin.

Insulin controls the level of glucose in the blood. If the level of glucose in Evie's blood falls too low she could go into a coma.

Evie is a teenager

Evie's ovaries are producing sex hormones because she has reached **puberty**.

- Her breasts are developing and her hips are wider.
- She is starting to grow hair in her pubic area and under her armpits.
- Her periods have started because her ovaries have started to release an egg every month.

Evie's older brother is also a teenager.

- His shape has changed because he has become more muscular.
- He shaves off his beard and moustache and he is proud of his hairy chest!
- His voice has 'broken' and so it is much deeper.
- His testes have started to produce sperm and his genitals have developed.

All these developments are called secondary sexual characteristics.

Control of blood sugar levels

After a meal containing carbohydrates, the digestive system breaks the large carbohydrate molecules down into simple sugars such as glucose. Glucose is carried in the blood plasma.

When the levels of glucose in the blood are too high, insulin converts some glucose into glycogen, which is stored in the liver.

Since Evie does not have enough insulin, a lot of her glucose is removed from her blood by her kidneys. Glucose is excreted in her urine.

Her body therefore does not have a store of glycogen to use later on. She needs to inject herself with insulin to keep her insulin levels as close to normal as possible. The size of the insulin dose that Evie needs depends on her diet and how much exercise she takes.

Evie's menstrual cycle

About every 28 days, Evie's ovaries release an egg. This is called **ovulation**. Egg release is controlled by oestrogen and progesterone.

The lining of her uterus (womb) changes in thickness. After an egg is released the uterus lining becomes thicker so that the egg can implant in it, should it be fertilised. This is controlled by progesterone.

If the egg is not fertilised the amount of progesterone decreases and the uterus wall breaks down. Another hormone, oestrogen, controls the repair of the uterus lining. This cycle of changes is called the **menstrual cycle**.

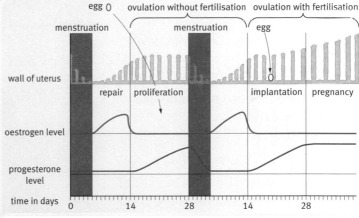

FIGURE 6: Does menstruation (periods) occur in pregnancy?

One method of contraception is the use of synthetic hormones. These block the production and release of eggs from the ovaries. There is a slight risk of side-effects, such as the formation of blood clots.

If later in her life Evie finds she is not releasing an egg each month, this can also be treated with female sex hormones.

QUESTIONS

11 What does insulin control?

12 Which organs make eggs?

13 Which organs make sperm?

QUESTIONS

14 Describe what happens to the levels of progesterone and oestrogen during pregnancy.

15 Suggest why the uterus wall is renewed every 28 days.

Gene control

You will find out:
- where your genes are
- what genes are made of
- how genes work

A great British scientist

Francis Crick died in July 2004. Every newspaper and TV programme reported his death.

This is because, together with James Watson, he worked out the structure of DNA. This explained many of the mysteries about inheritance.

He told his wife about his work saying he had found the secret of life and she said,

'You are always coming home and saying things like that'!

Crick was 37 and Watson was only 25 when together they worked out the structure of DNA.

DID YOU KNOW?

Plant cells also have chromosomes.

These are the chromosomes from a bluebell.

They have been stained with a dye so they show up when magnified under a microscope.

Characteristics

Calvin teaches a new class every year.

One of his new students is called Charlotte.

There are about seven billion people in the world, but there is only one Charlotte!

The information about Charlotte is in her **genetic code**. The code is a set of instructions. The instructions are like a recipe to make a cake.

The code is carried by her **genes**. Her genes are in **chromosomes** in the nucleus of every cell of her body.

The chromosomes have all the information to make Charlotte.

Genes are made of a chemical called **DNA**.

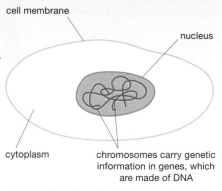

cell membrane

nucleus

cytoplasm

chromosomes carry genetic information in genes, which are made of DNA

FIGURE 1: What chemical are genes made of?

DID YOU KNOW?

- The fern *Ophioglossum* has 630 chromosomes in each cell!

- A worm called *Ascaris* has only two chromosomes in each cell.
- A human has 46 chromosomes in each body cell.

QUESTIONS

1. What is the code in Charlotte's genes called?
2. What do Charlotte's chromosomes carry?
3. Where in a cell are chromosomes found?
4. Who worked out the structure of DNA?

...A, T, C, G   ...chromosomes   ...deoxyribonucleic acid (DNA)   ...double helix

What are genes?

Calvin explains about genes to his class. He says, 'Making Charlotte is like following a recipe for a cake'!

The genetic code is a set of instructions. The instructions are in a chemical called DNA (**deoxyribonucleic acid**). Sections of DNA form a gene.

Watson and Crick worked out that DNA was shaped like a spring. They called the shape a **double helix**.

In DNA the two strands look like a twisted ladder.

The rungs of the ladder are made of four different chemicals called **bases**.

It is the specific arrangement of bases that makes up the unique genetic code (or recipe) that makes Charlotte.

WANT TO KNOW MORE?

To find out more about DNA and how its structure was discovered read the book *The Double Helix*, published by Touchstone.

It is a personal account of the discovery of the structure of DNA.

Charlotte's body is made up of one hundred million million cells!

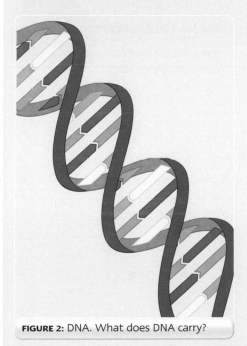

FIGURE 2: DNA. What does DNA carry?

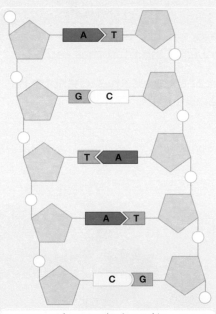

FIGURE 3: What are the 'rungs' in DNA called?

Switched on or off?

Charlotte's body is made up of one hundred million million cells (100 000 000 000 000)!

Each cell has a complete set of instructions contained in the DNA of its chromosomes.

Even a cell in Charlotte's big toe has information about her eye colour. Since this information is not needed in her big toe cells, these genes are **switched off**.

DNA bases

The four bases in DNA are shown by their initials **A**, **T**, **C** and **G**.

Watson and Crick realised that A only links with T, and C only links with G. This is important when DNA is copied. With only one side of the DNA ladder, the other side can be rebuilt. It is the specific sequence of bases that gives the genetic code.

QUESTIONS

8   Why is the sequence of bases in DNA important?

9   Suggest why many genes in a cell are switched off.

10 None of the genes in an egg or sperm cell are switched off. Suggest why.

QUESTIONS

5   What name did Watson and Crick give to the shape of DNA?

6   What makes up the genetic code?

7   How many different bases are there in DNA?

Making Charlotte

Each of Charlotte's body cells has 46 chromosomes. The chromosomes are arranged in matching pairs.

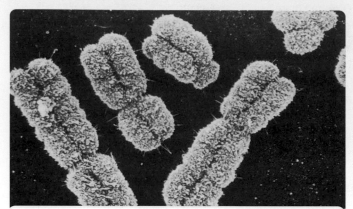

FIGURE 4: Human chromosomes. Stained and magnified using a microscope. How are chromosomes arranged inside the nucleus of a cell?

To make Charlotte, her mother made an **egg** and her father made a **sperm**. Eggs and sperm have half the number of chromosomes each.

The **fertilised** egg has the correct number of chromosomes. Charlotte has a mixture of her mother's and father's characteristics.

Clones

Scientists have found a way of making copies of living things without using sexual reproduction.

This is called **cloning**. In a clone all the genes come from only one parent. The clones look exactly like the parent. Plants and animals can be cloned.

It is easy to make a clone of a plant by taking a **cutting**.

- The shoot of a geranium plant is cut off.
- The shoot is then dipped in a special rooting powder and planted.

FIGURE 5: Will this geranium cutting grow to look exactly like its parent?

You will find out:

- about numbers of chromosomes
- how genes control who you are
- about clones

WOW FACTOR!

- Dolly the sheep was the first cloned mammal. She was born in 1996.
- Cc was the first cloned cat. She was born in December 2001.
- Snuppy was the first cloned dog, born in April 2005.

You can find out more about Cc at:

www.accessexcellence.org/ WN/SU/copycat.html

QUESTIONS

11 How many chromosomes are there in Charlotte's body cells?

12 Do eggs and sperm have half or double the full number of chromosomes?

13 How many parents does the cloned geranium have?

...clone ...cutting ...egg ...enzyme

Chromosome numbers

The number of chromosomes in a cell is usually an even number. This is because the paired chromosomes separate when eggs and sperm are formed.

- The camel has 70 chromosomes in each body cell.

- The squirrel has 40 chromosomes in each body cell.

- The mosquito has six chromosomes in each body cell.

Humans have 46 chromosomes, arranged in 23 pairs, in each cell.

Eggs and sperm (**gametes**) have only one chromosome from each pair. They combine to make a fertilised egg that has 46 chromosomes.

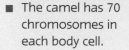
The number of chromosomes in a cell is usually an even number.

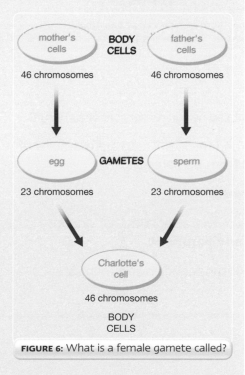

mother's cells — **BODY CELLS** — father's cells

46 chromosomes — 46 chromosomes

egg — **GAMETES** — sperm

23 chromosomes — 23 chromosomes

Charlotte's cell

46 chromosomes

BODY CELLS

FIGURE 6: What is a female gamete called?

How DNA controls characteristics

Calvin reminds his class of a cake recipe. Once the ingredients are mixed, reactions take place to produce the finished cake.

DNA contains codes for the production of specific **enzymes**. These in turn control cell reactions that produce specific chemicals, such as coloured eye pigments.

So DNA controls whether you have blue, brown or green eyes.

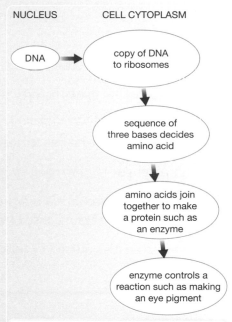

NUCLEUS — CELL CYTOPLASM

DNA → copy of DNA to ribosomes

sequence of three bases decides amino acid

amino acids join together to make a protein such as an enzyme

enzyme controls a reaction such as making an eye pigment

FIGURE 7: How many bases code for one amino acid?

QUESTIONS

16 Explain the importance of enzymes in controlling characteristics.

17 Enzymes are proteins. Suggest why this is important in explaining how genes work.

QUESTIONS

14 Explain why body cells of organisms usually have an even number of chromosomes.

15 Does a sperm contain a quarter, a half, three-quarters or all of the information to make a baby?

Who am I?

You will find out:

- about inherited characteristics
- about characteristics that are caused by the environment
- what makes a boy or a girl
- about mutations

The human blueprint

The Human Genome Project to identify all of the 30 000 human genes was finished in June 2000. The sites of many faulty genes are now known.

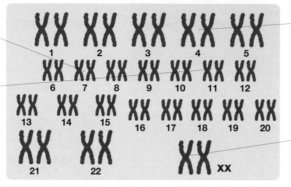

chromosome 7, causes excess mucus production (cystic fibrosis)

chromosome 4, causes on-going nerve damage (Huntington's disease)

chromosome 11, causes abnormal haemoglobin (sickle-cell anaemia)

chromosome X, causes lack of blood clotting factor (haemophilia)

Paired chromosomes. Chromosomes carry genes. Each chromosome pair is labelled with a number, except for the sex chromosomes that make a female or a male. These are labelled 'XX' in a female and 'XY' in a male.

Darren's characteristics

Calvin is a teacher. He draws his new students so he can remember their names.

This is Darren. He has red hair, blue eyes and freckles. These are examples of **characteristics** that he has **inherited** from his parents.

Each characteristic is controlled by his **genes**.

His scar and decayed tooth are examples of characteristics that are not inherited. They have been caused by his **environment**.

Other characteristics caused by both inheritance and environment are:

- height
- intelligence
- body mass.

People are not all the same

Human beings show **variation**.

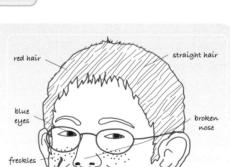

red hair · straight hair · blue eyes · broken nose · freckles · scar · ear without lobe · decayed tooth · large front teeth · rounded chin

FIGURE 1: Can you suggest another characteristic that Darren has on his face that is inherited?

FIGURE 2: What is meant by 'variation'?

:: QUESTIONS ::

1. Look at the picture of Darren. Write down **four** of his characteristics that are inherited.
2. What controls these characteristics?
3. Write down **three** of Darren's characteristics that are caused by his environment.

Sugar and spice and all things nice?

This is what little girls are supposed to be made of!

In the human population there are nearly the same number of males as there are females. Why is this?

All humans have 46 chromosomes, arranged in pairs, in their body cells. One pair of chromosomes is called the **sex chromosomes**.

- In a female the X sex chromosomes in a pair are identical and are called **XX chromosomes**.

- In a male the Y sex chromosome is shorter than and shaped differently from the X sex chromosome. The male sex chromosomes are called **XY chromosomes.**

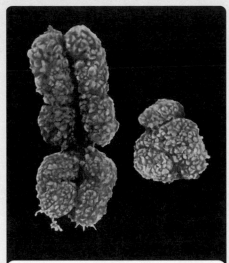

FIGURE 3: a X and **b** Y sex chromosomes magnified highly. How is the shape of the X chromosome different from that of the Y chromosome?

All the students in Calvin's class are unique. Even siblings in the school are not identical.

This is called variation. Variation is caused by:

- genes being mixed up in gametes
- genes coming from two parents (fertilisation)
- changes in genes or chromosomes called **mutations**.

There is a gene mutation that causes haemophilia. Blood does not clot so any wound can be fatal. This condition is inherited.

Not all gene mutations are harmful. In sickle-cell anaemia the red blood cells are the shape of a sickle and cannot carry oxygen as well as normal red blood cells. The malarial parasite cannot live so effectively in these damaged red blood cells and so people with sickle-cell anaemia are protected against malaria. This is a benefit from a mutation.

Mutations can occur spontaneously or be caused by:

- radiation
- chemicals such as mustard gas.

DID YOU KNOW?

Queen Victoria carried a mutant gene for haemophilia.

One of her sons, Leopold, was a haemophiliac and two of her daughters carried the mutant gene.

One daughter, Alice, married into the Russian royal family. This resulted in the famous haemophiliac, Alexis the last Tsarevitch (King).

A monk called Rasputin was supposed to have special powers to control Alexis' condition.

Male or female?

Each egg carries one type of sex chromosome (X). Each sperm carries an X or a Y sex chromosome.

There is always a random chance of which sperm fertilises an egg. During fertilisation the sex chromosomes mix.

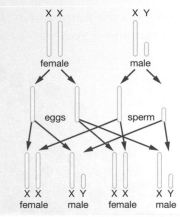

FIGURE 4: There should be equal numbers of males and females in the human population.

Nature versus nurture?

There is an on-going debate over the balance between genetic (nature) and environmental (nurture) factors in determining human attributes such as intelligence, sporting ability and health.

Could you produce an Olympic champion by long-term extensive training? Or is the ability controlled only by genes?

Scientists are discovering more about genes and how they work by studying twins. The Twin Research Unit now believes that inheritance plays a part in short-sightedness, osteoarthritis, acne and migraines.

The problem with mutations

A gene mutant causes a change in the **base sequence** in DNA. A change in the base sequence can prevent the normal protein from being made and change the structure of the protein made.

QUESTIONS

4 Will Darren's sex chromosomes be XX or XY?

5 What will Darren's sister's sex chromosomes be?

6 What is a mutation?

QUESTIONS

7 Suggest reasons why there are slightly fewer men in the world.

8 Suggest why twins are useful to study in genetic research.

Eye tests at school

Students in Calvin's class have their eyes tested.

■ They read letters from a chart to check how good their eyesight is.

■ Their colour vision is also tested. It is important to find out if they have red-green colour blindness. This would give them problems in recognising some colours.

If you see only the number 4 in the picture, you are 'green blind'. If you see only the number 2, you are 'red blind'.

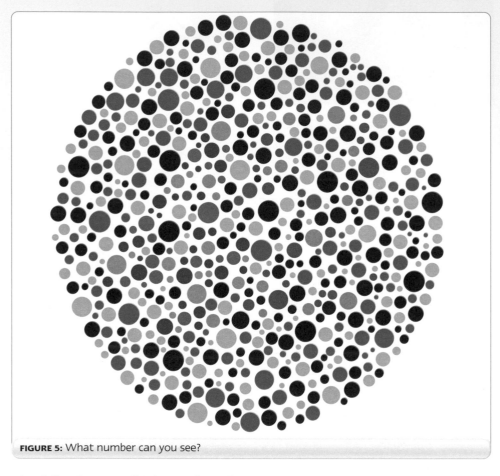

FIGURE 5: What number can you see?

The following are all inherited conditions:

■ red-green colour blindness

■ cystic fibrosis

■ sickle-cell anaemia

■ haemophilia.

Gender is an inherited characteristic.

QUESTIONS

9 Write down **three** inherited human conditions.

10 Suggest why it is important to know if you have red-green colour blindness. (Clues: riding a bicycle, choosing clothes, being an electrician.)

...allele ...base sequence ...cross-pollinate ...dominant ...generation ...genetic cross

Dominant and recessive characteristics

Calvin notices that some students have lobes to their ears and some have no lobes. This pair of characteristics is inherited.

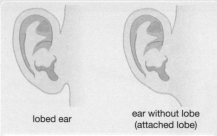

lobed ear

ear without lobe (attached lobe)

FIGURE 6: Why are there more students with lobed ears?

He finds out that there are more students with lobed ears than students without lobes. This means that lobed ears is a **dominant** characteristic over no lobes. No lobes (or attached lobes) is a **recessive** characteristic.

Other examples of dominant characteristics in humans are:

- ability to curl the tongue into a tube
- ability to taste a chemical called PTC
- a curved little finger.

Breeding tomato plants

Calvin's class does breeding experiments with two types of tomato plants. One type has only genetic information on green stems, another type has only genetic information on purple stems.

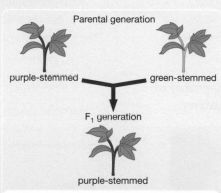

Parental generation

purple-stemmed   green-stemmed

F_1 generation

purple-stemmed

FIGURE 7: Breeding green- and purple-stemmed tomato plants.

The two plant types are grown to adulthood and **cross-pollinated** so that the male pollen and the female ovules (eggs) from both types are mixed. The seeds are collected and grown to form the next **generation.**

This generation (called the F_1) has purple stems. Purple stems are dominant over green stems.

QUESTIONS

11 Write down **three** dominant human characteristics.

12 What does cross-pollinated mean?

13 Suggest what colour stems the second (F_2) generation of tomato plants will have in the experiment.

A monohybrid cross

A **monohybrid cross** involves only one pair of characteristics. These are carried on a pair of chromosomes, one chromosome carrying the dominant **allele**, the other chromosome carrying the recessive allele. Alleles are different versions of the same gene.

Darren has no ear lobes. Symbols are used to work out the **genetic cross**.

Darren's mother   E e   **heterozygous**, lobes

Darren's father   E e   heterozygous, lobes

possible combinations of egg and sperm

mother (egg)

	E	e
E	EE	Ee
e	Ee	ee

father (sperm)

Darren is **homozygous**, no lobes

offspring

FIGURE 8: A genetic diagram.

Cystic fibrosis

Darren has cystic fibrosis, an inherited condition. He has difficulty in breathing because his body produces too much mucus, which collects in his lungs. It is a recessive characteristic.

When both healthy parents are heterozygous for the condition (they are Cc) there is a one in four chance of their baby being born with cystic fibrosis (cc).

Darren will have important decisions to make in later life.

- Will he accept the risk of passing cystic fibrosis to his children?
- Should he rely on new technology to select an embryo that does not carry the condition?

QUESTIONS

14 Using a genetic diagram work out the possible combinations if Darren's parents were Ee and EE in the ear lobes cross above.

15 Could parents with gene combinations of CC and Cc produce a baby with cystic fibrosis?

Module summary

Concept map

Blood is put under pressure by the heart. Blood pressure has two readings, diastolic and systolic pressure.

High blood pressure can damage the brain and kidneys.

Exercise keeps us fit

Our energy comes from aerobic respiration or anaerobic respiration.

A balanced diet should contain carbohydrates, proteins, fats, minerals and vitamins.

Feedback mechanisms help to maintain a constant internal environment.

Hormones, sense organs and reflexes keep us safe

Neurones carry electrical impulses.

A body temperature of 37 °C is the optimum temperature for enzymes.

Insulin controls blood sugar level.

Endocrine glands produce hormones, such as insulin and sex hormones.

Drugs can be harmful or keep us healthy

Fungi, bacteria, viruses and protozoa can cause disease.

Harmful drugs are classified as Class A, B or C.

Infectious diseases are easily passed on. Our immune system and immunisation protect us against infections.

All new drugs must be tested in trials.

Tobacco and alcohol are called 'social drugs'.

Genes make up chromosomes. Genes control protein production, such as enzymes.

Genes are us

Some human characteristics are inherited. Others are caused by the environment.

Genes are made up of a chemical called DNA. It is the sequence of bases in the DNA (the genetic code) that provides the information needed to make a specific protein.

Inherited disorders are caused by faulty genes.

Module quiz

1   A diet of carbohydrates, fats, vitamins, minerals, fibre and water isn't balanced. What needs to be added to make it a balanced diet?

2   Which **two** measurements are needed to calculate your BMI?

3   Write down the word equation for aerobic respiration.

4   Why is binocular vision important to us?

5   How does an impulse cross a synapse?

6   What do endocrine organs produce?

7   What conditions need to be controlled to keep a constant internal environment?

8   What is a pathogen?

9   Which vector carries malaria?

10 Which chemical in cigarette smoke is addictive?

11 How many chromosomes do we have:
    a in our body cells?   **b** in our gametes?

12 Name **three** inherited genetic disorders.

Numeracy activity

A new drug to treat arthritis has been tested by a large group of volunteers. All of the volunteers suffer from painful arthritis. Some of the volunteers were given the new drug. Others were given a salt solution. The volunteers did not know which treatment they were receiving.

Treatment	Level of pain relief each hour after treatment							
	1	2	3	4	5	6	7	8
new drug	4	6	5	4	2	2	2	1
salt solution	3	2	2	1	1	1	1	1

The volunteers were asked to estimate the level of pain relief, on a scale of 1 to 6, where level 1 means they feel no pain relief and level 6 means their pain has completely gone. They recorded their estimates every hour for 8 hours.

The results are shown in the table.

QUESTIONS

1   Was the new drug a successful treatment? Explain your answer.

2   How long did the pain relief last for:

    a   the new drug?   b   the salt solution?

3   How long did it take for the new drug to have maximum effect? Suggest why there was a time delay.

4   Why were some volunteers given a salt solution instead of the new drug?

5   Why were a large number of people used in the trials?

6   The new drug is thought to target synapses.

    a   Where are synapses?

    b   What happens in them?

Exam practice

Exam practice questions

1 The table shows the daily requirements for energy and protein for males and females of different ages. For each of these groups, the average body mass is also shown.

Male			
Age	Body mass (kg)	Daily energy requirement (kcal)	Daily protein requirement (g)
11-14	45	2500	45
15-18	66	3000	59
19-24	72	2900	58
25-50	79	2900	63
51+	77	2300	63

Female			
Age	Body mass (kg)	Daily energy requirement (kcal)	Daily protein requirement (g)
11-14	46	2200	46
15-18	55	2200	44
19-24	58	2200	46
25-50	63	2200	50
51+	65	1900	50

a For the age group 11-14, compare male and female daily requirements for:

   i energy. [1]

   ii protein. [1]

b **i** What is the relationship between age and daily energy requirement? [2]

   ii Explain your answer to the previous question. [2]

[Total 6 marks]

2 Copy and complete the following paragraph about the body's defence against disease-causing organisms using these words.

antibodies   **cells**   **antigens**
immunity   **engulfs**   **chemical**

Disease-causing organisms are called pathogens. These have proteins, called .... on their outer surface. If pathogens enter a human's body, they are destroyed, using white blood .... One type of white blood cell surrounds and .... the invading pathogens. Another type of white blood cell produces ....,

which attack the proteins of the pathogens. The body often 'remembers' how it has previously made a particular .... to attack the pathogens. This 'memory' allows the body to attack pathogens more quickly next time. This 'memory' is called .... [4]

[Total 4 marks]

3 The diagrams show the appearance of the front of the eye.

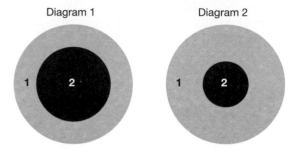

Diagram 1   Diagram 2

a Identify the numbered parts of the eye. [2]

b **i** Which of the diagrams shows the eye in dim light? [1]

   ii Explain your answer to the previous question. [2]

[Total 5 marks]

4 The table shows the proportion in each group who are smokers.

	Group	% of group who smoke
Adults	Male	25.2
	Female	20.0
Children	11-18 years	25.5
	5-10 years	10.5
Pregnant females		13.0

a Which group contains a larger proportion of smokers:

   i males or females? [1]

   ii young children or older children? [1]

   iii pregnant females or children aged 5-10 years? [1]

b Calculate the proportion of:

   i females who do not smoke. [1]

   ii children aged 5-10 years who smoke. [1]

[Total 5 marks]

This family tree ('pedigree chart') shows the inheritance of a dominant allele, T. Individuals who have this allele are 'tasters' (because they can taste certain chemicals).

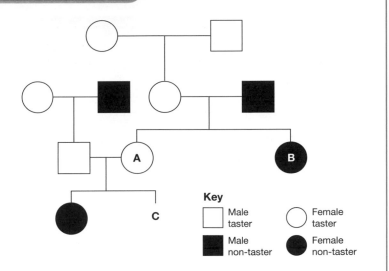

Key
- □ Male taster
- ○ Female taster
- ■ Male non-taster
- ● Female non-taster

a Copy and complete the following table using information from the pedigree chart.

Genotype	TT	Tt	
Phenotype	Taster		Non-taster

[2]

b What are the genotypes of female A and female B? [2]

c What is the chance that child C will be a taster? Show the possible genotypes. [2]

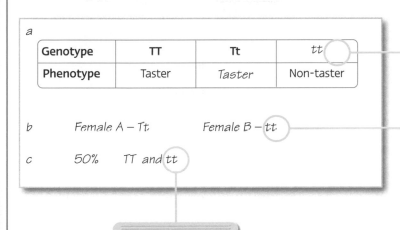

a

Genotype	TT	Tt	tt
Phenotype	Taster	Taster	Non-taster

b   Female A – Tt   Female B – tt

c   50%   TT and tt

Both answers are correct. You should be able to work out phenotypes from genotypes, or genotypes from phenotypes.

Both answers are correct. You can use the key to answer this question.

This is not correct. Child C's parents' genotypes are both Tt. The possible genotypes of their children are TT, Tt, Tt and tt. The ratio of tasters is 3:1, or 75%.

Overall Grade: C

How to get an A

Reading pedigree charts can be tricky, so make sure you give yourself plenty of practice before the exam. A fun way to practise is to work out your own family's genotypes based on eye and hair colour.

B2 Understanding our environment

To be a successful predator, an animal needs to have:

- sharp teeth and claws
- camouflage to make it hard to see
- a body built for speed
- eyes to the front of the head, to help judge distances.

Our environment is full of a huge variety of living things. We need to understand how they interact with each other and with us. By doing this we can protect all living things and their habitats for future generations.

Cheetahs are the fastest mammal on Earth. They can reach speeds of 112 kilometres per hour, but can only run for short periods.

Gazelles cannot run as fast as Cheetahs, but they can turn quickly and run for a long time. This makes them difficult to catch.

Ecology in our school grounds

You will find out:
- about ecosystems
- that some ecosystems are still unexplored
- about controlling artificial ecosystems

How many lions are there in Africa?

How many lions do you think there are in Africa?

Twenty-five years ago there were thought to be about 100 000 lions and now there are probably more like 30 000. This is only an estimate as it would be very difficult to catch and count every one.

What are ecosystems?

A garden is an example of an **ecosystem**.

All the living things in the garden and their surroundings make up the ecosystem.

All the animals and plants living in the garden make up the **community**.

Like all communities, the members of the community affect each other's lives. Flowers provide nectar for the bees to eat and bees carry pollen from one flower to the next.

Where an animal lives is called its **habitat**. In the garden, the worm's habitat is the soil.

Ecosystems can be **natural** such as a lake, or **artificial** such as an aquarium.

FIGURE 1: What is the difference between a natural ecosystem and an artificial ecosystem?

 An ecosystem describes living things and their environment.

A habitat describes the place where the living things live.

▪ QUESTIONS ▪

1 Copy the list of words and write the correct description beside each one.

Word	Description
community	a place where animals and plants live
habitat	a group of living things and their environment
ecosystem	all the animals and plants in an ecosystem

2 Name **three** animals that live in a woodland ecosystem.

...*artificial* ...*biodiversity* ...*community* ...*ecosystem* ...*fertiliser*

Ocean ecosystems

We know more about the surface of the Moon than we do about the deepest oceans.

Animals from the deep cannot live near the surface; they are rarely seen. In 1938 a coelacanth fish was caught off the East Coast of South Africa. This dinosaur fish was thought to have been extinct for millions of years! It is now known to live 700 m below sea level, making its capture an extremely rare event.

Another example is the giant squid. This can grow up to 20 m long but has never been found alive near the surface. It is thought that the squid can only take in oxygen from cold water. When it gets to the warmer surface water it suffocates.

FIGURE 2: a Coelacanth fish. **b** Giant squid. What other ecosystems are difficult to explore?

To see these animals in their natural habitat requires very expensive submarines. A human would be crushed due to the increased pressure at such depths.

QUESTIONS

3 There are still new species to discover in the world. Where would you expect to find these new species?

4 Give **two** reasons why it is difficult to find animals at the bottom of the ocean.

5 What problems might an animal living at the bottom of the ocean face?

Artificial ecosystems

Oceans are natural ecosystems; they exist without any help from humans.

There are many artificial ecosystems controlled by humans.

A field of wheat is mainly artificial. Farmers try to control what grows and lives there.

- They use **herbicides** to remove weeds.
- They use **pesticides** to control pests.
- They can increase the crop yield by adding **fertilisers**.

Biodiversity describes the range of living things, both plants and animals, in an ecosystem. When the farmer uses herbicides and pesticides he decreases the biodiversity of his farm.

FIGURE 3: Do the control methods used by the farmer increase or decrease the biodiversity of the farm?

QUESTIONS

6 Why are wheat fields artificial ecosystems?

7 Describe how you would control an ecosystem such as a greenhouse. Include ways you could control both living and non-living factors.

Collecting living things

Sam wanted to find out what animals lived on the school field. He and his classmates tried to catch the animals using:

- **pooters**
- nets
- **pitfall traps.**

He identified the animals using a key.

FIGURE 4: Animals must be handled carefully and released back into their habitat at the end of the experiment.

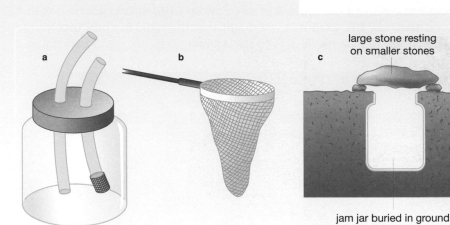

large stone resting on smaller stones

jam jar buried in ground

FIGURE 5: **a** Pooter. **b** Net. **c** Pitfall trap.

These are the animals that Sam and his classmates found.

He identified the animals using a **key.**

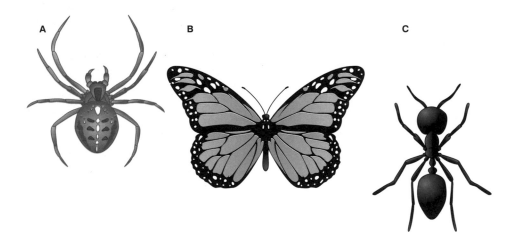

A   B   C

Does it have six legs?

yes → no

Does it have coloured wings?   Does it have eight legs?

yes → no   yes → no

butterfly   ant   spider   centipede

FIGURE 6: A simple key.

To find out which plants were growing, Sam used a square frame called a **quadrat**. He threw the quadrat over his shoulder and counted how many of each type of plant was inside it.

FIGURE 7: What did Sam do to make sure his sample was random?

QUESTIONS

8   Use the key to identify the **three** animals Sam caught.
9   Which of Sam's catching methods do you think caught the butterfly?
10 Ants crawl along the ground. Which method do you think Sam used to catch the ant?

...*estimate* ...*key* ...*pitfall trap*

Counting animals

Counting one type of animal in a habitat is difficult, as they do not stand still. To **estimate** a species **population** scientists can use a method called 'mark and recapture'.

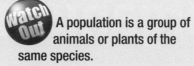 A population is a group of animals or plants of the same species.

A community is lots of different species living in the same ecosystem.

- The animals are trapped and marked in some harmless way.
- They are then released and the traps are set again a few days later.

FIGURE 8: Why is this moth trap hanging above the ground?

To estimate a population the following formula is used.

$$\frac{\text{number of animals caught first time} \times \text{number of animals caught second time}}{\text{number of marked animals caught second time}} = \text{population}$$

This can only be an estimate as not all the animals are counted.

Population sizes are always changing because:

- animals are being born and others are dying
- there is movement of animals in and out of an ecosystem.

To increase the accuracy of an estimate: the process is repeated several times and the sample size is as large as possible.

Counting plants

To estimate a plant population scientists can use quadrats.

- The quadrat is put on the ground and the percentage cover of each plant is recorded.
- The quadrat is placed in a random way to ensure a fair representation of an area.

This can be achieved by dividing the habitat into squares and using pairs of numbers as coordinates. For example, if the numbers were six and three, you would start from a point and count six squares along and three across.

To increase the accuracy of an estimate the process is repeated several times and the sample size is as large as possible.

Scientists have to remember that their samples may be unrepresentative of the population as a whole.

QUESTIONS

11 Scientists want to know the number of moths living in a wood. They set traps and catch 200 moths. They mark the moths' under-wings with a harmless spot of red paint and release them. Two days later they set the traps again and catch 150 moths. Fifty of them have paint on their under-wing.

a Suggest why the paint is not put on the upper surface of the wing.

b Estimate the population of moths.

12 Suggest **two** ways in which a population may increase overnight.

13 Explain the difference between a population and a community.

QUESTIONS

14 When estimating the population of plants in a habitat, suggest why it is unreliable to place just one quadrat.

15 a Describe how numbers are used to place a quadrat in a random way.

b Suggest why it is important to place quadrats in a random way rather than choose an area.

Grouping organisms

You will find out:

- how to classify animals and plants into different groups
- about the characteristics of the vertebrate groups

Which is the odd one out?

Three of them can fly. Which is the odd one out?

Three of them have feathers. Now which is the odd one out?

You can see that how you group things depends on the characteristics you select.

Scientists put living **organisms** into groups because they are similar in some way. They put birds into a group because they all have feathers and a beak. Grouping organisms is called **classification**.

The plant and animal kingdoms

Organisms can be sorted into the **plant kingdom** and the **animal kingdom**.

We are part of the animal kingdom. Some other animals we share the animal kingdom with are the lion, tiger and fish.

The animal kingdom is split into two groups called **vertebrates** and **invertebrates**.

Vertebrates are animals that normally have a backbone. All the vertebrates in the world can be put into one of five groups.

Invertebrates are animals without a backbone. Some of the invertebrate groups are shown in Figure 1.

FIGURE 1: How do scientists sort living organisms into groups?

■ QUESTIONS ■

1. Sort the following living organisms into an animal group or a plant group.
   tulip   wasp   caterpillar   mouse   oak tree
2. Name the **five** vertebrate groups.
3. Give **two** examples from each of the vertebrate groups.

...amphibian   ...animal kingdom   ...bird   ...classification   ...fish   ...fungi   ...insect

Animal or plant?

	Food	Shape	Movement
plants	make their own food using chloroplasts to trap energy from the Sun	spread out to collect plenty of water and nutrients from soil	stay in one place, they cannot get up and move somewhere else
animals	cannot make their own food, so they need to eat	more compact than plants to help them move around	able to move around to find food

There are more than 1.5 million animal species in the world. There are fewer vertebrates than invertebrates.

Vertebrates

New animals are discovered all the time. In 2000, a Dutch zoologist named Marc Von Roosmalen found a new monkey in the Amazonian rainforest in Brazil. He called it the Manicore Marmoset, named after the Manicore river close to where he discovered the monkey. This new monkey is just one of many different types in the world.

FIGURE 2: A Manicore Marmoset. What characteristics do all mammals have?

Monkeys belong to a very large group of vertebrates called **mammals**. All mammals:

■ have fur

■ produce milk for their young.

The other vertebrate groups have different characteristics.

■ **Reptiles** have dry scaly skin.

■ **Amphibians** have a moist permeable skin, which means they can absorb oxygen through their skin when they are in water. On land they use lungs to extract oxygen from the air.

■ **Birds** all have feathers and beaks but not all of them can fly.

■ **Fish** have wet scales and gills to absorb oxygen from the water.

Invertebrates

There are more than one million invertebrates. The **insect** group makes up the majority of the invertebrates. To classify as an insect an animal needs to have six legs and a body divided into three parts: the head, thorax and abdomen.

▒▒▒▒ QUESTIONS ▒▒▒▒

4 Describe **two** characteristics of plants.

5 Describe **two** characteristics of animals.

6 Copy the vertebrate groups below and write the correct description next to each one.

Vertebrate group	Description
mammal	has dry scaly skin
reptile	has feathers and a beak
amphibian	has fur and feeds young on milk
fish	has moist permeable skin
bird	has scales and gills

Odd ones out!

Some organisms just do not fit into the animal kingdom or plant kingdom.

Fungi

Mushrooms cannot move like an animal and they cannot make food like a plant. They, together with toadstools, have their own kingdom called **fungi**.

Protoctista

Euglena are single-celled organisms. Like plants, they make their own food using light energy. However, like animals, they can survive in the dark if they are given food. They belong in the kingdom called protoctista.

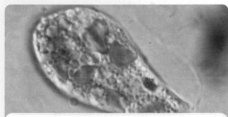

FIGURE 3: In what ways is Euglena like a plant and like an animal?

Reptile or bird?

In the mid-19th Century a fossil was found showing an animal with a jaw like a reptile and the feathers of a bird. It was called Archaeopteryx.

This creature is thought to represent the evolutionary link between reptiles and birds.

FIGURE 4: How is Archaeopteryx like a reptile and how is it like a bird?

▒▒▒▒ QUESTIONS ▒▒▒▒

7 Discuss the problems of classification of organisms such as Euglena.

8 What problems might scientists encounter when classifying new species?

...invertebrate ...mammal ...organism ...plant kingdom ...reptile ...vertebrate

Dogs and cats

Dogs and cats can both be kept as pets. They also have other characteristics in common:

- they eat meat
- they have fur
- they give birth to live young.

Dogs and cats are in the same group, the mammals, because they share these characteristics.

But dogs and cats are also very different. They are different **species.**

All the dogs we keep as pets belong to the same species. But they can look very different. This is because humans have bred lots of different types of dogs.

WOW FACTOR!

There are more than 1000 different breeds of dogs in the world.

FIGURE 5: How have humans made lots of different types of the dog species?

The dogs in the picture are very different, but they belong to the same species. They all:

- have fur
- eat meat
- have sharp claws and teeth
- can mate and give birth to a litter of puppies.

WANT TO KNOW MORE?

Find out more about dog breeds from:

www.the-kennel-club.org.uk

QUESTIONS

9 Describe **two** characteristics shared by cats and dogs.

10 Look at the pictures of the labrador and the poodle. Describe **one** way in which they look different.

...breed ...family ...fertile ...hybrid

What is a species?

A tiger and a lion are both cats. However, they are two different species. Lions look different from tigers; the most obvious difference being their lack of stripes.

Members of the same species can **breed**. Lions breed with other lions to make young lions. These young lions will be **fertile**. This means they can grow up and have young of their own.

Members of different species cannot naturally breed together. A lion will not naturally breed with a tiger.

However, scientists have artificially mated a lion with a tiger to produce a tigon. The tigon is **sterile**. This means that it cannot **reproduce**.

tiger   lion   tigon

FIGURE 6: Will the tigon be able to have young?

All cats belong to the same **family**. The family is called *Felidea*. Each species of cat is given its own scientific name. Lions have the name *Panthera leo*. Tigers are called *Panthera tigris*. They both have the same first name, which means they are closely related. This close relationship is the reason why scientists can breed from them.

The lion and the tiger share a recent ancestor but have evolved to live in different habitats. Lions live in open grassland while tigers prefer forest.

Their different coat patterns are part of their adaptation to their habitats, and act as camouflage. This means they blend in with their surroundings, making them difficult to see. Because of this, they are able to surprise their prey during a hunt.

WOW FACTOR!

What do you get if you cross a zebra with a horse? A zorse.

What do you get if you cross a zebra with a donkey? A zonkey.

It may sound like a joke, but these animals can exist.

Zorses and zonkeys are not classed as species because they cannot reproduce.

QUESTIONS

11 Explain why a lion and a tiger are different species.

12 Suggest **one** reason for the different coat patterns of a lion and a tiger.

More odd ones out!

Dolphins and whales

Dolphins and whales are special animals. They have many of the characteristics of mammals, yet they look and live like fish such as sharks.

Their ancestors lived on land, but gradually evolved to live in the sea. However, they are still classed as mammals because they give birth to live young and produce milk to feed them.

Mules

Hybrids are the result of breeding two animals from different species, such as the tiger and the lion to produce a tigon.

One of the first successful hybrids was produced from a male donkey and a female horse. This produced a mule. It was bred to provide a strong powerful animal.

FIGURE 7: How is a mule useful to man?

However, because hybrids cannot breed (they are sterile), a mule is not a species and therefore is difficult to classify.

QUESTIONS

13 Explain what is meant by the term hybrid.

14 Discuss the problems of classifying hybrids.

15 Would you expect dolphins to have lungs or gills? Give reasons for your answer.

The food factory

You will find out:
- how plants make food using photosynthesis
- what plants need for photosynthesis
- how plants use the products of photosynthesis

Killer trees

One of the most dangerous trees in the world grows in the Caribbean. It is called the Manchineel tree. It looks like an apple tree but its small green fruit can kill.

Contact with the sap causes an eruption of blisters and can cause blindness if it gets into the eyes. The sap was used by the Carib Indians to poison their arrow tips for hunting.

However, like all trees, the Manchineel tree does a useful job, it photosynthesises.

The Manchineel tree.

WOW FACTOR!

The largest carrot ever grown weighed a whopping 8.61 kg.

That's about the weight of a cat!

Plants and photosynthesis

Ben likes to grow carrots to enter in the local garden show. He knows that to grow well his carrots need to carry out lots of **photosynthesis**.

Photosynthesis means using light (*photo-*) to make food (*-synthesis*).

The carrots' leaves carry out photosynthesis using light energy from the Sun.

How do leaves carry out photosynthesis?

Leaves contain **chlorophyll** which is a green-coloured substance. The green leaves use the chlorophyll to trap **light**. They use the light energy to turn **carbon dioxide** and **water** into **glucose**. This is photosynthesis.

The glucose is then used for **energy** for the plant to grow, or it can be stored. To store the glucose it has to be turned into **starch**. Bens' carrots store the starch in their large orange roots.

A plant also makes **oxygen** during photosynthesis. This oxygen is very important to both plants and animals. They need it for **respiration**.

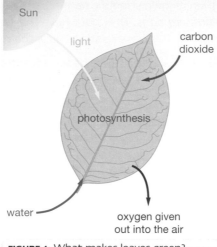
FIGURE 1: What makes leaves green?

□ QUESTIONS □

1   Copy and complete the following sentence.
    Plants need c _ _ _ _ _ dioxide, l _ _ _ _ and w _ _ _ _ for photosynthesis.
2   Name the **two** things plants make during photosynthesis.
3   What do plants do to glucose before they store it?

...carbon dioxide   ...cellulose   ...chlorophyll   ...energy   ...fat   ...glucose   ...insoluble

Products of photosynthesis

Photosynthesis can be described using the following word equation:

carbon dioxide + water $\xrightarrow[\text{(chlorophyll)}]{\text{(light energy)}}$ glucose + oxygen

The products of photosynthesis are glucose and oxygen.

The glucose can be used by the plant to make energy. To release the energy, glucose reacts with the oxygen in respiration.

Other uses of oxygen and glucose

Not all of the oxygen and glucose is used up in respiration. A lot of the oxygen is released into the air for use by animals.

- Glucose is **soluble** so it can be dissolved in water and transported to parts of the plant where it is needed.
- Glucose can be converted into starch for storage. Starch stores better than glucose because it is **insoluble**.
- When a plant grows it needs to turn glucose into **cellulose** to make new cell walls.
- During growth or repair of cells the plant will need to convert the glucose into **proteins**.
- **Fats** and **oils** can also be made from glucose. These are then stored for future use. This is how we get vegetable oil, used for cooking.

FIGURE 2: Harvesting olives.

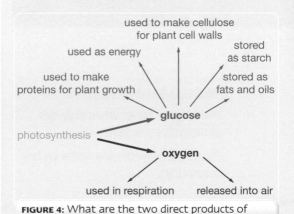
FIGURE 4: What are the two direct products of photosynthesis?

FIGURE 3: Olive oil. What do plants make oils from?

Balancing the photosynthesis equation

The chemical symbol for glucose is $C_6H_{12}O_6$.

Therefore the overall balanced chemical equation for photosynthesis is:

$6CO_2 + 6H_2O \xrightarrow[\text{(chlorophyll)}]{\text{(light energy)}} C_6H_{12}O_6 + 6O_2$

Glucose ($C_6H_{12}O_6$) is a small, soluble molecule unsuitable for storage. This is because it could easily dissolve and be lost from the cell. If it does dissolve it increases the strength of the fluid in the cell, which could damage the cell.

For storage, the glucose joins together to make larger molecules of starch. Starch is:

- insoluble and therefore not easily lost from the cell in solution
- not very reactive making it a good storage molecule.

starch is insoluble and is made up of many glucose molecules joined together

glucose molecules are soluble

FIGURE 5: Starch is a large molecule and glucose is a small molecule.

4 Why can glucose be carried around the plant easily?
5 Why is starch stored rather than glucose?
6 Why does photosynthesis stop in the dark?
7 Apart from starch, name **three** substances that glucose can be converted to by plants.

8 Explain why being insoluble makes starch a better storage molecule than glucose.
9 Name the elements present in a molecule of starch.

You will find out:

- what factors increase the rate of photosynthesis
- when plants carry out respiration

Summer growth

Ben also grows peas in his garden.

He likes to harvest the peas in June, so he needs to plant the seeds in February.

February can be very cold so the pea seeds have to be covered by glass to keep them warm. Ben does not see much growth at first.

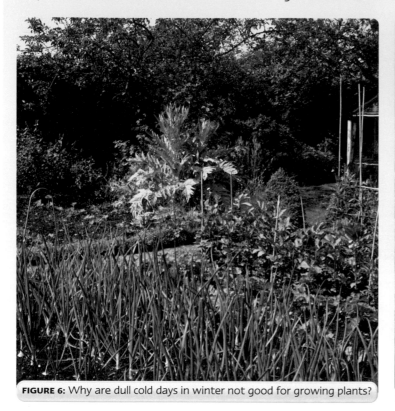

FIGURE 6: Why are dull cold days in winter not good for growing plants?

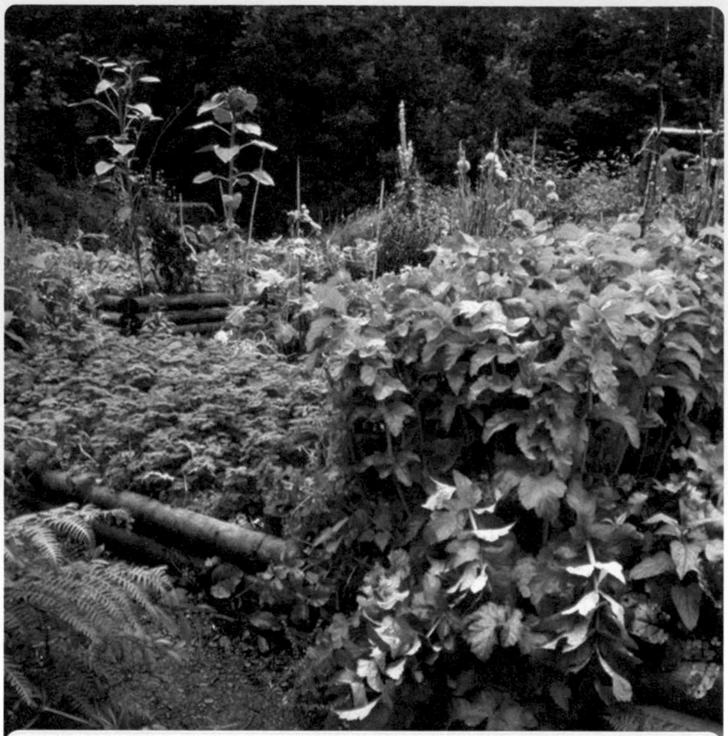

FIGURE 7: Why are bright warm days good for growing plants?

When spring and summer arrive the pea plants get more light for **photosynthesis**. The extra light and warmth help the peas grow faster, ready for picking in June.

EXAM HINTS AND TIPS

Plants grow faster when they can photosynthesise faster.

Plants photosynthesise faster on hot sunny days.

QUESTIONS

10 Give **two** reasons why plants grow faster in the spring and summer months.

11 Why do the pea plants need to be covered by glass during February?

Conditions that speed up photosynthesis

Ben has a greenhouse in his garden. Plants grow better in a greenhouse. This is because Ben is able to help the plants carry out photosynthesis better. The following actions increase the rate of photosynthesis:

- keeping the greenhouse warm
- providing the greenhouse with extra carbon dioxide
- increasing the amount of light in the greenhouse.

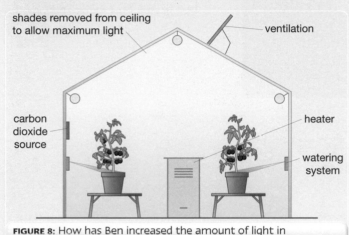

FIGURE 8: How has Ben increased the amount of light in his greenhouse?

Plants and respiration

Respiration uses oxygen to release energy from glucose. At the same time it releases carbon dioxide and water. This makes respiration the reverse of photosynthesis.

Unlike photosynthesis, respiration never stops because the plant needs the constant supply of energy it releases.

 Plants carry out respiration 24 hours a day, not just at night.

If they stopped respiring they would have no energy and die.

QUESTIONS

12 Paraffin burns to release carbon dioxide. Give **two** reasons why a paraffin heater would be useful in a greenhouse.

13 What would happen to a plant if it stopped carrying out respiration?

Factors that limit photosynthesis

Experiments can be done to find out what speeds up photosynthesis and what slows it down. Some results are shown in the graph.

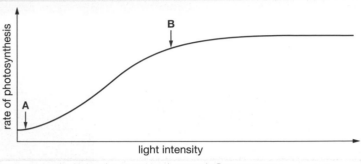

FIGURE 9: Why does the curve in the graph flatten out?

Scientists found that:

- the rate of photosynthesis increases as the light intensity increases until point B is reached
- at point B, the rate of photosynthesis stays the same, because something else is limiting it
- the limiting factor could be carbon dioxide level or temperature
- carbon dioxide, light intensity and temperature are all **limiting factors** of photosynthesis.

Gas exchange

As long as a plant is photosynthesising it needs to take in carbon dioxide through its leaves. At the same time it will release oxygen.

At night the plant still needs oxygen for respiration. It takes in oxygen from the air and releases carbon dioxide.

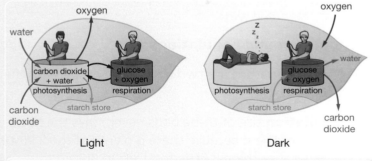

FIGURE 10: Why do plants not photosynthesise at night?

QUESTIONS

14 Name **three** factors that could limit photosynthesis.

15 Copy the graph showing the effect of light intensity on photosynthesis. Sketch a line to show the results you would expect if the experiment was repeated at a higher carbon dioxide level.

16 A plant produces carbon dioxide from respiration 24 hours a day. Explain why it only releases the carbon dioxide when it is dark.

Compete or die

You will find out:
- what animals and plants compete for
- how competition changes a population

Keeping a mate

Male elephant seals keep several females to mate with. They have to stop other males from trying to steal them.

They do this by fighting each other.

WOW FACTOR!

A male elephant seal can weigh 2700 kg.

That is about the same as 35 men.

What do animals and plants compete for?

Plants and animals **compete** to survive. If they do not, their species will die out.

Plants compete for:
- light for photosynthesis
- water and minerals
- space to grow.

Animals compete for:
- shelter from bad weather
- food and water
- a mate to breed with.

Competition and populations

Swallows and martins are two birds that compete for the same insect food.

The **population** size of these birds never stays the same. In summer, you will see lots of them because there is plenty of food. In winter, they must fly south because there is little food left in Britain.

FIGURE 1: House martins (top) and barn swallows (bottom) compete for the same food. Can you tell from their names where they build their nests so as not to compete for the same nest sites?

Plants and animals compete to survive. If they do not, their species will die out.

QUESTIONS

1. List **three** things a plant needs to compete for.
2. List **three** things an animal needs to compete for.
3. Why is it unusual to see a swallow during a British winter?

...compete ...competition ...ecological niche

Plant competition

If you go for a walk in a beech wood in spring, you will find lots of different plants growing. Yellow primroses and bluebells are two examples.

These plants grow and flower in spring to catch as much light as possible before the beech tree leaves are fully out. In summer the plants find it difficult to grow as the larger trees take most of the light, water and minerals. The plants and the beech trees are in **competition** with each other.

Animal competition

Bowerbirds live in Australia. The male bowerbird likes to collect brightly coloured objects. He then spends hours arranging them in his display area, called a bower.

He does this to attract a mate. Like other animals, his species will die out if its members do not breed. The bowerbird is competing with other males of his species.

The male with the best bower attracts the females first. Often a male will steal objects from another male when it is away from its bower.

Competition for food

Animals of different species often eat the same food. Lions and cheetahs live in the African grasslands and compete for similar prey. However, the smaller cheetah tends to keep to its own small area away from the lion, who would try to steal its food.

When cheetah cubs grow up they have to move away from their mother's territory so they are not competing with her for food. If they stayed, the population of the area would grow too large and there would not be enough food to go round.

FIGURE 2: What plants are in competition in this picture?

FIGURE 3: Why does the male bowerbird collect brightly coloured objects?

EXAM HINTS AND TIPS

If you are asked about animals or plants you have never heard of, don't be put off.

All animals and plants compete for similar things.

Ecological niches

All organisms have a role to play in an ecosystem. For example, the role of a squirrel is to live in woods and eat acorns. This role is called the squirrel's **ecological niche**.

Different species living in a **habitat** normally have a slightly different niche. This helps to reduce competition. Badgers also live in a wood but they feed on small animals not nuts.

Close competition

FIGURE 4: **a** Red squirrel. **b** Grey squirrel. What has happened to the size of the red squirrel population in recent years?

In Britain, there are two types of squirrel:

- the native red squirrel
- the American grey squirrel.

At one time they both occupied the same niche, but in different countries. Now they compete for the same niche in Britain. This has resulted in a decline in the numbers of red squirrels.

QUESTIONS

7 What do we mean by the term 'ecological niche'?

8 Explain why introducing the grey squirrel to Britain caused a fall in the red squirrel population.

QUESTIONS

4 Explain why bluebells grow before the trees in the wood are in leaf.

5 Describe **two** ways in which males of a species can compete for a mate.

6 Pandas are unusual animals because they only eat bamboo. Suggest **one** reason why a panda could not live in a beech wood.

Friend or foe?

In any habitat there are lots of different animals living together.

Some of these animals help each other out (friend). Other animals hunt another animal for food (foe).

Friends

An oxpecker is an African bird that feeds on insects.

The buffalo is a large mammal that feeds on grass.

The two animals are not in competition. Instead, they help each other out.

Oxpeckers sit on buffalo. They feed on the insects that live on the buffalo's skin. The oxpeckers help to clean the buffalo by getting rid of ticks and fleas. In return the oxpeckers get plenty of food. Both animals are happy.

Foes

A **food chain** shows who eats who. In this food chain the badger eats the shrew. The badger is called a **predator** and the shrew its **prey**. These two animals are foes.

FIGURE 5: The oxpecker is sometimes called a 'cleaner species'. Why?

Watch Out In a food chain the arrow points at the animal that is doing the eating.

lettuce ⟶ snail

The snail eats the lettuce. The lettuce does not eat the snail!

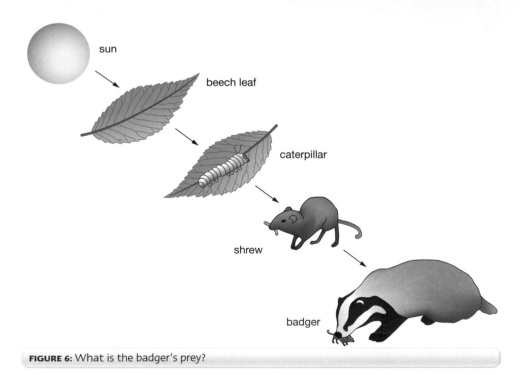

sun

beech leaf

caterpillar

shrew

badger

FIGURE 6: What is the badger's prey?

▥ QUESTIONS ▥

9   How is an oxpecker helpful to a buffalo?

10 Look at the following food chain.

    lettuce ⟶ snail ⟶ hedgehog ⟶ fox

    a Name a predator.

    b Name the fox's prey.

...cleaner species   ...cyclic fluctuation   ...food chain   ...host   ...legume   ...mutualism

Animal relationships

There are many ways in which animals of different species interact.

Predator–prey relationships

The badger is a predator. It hunts shrews as its prey. The number of shrews in a population will affect the number of badgers.

When there are more shrews, the badgers have more food so they can raise more young. This helps the badger population increase. The following year, the increased badger population eats more shrews so the shrew population decreases.

Parasites

The tapeworm is a **parasite**. It lives in the digestive system of other animals, including humans. The tapeworm takes food away from its **host** so it can grow.

The tapeworm is unlikely to kill its host as the tapeworm would also die. However, the host is likely to lose weight.

WOW FACTOR!

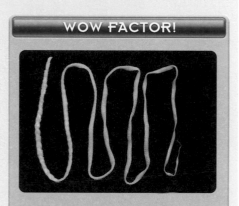

- Tapeworms were used by some 1930s Hollywood actresses as a 'slimming aid'.

  Not to be recommended!

- A tapeworm can grow to 5 m in length!

Cleaner species

The sharksucker is a fish that attaches itself to sharks. It cleans the shark's skin by eating its parasites. In return, the shark protects the sharksucker from predators. A relationship where both animals benefit is called **mutualism**.

QUESTIONS

11 Explain how a decrease in the shrew population results in a decrease in the badger population.

12 Fleas live on the skin of dogs and feed on their blood.
   a Explain how fleas benefit from dogs.
   b Suggest how fleas may harm dogs.
   c What type of relationship is this an example of?

13 Explain how the shark and the sharksucker benefit from their relationship.

More about relationships

Populations and cyclic fluctuation

Predator-prey relationships play an important part in controlling populations.

The lemming is a small hamster-like animal that lives in the Arctic. Its population size can decrease and increase dramatically.

In years when there is a lot of food lemmings reproduce rapidly. If the population grows too large, food becomes scarce and the female lemmings do not reproduce so rapidly.

The snowy owl hunts lemmings. In years when there is more lemming young, there is more prey and the owls successfully raise more young. The owl population increases, so the following year the lemming population decreases as there are more owls to hunt them.

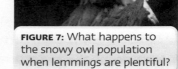

FIGURE 7: What happens to the snowy owl population when lemmings are plentiful?

This 'up and down' pattern or **cyclic fluctuation** can be shown on a graph. The numbers increase and decrease cyclically, but on average the populations of the lemmings and snowy owls stay the same.

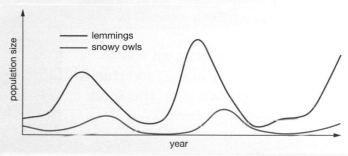

FIGURE 8: Why are the peaks in the snowy owl population slightly behind the peaks in the lemming population?

Mutualism

Some species are totally dependent on others. They cannot live without them. The pea plant is a **legume**. It has structures on its roots called **root nodules**. A type of bacteria live inside the nodules and convert nitrogen into nitrates. They are called **nitrogen-fixing bacteria**.

The bacteria give the pea plant extra nitrates to help it grow. The pea plant gives the bacteria sugar, which they turn into energy.

QUESTIONS

14 Explain why the population of snowy owls falls soon after the population of lemmings falls.

15 Explain why it is important that the lemming population does not increase too much.

16 Describe **two** examples of mutualism.

Our day at the seaside

SELF-CHECK ACTIVITY

CONTEXT

Andy and Barney are down on the beach during their May half-term holiday. Their parents are having a barbeque and the food is taking longer to cook than they'd expected, so Andy and Barney go off to explore the rock pools at the water's edge.

One large rock pool that they spend quite a lot of time looking in has lots of living things in it.

By looking carefully and thinking about what they already know about some of the creatures, they sketch a simple food web in their notepad.

STEP 1

Shrimps play an important role in this web. See how many food chains you can write down from this food web that include shrimps.

STEP 2

The boys start to fish the shrimps out and put them in their bucket. In fact they are going to return them to the same rock pool shortly, but if they did not, what other organisms in the rock pool would be affected and in what way?

STEP 3

One day, early in the autumn, hungry gulls with no more beach picnic scraps to feed from, eat large numbers of crabs. Explain what you think will happen to the populations of the other organisms in the rock pool over the next few months.

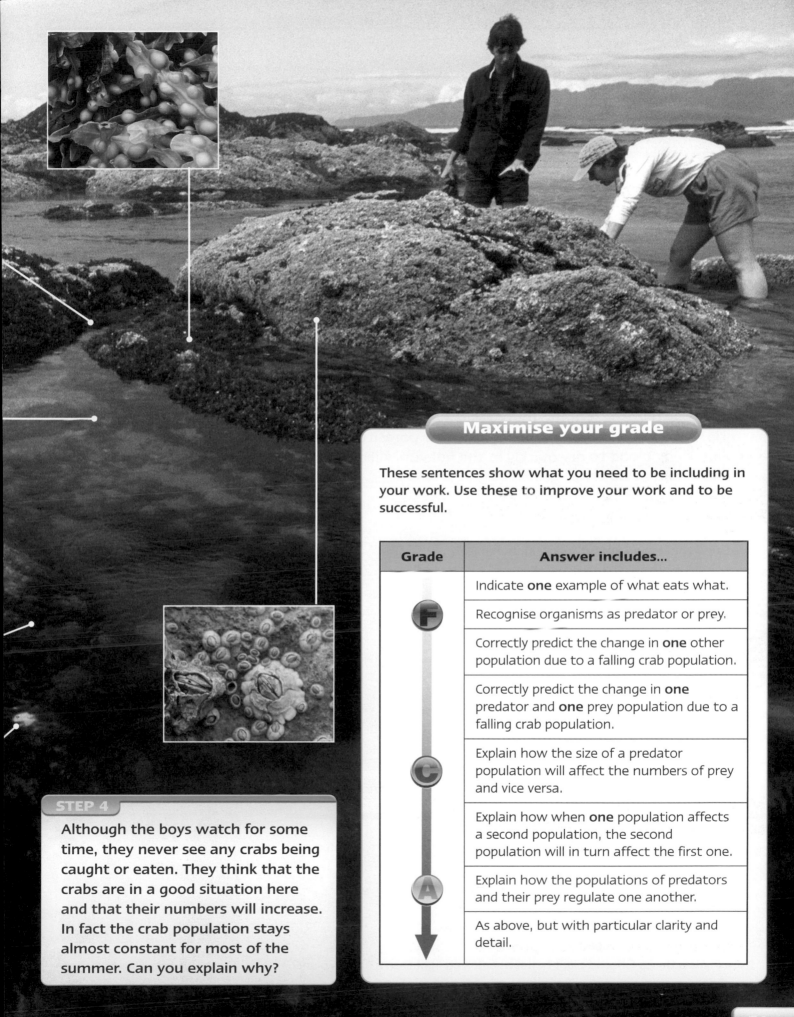

These sentences show what you need to be including in your work. Use these to improve your work and to be successful.

Grade	Answer includes...
F	Indicate **one** example of what eats what.
	Recognise organisms as predator or prey.
	Correctly predict the change in **one** other population due to a falling crab population.
	Correctly predict the change in **one** predator and **one** prey population due to a falling crab population.
C	Explain how the size of a predator population will affect the numbers of prey and vice versa.
	Explain how when **one** population affects a second population, the second population will in turn affect the first one.
A	Explain how the populations of predators and their prey regulate one another.
	As above, but with particular clarity and detail.

STEP 4

Although the boys watch for some time, they never see any crabs being caught or eaten. They think that the crabs are in a good situation here and that their numbers will increase. In fact the crab population stays almost constant for most of the summer. Can you explain why?

Adapt to fit

You will find out:
- how animals and plants are adapted to their environment
- how a camel is adapted to live in the desert
- how a cactus is adapted to live in dry places

Adapted to eat the dead

Ever wondered why a vulture has a long neck and a bald head?

The answer is simple; a vulture feeds on dead bodies that predators leave.

It needs a long neck to reach far inside the body to get at whatever meat is left.

If vultures had feathers on their head, the feathers would get covered in blood and flesh every time they ate. Head feathers are difficult for the bird to clean and would quickly become a home for parasites and bacteria. A bald head offers no hiding place for parasites and allows any blood to dry quickly in the hot sun, killing any parasites that do try to grow.

Vultures feeding.

Adapting to habitats

Every living thing is **adapted** to live in its habitat.

- Birds have feathers, lightweight bones and strong flight muscles so they can fly.
- Fish have gills so they can live in water.
- Earthworms can move soil through their bodies so they can make underground burrows.
- **Cacti** have stems that store water to be able to survive the heat of the **desert**.
- Rubber plants have large deeply divided leaves to let the water run off easily and to catch what little light there is in the rainforest.

FIGURE 1: How has the cactus adapted to survive in the desert heat?

QUESTIONS

1 Match up the following living things with the habitat they are adapted to live in.

Living thing	Habitat
polar bear	soil
cod fish	Arctic
cactus	sea
earthworm	desert

2 Why is a Swiss Cheese plant better at catching light than a cactus plant?

FIGURE 2: Monstera (Swiss Cheese) plant. How has this plant adapted to live in the rainforest?

Adapting to the desert

The desert is a very difficult place in which to live. Temperatures can reach as high as 40 °C during the day and then drop below freezing at night.

To live in the desert, an animal has to be well adapted to survive the heat and scarcity of water.

Camels are well adapted to life in the desert.

- The only body fat a camel has is in its hump. Fat all over its body would insulate the camel, causing it to overheat.

- The stored fat in the hump can be used when there is no other food available.

- Camels do not need to sweat. Their body temperature can rise above normal without harming them.

- Camels have bushy eyelashes and hair-lined nostrils to stop sand getting in.

- Camels have large feet to spread out their weight. This stops them sinking into the sand.

FIGURE 3: What special features make camels suited to living in the desert?

Cacti and the desert

Cacti are plants that live in the desert. They are well adapted to hot dry conditions.

- They have very long roots to reach as much water as possible.

- They are covered with a thick waterproof **cuticle** to reduce water loss.

- Water is stored in a fleshy stem.

- The leaves have become spines to reduce water loss and to stop animals getting at the water in the stem.

FIGURE 4: What functions do the cactus' spines have?

- Photosynthesis takes place in the green stem.

- The round shape reduces the plant's **surface area**. This cuts down water loss through evaporation.

QUESTIONS

3 Deserts are very dry places. Why is the fact that camels do not need to sweat an advantage to them?

4 Explain how large feet help a camel to walk in the desert.

5 Camels are used for transport in many hot places. Explain why they are better adapted than horses for crossing the desert.

QUESTIONS

6 Explain **three** ways in which a cactus is adapted to reduce water loss.

7 Explain why there are lots of cacti in the desert but no roses.

Adapted to hunt

FIGURE 5: How is the Alaskan brown bear adapted for fishing?

You will find out:

- why predators are good at catching prey
- why prey are good at getting away from predators
- how polar bears cope with the cold
- how plants are adapted for pollination

WOW FACTOR!

A brown bear can weigh as much as 635 kg.

That is about the weight of seven men weighing in at 91 kg each.

Alaskan brown bears like to catch salmon. They can be seen standing in rivers waiting for the salmon to swim past. To be good fishers they have to be well adapted.

- The bear has eyes at the front of its head. This helps it to judge distance. It knows how far to reach for the salmon to catch it.
- The bear has sharp claws to grab the salmon.
- The bear's sharp teeth tear into the salmon's flesh.

Adapted to escape

The salmon needs to swim past the bear to escape. It is adapted to do just that.

- It has a **streamlined** shape to help it swim fast.
- The colour of the salmon gives it **camouflage** in the water.
- A lot of salmon swim up the river together so only a few get caught.
- Salmon have eyes on the side of their heads. This gives them a wide field of view. They have more chance of seeing the bear.

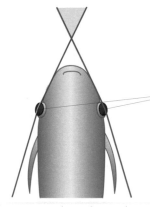

eyes at the side of the head give a large range of vision (and a smaller area of binocular vision)

FIGURE 6: Salmon have a large range of vision. How does this help them escape the bears?

▪ QUESTIONS ▪

8   Copy and complete the sentences using the following words.

   claws   prey   predators

   Bears are_____. They have sharp _____ to help them catch their _____.

9   What can judge distance better – a cheetah or a salmon?

10 How is a wasp adapted to avoid being eaten?

...Arctic   ...blubber   ...camouflage   ...nectar

Adapting to the cold

Living in the **Arctic** is not easy. It is always covered in ice and the temperature can drop to below −30 °C. The polar bear has to be very well adapted to live there.

FIGURE 7: Why do polar bears have small ears?

To give the polar bear good insulation it has:

- thick fur
- a layer of fat over its body called **blubber**
- fur on the soles of its paws
- a large body compared to its surface area, to stop it losing too much heat
- small ears, to reduce the surface area from which heat can be lost.

To help the polar bear cross the ice and catch prey it has:

- white fur for camouflage
- sharp claws and teeth for seizing and eating prey
- strong legs for running and swimming
- large feet to spread its weight on the snow
- fur-covered soles on its paws to help it grip.

Different bears for different habitats

Brown bears and polar bears live in different habitats. Brown bears would find it difficult to exist in the polar bear's habitat because of the way in which they are adapted.

- Polar bears hunt mainly seals. They wait at the water's edge for the seal to surface. When a seal appears the polar bear bites into the seal's head.
- Brown bears could not hunt in this way as their colour would make them stand out in the snow. The seals would see them from under the water and would not surface.

QUESTIONS

11 Give **two** reasons why a polar bear has fur-covered soles on its paws.
12 There is very little food in the Arctic. Explain how the polar bear is better adapted to catch seals than the brown bear.

Plants and pollination

Animals and plants not only adapt to survive, they also adapt to reproduce.

In order to reproduce, plants need to transfer pollen from one plant to another. The process they use is called **pollination**. Plants have adapted to carry out pollination in two ways.

Wind pollination

- The **pollen** is small and light so it can be carried by the wind.
- The plants have feathery **stigmas** which hang outside the plant providing a large surface area to catch passing pollen.

FIGURE 8: Why do the stigmas on the sweetcorn hang outside the plants?

Animal pollination

- The plants make sticky pollen that sticks to the hairs of visiting insects.
- To attract insects, the flowers have brightly coloured petals and a sweet, sugary substance called **nectar** at the base of the flower that insects love to eat.

FIGURE 9: The plant has adapted by having a brightly coloured flower to attract the insect. How has having a long 'tongue' helped the insect?

QUESTIONS

13 Describe the **two** ways in which plants have adapted to carry out pollination.

...pollen   ...pollination   ...stigma   ...streamlined

Survival of the fittest

You will find out:
- how fossils are formed
- how fossils show us how animals and plants have evolved

Perhaps 'Hobbits' were real!

Scientists in Indonesia recently discovered the 12 000 year old remains of an adult human just one metre tall. These tiny people have been nicknamed 'Hobbits'.

The Hobbits had skulls the size of a grapefruit but were still intelligent enough to make tools.

Their skeleton showed that they had extremely long arms, leading scientists to think they may have lived in trees.

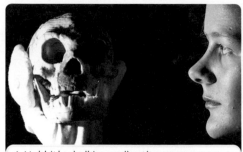
A Hobbit's skull is smaller than ours.

Artist's impression of a Hobbit.

Fossils – a link with the past

The Earth was a very different place 200 million years ago. Most of the animals found today did not exist. Instead, dinosaurs walked on Earth.

How do we know this? We have **fossils** as evidence. Fossils are the preserved parts of dead plants and animals that have turned to stone over millions of years. The bones of dinosaurs turned into fossils. Scientists now find them buried in rocks. They use the fossils to decide what a dinosaur may have looked like and how long ago it might have lived.

Fossils and evolution

Scientists study fossils of animals found in rocks of different ages. The deepest rocks in the Earth contain the oldest fossils. The fossils found in higher layers of rock are of animals that died more recently.

By comparing old and newer fossils, scientists can see how animals have changed over time. This change is called **evolution**.

FIGURE 1: The fossilised skull of a Dinogorgon Rubidgei.

QUESTIONS

1 What are fossils?
2 Copy and complete the sentences using the following words.
   changed   deeper   evolution   rocks
   Animals and plants have _____ over time.
   This change is called _____.
   Fossils found in _____ of different ages can show this change. The oldest fossils are usually found _____ in the ground.

...amber ...cast ...creationist ...evolution

How fossils are formed

Fossils are often formed from the hard parts of living things, such as the shells and bones of animals. These hard parts decay much more slowly than soft tissue.

If dead animals are covered with sediment and buried, the hard parts can be replaced by minerals. The minerals turn to stone, forming a fossil.

In some cases the dead animal sinks into mud, which sets very quickly. The body then decays, leaving a **cast** or **impression**.

Sometimes when an animal or plant dies it does not decay.

- A complete woolly mammoth has been found frozen in ice.

- The body of a woman has been found preserved in a peat bog. Bacteria that normally decay the soft parts cannot live in the acid bog.

- Insects can become trapped in tree sap. The sap turns into solid **amber** preserving the whole insect.

FIGURE 2: Why did Peat Bog Woman not decay?

FIGURE 3: How did this spider become trapped in amber?

The fossil record

The horse, like many animals, has changed over time. The **fossil record** of the horse shows this change.

Not all living things have such a complete fossil record. There are different reasons for this.

- Some body parts decay quickly. Soft tissue often decays before it can be fossilised.

- Fossilisation is rare. Most living things will completely decay.

- There may still be fossils we have not found.

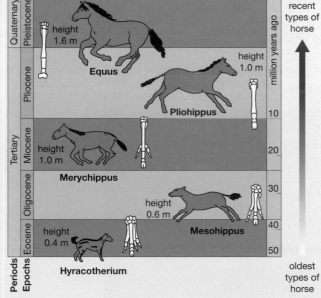

FIGURE 4: Has the shape of the horse's foot evolved over time?

You can find out more about Creationists from:

www.pilgrimtours.com/creation/paleontology.htm

Interpretation of the fossil record

Not everyone has the same view of the fossil record.

It is often used to show how animals and plants evolved. However, other scientists have used the gaps in the fossil record to argue against the theory of evolution.

Many complex organisms in the fossil record appear and then disappear. Unlike the horse, they show no gradual change.

Creationists interpret this to mean that organisms were created and did not evolve.

QUESTIONS

7 Creationists believe that each living thing was created individually and did not evolve.

  a What argument might they put forward to back up their theory?

  b Explain why the fossil record of the horse is an argument against the creationist theory.

QUESTIONS

3 Describe how skeletons become fossils.

4 Explain how organisms can be preserved in a peat bog.

5 Describe how the structure of the horse's leg has changed over time.

6 Suggest **one** reason why the fossil record for some animals is incomplete.

Adapt or die

Large numbers of penguins live together in the Antarctic. The penguins lay their eggs in the same place.

FIGURE 5: Why do penguins live in large groups?

Not all the penguins are the same. Some of them will be better **adapted** to the cold.

- Some penguins will be able to live and breed closer to the South Pole and survive really bad weather.
- Others are better swimmers and can catch more fish.

When the penguins leave the land and swim in the sea to catch fish, predators such as killer whales and leopard seals try to catch them.

The faster swimmers have more chance of getting away. Being better adapted to swimming helps penguins to survive.

WOW FACTOR!

Emperor penguins are the tallest species of penguin. They measure in at up to 130 cm tall!

Penguins may swim up to 15 to 20 km a day searching for small fish to eat.

One penguin travelled 100 km in a single day!

FIGURE 6: In what way is the penguin adapted to help it get away from leopard seals?

QUESTIONS

8 Give **two** reasons why a penguin that swims faster has more chance of surviving.

9 Suggest **one** way in which penguins are adapted to the cold.

...adapted   ...acquired characteristics   ...Darwin   ...extinct

Natural selection

Over millions of years, plants and animals have become adapted to their environment. Environments can change, leaving the animals and plants in the environment no longer suited to living there.

To survive, a species needs to adapt and evolve. If it does not evolve it will become **extinct**. In any species, it is only the best adapted or fittest that survive.

This **survival of the fittest** is called **natural selection**. Natural selection is not just part of history, it is still happening today.

Genes pass on the successful characteristics of a species to the next generation.

Examples of natural selection

Peppered moths

- Genes control the colour of the peppered moth. Some moths are dark and some are pale.

- In parts of the country that have high pollution, lichen growing on the bark of trees is killed by the pollution. Dark moths are camouflaged on dark tree bark, so there are more dark moths in polluted areas.

- In cleaner regions, pale coloured lichen grows. Dark moths stand out so are more likely to be eaten. It is the pale form of the moth that survives to pass on its genes to the next generation.

FIGURE 7: How many moths are there in this picture?

Rats

Rats have evolved to become resistant to the poison warfarin.

Bacteria

- To destroy harmful bacteria that invade our bodies, doctors give us antibiotics.

- More and more bacteria are developing resistance to antibiotics.

FIGURE 8: How will this rat pass on its resistance to warfarin to the next generation?

- If an antibiotic does not kill all the bacteria, the surviving bacteria reproduce and pass on their resistance to the next generation.

Theories of evolution

FIGURE 9: Charles Darwin proposed the Theory of Natural Selection.

Charles **Darwin** sailed around the world from 1831 to 1836 on board the ship HMS Beagle. He developed the theory of natural selection.

- Within any species there is **variation**.

- Organisms produce far more young than will survive.

- There will be competition for limited resources such as food.

- Only those best adapted will survive, called survival of the fittest.

- Those that survive pass on their successful adaptation to the next generation in their genes.

- Over time, the changes may result in a new species.

- Where different species are competing, the less well adapted species may become extinct.

Jean Baptiste de **Lamarck** had a different theory, called the law of **acquired characteristics**. Giraffes acquired long necks to feed and this characteristic was passed on.

Now that it is known that genes pass on characteristics, Lamarck's theory of acquired characteristics has been discredited.

QUESTIONS

10 What might happen to a species if it does not adapt to a changing environment?

11 How is the colour of a peppered moth passed on to its offspring?

12 Suggest **one** reason why warfarin resistance in rats is a problem to humans.

QUESTIONS

13 Darwin suggested humans evolved from apes. Why might some people object to this?

14 Explain how Darwin's theory differs from that of Lamarck.

Population out of control?

You will find out:
- about increases in the human population
- how the increase in population is causing more pollution

On course for a world drought?

The world is running out of water. In Beijing, China, more than one third of the wells have run dry. The countries of the Middle East and North Africa face similar problems. In all these cases, the situation can only get worse because the human population continues to increase.

The situation is so bad, that the Chinese have thought about towing icebergs from the Arctic!

A different kind of Chinese takeaway!

More people = more resources

The world population is increasing. In 1800, there were about 1 billion (1000 million) people. Now there are about 6 billion. All these people are using more and more of the Earth's **resources**.

- **Fossil fuel** resources such as coal, oil and gas are burned for energy and heat.
- **Mineral** resources, such as limestone, are used for building. Aluminium ore is mined to make foil for drinks cans and takeaway trays.

FIGURE 1: An oil rig. What are fossil fuels used for?

FIGURE 2: Quarrying for minerals or rocks creates huge scars in the landscape.

Using more and more resources

As more people use more resources, more waste is produced. All this waste is **polluting** the Earth.

- Household rubbish is piling up in landfill sites.
- Sewage can end up in rivers killing fish.
- Burning fossil fuels releases carbon dioxide and sulfur dioxide.

FIGURE 3: Landfill sites are overflowing as our increasingly wasteful lifestyles create more and more rubbish.

▪▪ QUESTIONS ▪▪

1 Name **one** of the Earth's resources that is used for building.
2 Name **two** fossil fuels.
3 Why is there more household rubbish now than there was in 1800?

...acid rain   ...CFCs   ...exponential growth   ...fossil fuel   ...global warming

The effects of pollution

Global warming

An increase in the use of fossil fuels has resulted in an increase in carbon dioxide in the atmosphere. The higher carbon dioxide levels are contributing to **global warming**. Scientists are concerned that global warming is changing the climate, which could lead to a rise in sea levels.

Ozone layer depletion

The **ozone layer** is a layer of the Earth's atmosphere that protects us from the Sun's harmful ultraviolet (UV) rays.

An increase in the use of chemicals called **CFCs** has led to a depletion of this layer. More people are suffering from skin cancers as a result of more UV rays reaching Earth and damaging their skin.

Acid rain

Sulfur dioxide is produced when fossil fuels burn. Sulfur dioxide reacts with rainwater making it more acidic. The **acid rain** falls on the Earth killing trees and making lakes acidic, causing fish to die.

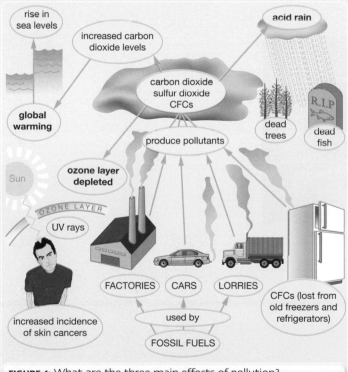

FIGURE 4: What are the three main effects of pollution?

QUESTIONS

4 Which gas contributes to global warming?

5 How has the use of CFCs led to an increase in skin cancer?

6 Name **one** gas that causes acid rain.

Population and pollution

The graph shows the past, present and predicted future world human population.

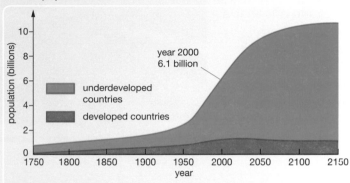

FIGURE 5: What type of population growth does this graph show?

Human population still seems to be in the growth phase. The population is growing at an ever-increasing rate. This is called **exponential growth**.

The increasing population is quickly using up the Earth's resources and increasing the amount of pollution.

Who is causing the problem?

The world population figures show the greatest rise in population is occurring in underdeveloped countries, such as Africa and India.

However, if the countries that use the most fossil fuels are considered, it turns out to be the developed countries, such as the USA and Europe, that are causing the problem.

America is the heaviest user of oil, using about 50 litres per person each day.

WOW FACTOR!

The world's oil producers make 76 million barrels a day.

America, with 5% of the world's population, uses 20 million barrels each day, that's 26% of the world's total!

QUESTIONS

7 a Suggest **one** reason why there is a greater demand for oil now than there was 200 years ago.

   b Explain why this demand is likely to increase even more in the future.

8 Suggest **one** reason why a developed country such as America uses more oil than a poorer country such as Ethiopia.

Gone fishing...

Kevin likes to go fishing. He has fished in the same canal for 20 years. The last time Kevin went, he found lots of dead fish.

Kevin found out that a local factory had emptied waste into the canal. The fish could not survive the **pollution** and died.

You will find out:
- about living things and pollution
- about indicator species

FIGURE 6: Why have these fish died?

In another of Kevin's fishing spots there is a much happier story.

The river has been cleaned up. There are a lot more fish for Kevin to catch. It is not just Kevin who is happy, otters and herons have returned to enjoy the fish too.

FIGURE 7: a Heron. **b** Otter. What food source do these animals need?

⊞ QUESTIONS ⊞

9   What can pollution in a river do to fish?

10 How did cleaning up the river help the otters?

...indicator species

Using indicator species to test for water pollution

Animals have different sensitivities to environmental conditions. In rivers and ponds, different animals can tolerate different pollution levels.

- The sludge worm can live in polluted water. This is because it can cope with the low oxygen levels that occur.
- The alderfly cannot live in polluted water. It cannot tolerate low oxygen levels.

Water that contains lots of different species is usually a healthy environment.

Animal	Sensitivity to pollution
stonefly larva	sensitive
water snipe fly	sensitive
alderfly	sensitive
mayfly larva	semi-sensitive
freshwater mussel	semi-sensitive
damselfly larva	semi-sensitive
bloodworm	tolerates pollution
rat-tailed maggot	tolerates pollution
sludge worm	tolerates pollution

EXAM HINTS AND TIPS

You only need to remember that indicator species are used.

You do not have to remember the level of pollution each species tolerates.

Indicator species

The presence or absence of an **indicator species** is used to estimate levels of pollution.

- The stonefly larva is an insect that can only live in clean water.
- The bloodworm, water louse, sludge worm and rat-tailed maggot are animals that can live in polluted water.

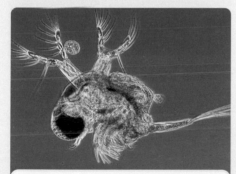

FIGURE 8: The water louse is an indicator species. Can it live in polluted water?

- Lichen grows on trees and rocks, but only when the air is clean. It is unusual to find lichen growing in cities. This is because it is killed by the pollution from cars.

FIGURE 9: Clear mountain rivers contain lots of living organisms.

FIGURE 10: Do polluted ponds support much life?

QUESTIONS

11 A water sample from a river contained bloodworms but no stonefly larvae. Is the water polluted? Explain your answer.

12 Explain why it is unusual to find lichen growing in cities.

QUESTIONS

13 The animals in three different water samples were identified.

Sample	Animals found
A	stonefly larva, water snipe fly, alderfly, mayfly larva, damselfly larva
B	rat-tailed maggot, sludge worm, bloodworm
C	sludge worm, freshwater mussel, damselfly larva

a Which sample had the largest variety of animals?
b Place the samples in order from cleanest to most polluted.
c Which water sample contained little dissolved oxygen?
d Suggest which sample could be from a fast-running stream. Explain your answer.
e Suggest which sample could be from a polluted pond. Explain your answer.

Sustainability

You will find out:
- why species become endangered
- how species become extinct
- how species can be saved from extinction

Whaling in Whitby

In the 18th and 19th centuries, Whitby, in North Yorkshire, was the biggest whaling port in England.

'The Volunteer' was a typical Whitby whaling ship. In the year of 1811, it caught 23 whales.

On its return to port, the barrels of **blubber** were used to produce many tonnes of oil. The horrible stench of the oil could be smelled all over the town.

As dead as a dodo

Sailors discovered the dodo on the island of Mauritius in 1598. By 1681 it was **extinct**.

The dodo is just one of many animals that no longer exist. Other examples are the sabre toothed tiger and the mammoth.

Endangered species

Many animals and plants are in danger of becoming extinct. A species is **endangered** when its numbers are so low it is difficult for the population to rise.

In Britain, people are protecting endangered species such as the red squirrel, red kite and osprey. This is called **conservation**. It is important to save these animals so future generations can see and enjoy them.

In other countries the panda and gorilla are endangered.

The dodo.

FIGURE 1: The gorilla has lost a lot of its habitat to building and farming.

FIGURE 2: The red kite is endangered and has been put into an area of the Chiltern Hills in Oxfordshire where it is protected.

FIGURE 3: The osprey is endangered and its nests are protected from people who collect its eggs against the Law.

▥ QUESTIONS ▥

1. Name **three** extinct animals.
2. When is an animal endangered?
3. Gorillas live in the jungle. How does cutting down the jungle harm the gorilla?

...artificial ecosystem ...blubber ...captive breeding

Why animals become extinct

If an environment changes, an animal may not be as well adapted. It will be forced to compete with other species. This may result in species becoming endangered or extinct.

The environment can change in two ways.

- Naturally, such as an ice age.
- Artificially, normally as a result of human activities, such as destruction of habitats for farming or building and pollution of rivers or lakes by industry.

Other animals, such as the great auk, have become extinct because humans have hunted them. The great auk was hunted for food. As the birds became scarce, they were also hunted for a well-paid trade in skins and eggs. The last known living pair and one egg were stolen in Iceland in 1844.

FIGURE 4: The great auk. Why did it become extinct?

The Tasmanian Tiger, or Thylacine, was hunted to extinction because it was considered a danger to man.

Saving animals from extinction

The giant panda is one of the best known endangered animals. It has been the symbol for the WWF (formerly World Wildlife Fund) since 1961.

The panda lives in the forests of China. It eats bamboo. To help with its conservation, large areas of forest are now protected. Hunting the giant panda is illegal.

Only 61 per cent of the panda population is protected. Outside of the reserves, panda habitat is still being destroyed and poaching remains a problem. To stop this, people need to be educated as to the importance of saving the panda.

Many pandas live in **captivity**. Zoos around the world help to increase the panda population by breeding them. Zoos often exchange pandas for **captive breeding** programmes.

It is also possible to set up **artificial ecosystems** where pandas can live safely.

FIGURE 5: How is the giant panda being protected?

WANT TO KNOW MORE?

You can find out more about panda conservation from:

http://www.panda.org/

Why save the panda?

Pandas have a highly specialised diet – they eat only fresh green bamboo shoots, so they have a limited habitat in which to live.

Panda habitat is found at the top of the Yangtze Basin in China, in an area populated by millions of people. The area contains many rare plants and animal species. Some of the plant species could be of important medicinal value.

Protecting the panda will ensure its habitat remains, which also benefits the local people.

Tourism could become an important economic benefit to local people and lead to improved transport and water resources. By protecting the environment the local people will still be able to collect food and other resources as their ancestors have done for millions of years.

QUESTIONS

7 Suggest **three** reasons why tourists visiting pandas in the wild would benefit the local people.

8 How will protecting the panda help:

a medical research?

b preserve traditions of the local people?

QUESTIONS

4 Describe **three** ways in which an animal could become extinct.

5 How are zoos helping to increase panda numbers?

6 What problems do pandas living outside the reserves face?

...*captivity* ...*conservation* ...*endangered* ...*extinct*

Different types of whales

Whales are mammals that live in saltwater. There are two types of whales.

- The baleen whale eats small animals called krill. The whale sieves the water through baleen plates in its mouth trapping the krill.

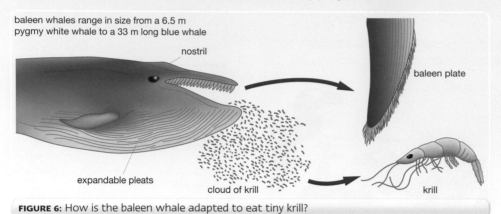

baleen whales range in size from a 6.5 m pygmy white whale to a 33 m long blue whale

nostril

baleen plate

expandable pleats

cloud of krill

krill

FIGURE 6: How is the baleen whale adapted to eat tiny krill?

- Toothed whales, such as the sperm whale, have lots of teeth to trap food such as squid.

Where whales live

Different whale species are found in different seas. This is because they eat different food. Some whales even move from place to place following their food. This is called **migration**.

Minke whales are close to extinction

Whales have been hunted for many years for oil and meat. Minke whales are still hunted. If too many more minke whales are caught they could become extinct.

long rows of sharp teeth

FIGURE 7: How is the sperm whale adapted to eat larger animals?

Sustainable resources

It is important not to take too many things from the environment.

Whales, fish and trees are all **sustainable resources**. If only a few of the resources are taken they will never die out. This is because the ones left behind will be able to reproduce enough so that they do not become extinct.

FIGURE 8: Why is it important not to hunt too many minke whales?

Oil is not a sustainable resource. It takes millions of years to form, yet we have used up most of it in only 150 years.

FIGURE 9: No one knows how many whales there are left in the seas. They are still being hunted, with some countries saying they are catching them for scientific research when really they are being used to make money.

QUESTIONS

9 Why do different whale species live in different places?
10 Why may minke whales become extinct?
11 Why are fish a sustainable resource?

...*captivity* ...*migration* ...*quota*

What are whales used for?

Whales have been hunted for hundreds of years. Their parts have many uses. Selling the whale parts earns the hunters money.

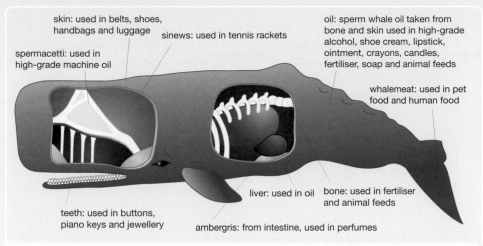

skin: used in belts, shoes, handbags and luggage

sinews: used in tennis rackets

spermacetti: used in high-grade machine oil

oil: sperm whale oil taken from bone and skin used in high-grade alcohol, shoe cream, lipstick, ointment, crayons, candles, fertiliser, soap and animal feeds

whalemeat: used in pet food and human food

liver: used in oil

bone: used in fertiliser and animal feeds

teeth: used in buttons, piano keys and jewellery

ambergris: from intestine, used in perfumes

FIGURE 10: Do you think we could do without or use different materials to make all these things?

When whaling was first stopped in 1986 (it has now started again), many owners of whaling ships had to find new employment. Tourist whale-watching trips have given whales new commercial value.

Whales in captivity

Some whales are kept in **captivity**. This can be for important reasons like research or captive breeding programmes, or just for our entertainment. However, many people object when whales lose their freedom.

Sustainable development

To ensure we do not run out of important resources we need to plan for the future. **Sustainable development** is a way of taking things from the environment but leaving enough behind to ensure a supply for the future and prevent permanent damage.

Fishing quotas

Scientists have worked out how many fish can be taken from the sea and leave enough to reproduce and maintain the population. Fishermen have then been set **quotas**.

Many fishermen see the quotas as a threat to their livelihood. They need to be educated as to the importance of quotas. Without them there will not be enough fish for future generations.

Managed woodland

In managed woodland, trees are only cut down if other trees are planted to replace them. The number of trees cut down will also depend on how long it takes the new trees to grow. Pine trees grow faster than oak trees, so it is easier to maintain their numbers.

> **QUESTIONS**
>
> 12 What commercial value do live whales have?
> 13 Suggest arguments for and against keeping whales in captivity.
> 14 Why are fishermen set quotas?

Reasons for whaling

In 1986, a halt to whaling was agreed by the International Whaling Commission. This caused problems for countries such as Norway, Iceland and Japan. Many small communities in these countries rely on whaling for food and income. In the 1990s, they started whaling again.

Scientists also see a need to kill some whales. They believe it will help them to find out more about how whales can survive at extreme depths. However, they could study the whales without killing them. Migration patterns and whale communication can only be investigated if the animal is alive.

Sustainable development and world population

As the world population increases it is even more important to carry out sustainable development.

Fossil fuels will run out, yet there is an increase in demand for them. Therefore we must manage alternative fuels such as wood.

The demand for food and other resources could lead to an increase in whaling. The whaling nations will need to work together to prevent extinction.

When whaling quotas are set, other factors will need to be taken into account. These include:

- pollution levels
- over-fishing of the whales' food source.

> **QUESTIONS**
>
> 15 Suggest why it is difficult to police whaling.
> 16 Waste products of industry are often dumped at sea. Suggest why this could make maintaining fish numbers difficult.

Module summary

Concept map

Ecosystems
An ecosystem is made up of all the living things and their surroundings.

The animal and plant populations in a habitat can be counted using pooters, nets, pit-fall traps and quadrats.

Ecosystems can be artificial (for example a fish pond), or natural (for example a lake).

Keys can be used to identify the animals and plants in a habitat.

Many ecosystems are still unexplored and could contain new species.

Classification

The animal kingdom is split into two groups, vertebrates and invertebrates.

There are five vertebrate groups:
- fish
- amphibians
- reptiles
- birds
- mammals

Plants can make their own food by a process called photosynthesis.

$$\text{carbon dioxide + water} \xrightarrow[\text{(chlorophyll)}]{\text{(light energy)}} \text{glucose + oxygen}$$

Competition and survival

Animals and plants within a habitat compete for limited resources, such as food and water.

Animals and plants adapt to their habitats. The survival of a species depends on how well it can adapt to changes in its habitat. Those which are better adapted are more able to compete for resources. Species that cannot adapt may become extinct.

The increase in human population is leading to an increase in pollution and loss of habitat. As habitats become smaller, species are unable to compete and become extinct. Species can be protected from extinction if resources are carefully managed. This is called sustainable development.

Some animals are adapted to be successful prey.

The number of predators in a habitat can affect the number of prey, and vice versa.
Survival may also depend on the presence of another organism – mutualism and parasitism.

Some animals are adapted to be successful predators.

Module quiz

1. Is woodland a natural or artificial ecosystem?

2. Is an aquarium a natural or artificial ecosystem?

3. Name the **five** vertebrate groups.

4. What is the name of the green pigment in leaves?

5. Write down the word equation for photosynthesis.

6. Name **one** condition that will increase the rate of photosynthesis.

7. What do animals compete for?

8. What do plants compete for?

9. A badger hunts shrews. Which is the predator and which is the prey?

10. Why do camels have bushy eyelashes?

11. What adaptation does a polar bear have to help it grip on the snow?

12. What are fossils?

13. Which scientist produced the theory of natural selection?

14. Which chemicals have caused depletion in the ozone layer?

15. What is sustainable development?

Citizenship activity

Oil from Ecuador

The Yasuni National Park in Ecuador is home to more than a thousand different species of tree, and hundreds of thousands of different species of insect. Along with all the different birds and animals, this makes the park one of the world's most species-rich forests.

However, the park is under threat because of the extraction of oil. The Brazilian National Oil Company intends to build roads and drilling platforms within the park, destroying large areas of habitat. The Ecuador government hope to raise £50 million from the oil, however many of the people living there object to the plans.

Ecuador is destroying large areas of rainforest every day. Scenes like this could disappear, along with the animals and birds that live there.

QUESTIONS

1. Use the following website to find out more about deforestation in Ecuador:
www.amazonwatch.org

2. Suggest arguments for and against extracting oil from the Yasuni National Park.

Exam practice

1 The graph shows the relative population sizes of a predator and its prey over several breeding seasons.

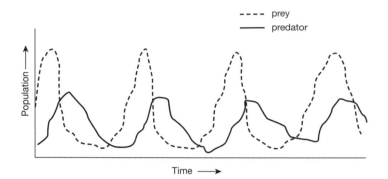

- - - - prey
———— predator

a i Which one of the two species generally has a higher population, the prey or the predator? [1]

ii Explain why this species generally has a higher population. [2]

b Explain the effect of the prey species on the predator population. [3]

[Total 6 marks]

2 The following food chain occurs in some fresh water ponds:

The table shows the amount (g) of biological material for this food chain. Only one of the options is correct.

Option	Microscopic plants	Water fleas	Fish
A	5	15	60
B	60	5	30
C	30	60	15
D	60	30	5

a Which is the correct option, A, B, C or D? [1]

b Explain your answer to the previous question. [2]

[Total 3 marks]

3 The table shows some of the adaptations of a polar bear to the cold arctic conditions in which it lives. Copy and complete the table by writing a brief explanation in the empty boxes. One has been done for you.

Feature	Why the feature is an adaptation to cold arctic conditions
White colour of fur	
Layer of fat (blubber) under the skin	*Insulates the animal against the extreme cold*
Large feet	
Fur on soles of paws	
Small ears	

[4]

[Total 4 marks]

4 a Which of the following statements is not a description of fossils? [1]

	Description
A	The frozen remains of dead organisms in ice
B	The imprints left in sedimentary rock by dead organisms
C	The complete record of all organisms that lived millions of years ago
D	The preserved remains of dead organisms in waterlogged bogs

b Explain your answer to the previous question. [2]

[Total 3 marks]

Worked example

A scientist surveyed five rivers, near where they passed through a town. The results are shown in the table.

Town	Number of bacteria	Oxygen concentration	Amount of green plants	Amount of fish
A	High	High	Low	Low
B	High	High	Low	High
C	High	Low	Low	Low
D	Low	High	High	High
E	Low	Low	High	Low

The scientist knows that one of the towns is discharging untreated sewage into the river.

a Which town appears to be situated on a **polluted** river? [1]

c Which town appears to be situated on an **unpolluted** river? [1]

b Explain your answer to the previous question. [2]

d Explain your answer to the previous question. [2]

---

a C

This is correct.

b It is town C because untreated sewage has to be broken down by bacteria, so they increase in numbers. The bacteria need oxygen to work, so they use up a lot of oxygen. Green plants get killed by the pollution, and so do the fish.

This is mostly correct. The last part of the answer is vague, but the first part is well written.

c D

This is correct.

d It is town D because oxygen is high (because there are less bacteria). Also, there are lots of plants and fish because there is more oxygen and less pollution in the water.

This is mostly correct. The student has a good understanding of the effect of bacteria numbers on oxygen content of the water.

Overall Grade: B

How to get an A

Even students with a good understanding of the subject can lose marks by not expressing themselves clearly enough. Use the number of marks allocated for each question as a guide to how much to write for each answer.

Oil fires create soot, heat and toxic gases. Carbon monoxide may also be produced if combustion is incomplete.

Burning too much fuel causes an increase in carbon dioxide. Carbon dioxide is a greenhouse gas. It absorbs infrared radiation, which warms the Earth. This contributes to global warming.

Essential to life, carbon is the central element for living processes, new non-living materials and fossil fuel energy sources. Fossil fuels provide energy for cooking, transport and heating. Crude oil provides the basic material for plastics and medicines.

Oil is a fossil fuel, which is essential for transport and heating. When it runs out, we have no way of making more. It is a non-renewable fuel.

Complete combustion happens when fuel burns in plenty of oxygen. Carbon dioxide and water are produced.

CONTENTS

Cooking

You will find out:

- that some foods can be eaten raw and others must be cooked
- about the different ways used to cook food
- how to recognise when a chemical change takes place
- about what happens to protein when food is cooked

A burning discovery

Ancient Man's discovery of how to make fire was enormously important.

Not only could he now keep warm but he could also cook food.

Ways to cook food

There are different ways to cook food:

- on a barbeque
- in an oven
- on an electric ring
- on a gas ring
- in a microwave.

A food changes when it is cooked. It cannot go back to its raw state.

The change is **irreversible**.

These **chemical changes** happen when the chemicals in food are **heated**.

An **energy change** takes place in the food.

FIGURE 1: Meat has different chemicals in it. When it is cooked irreversible changes happen to the chemicals.

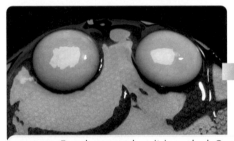 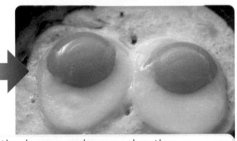

FIGURE 2: Egg changes when it is cooked. One of the changes can be seen when the transparent liquid 'white' of a raw egg turns to a solid opaque white when it is cooked.

⬛ QUESTIONS ⬛

1. Write down **three** ways that food can be cooked.
2. Write down the word that means 'it cannot change back'.
3. Which diagram **A**, **B**, **C** or **D** does not show a chemical change?

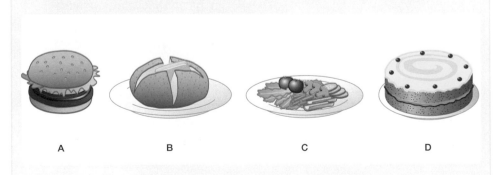

Watch Out Don't forget that an electric or gas ring can be used for boiling, steaming or frying food.

A grill or a barbeque is used for grilling.

An oven can be used for baking or roasting.

...*chemical change* ...*denature* ...*energy change*

Why do we cook food?

- High temperature kills harmful microbes in food.
- Texture of food is improved.
- Taste of food is improved.
- Flavour of food is enhanced.
- Food is easier to digest.

Proteins

Cooking is a chemical change because a new substance is made.

Many of the chemicals in food are **proteins**.

Meat and eggs are good sources of proteins. Proteins are large molecules that have definite shapes.

The white of the egg is made of a protein called albumin. Albumin molecules change shape when the egg is cooked.

The protein molecules of meat also change shape when it is cooked.

FIGURE 3: a Raw chicken and **b** the chicken cooked.

QUESTIONS

4 Give **two** reasons why certain types of food need to be cooked.

5 What evidence is there that cooking produces a chemical change?

6 What happens to the protein molecules in an egg when it is cooked?

More on proteins

A protein is a large molecule that has a definite shape.

When a protein molecule in egg or meat is heated during cooking it changes shape.

The shape change is irreversible.

The protein molecule is **denatured**.

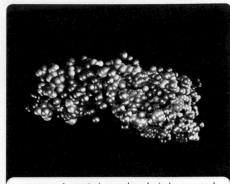

FIGURE 4: A protein molecule is large and has a definite shape.

DID YOU KNOW?

A protein is a long molecule that has **four** types of structure.

- **Primary:** this is the sequence of amino acids in a protein chain.

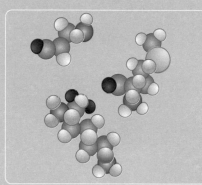

- **Secondary:** this is when a protein coils into a helix shape.

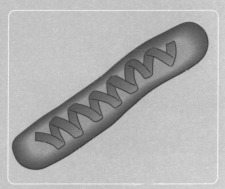

- **Tertiary:** this is when a protein has a folding structure as new bonds are formed.

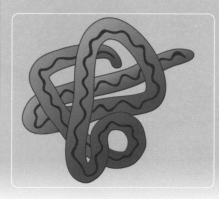

- **Quaternary:** this is when more than one protein chain joins to form a large protein such as haemoglobin.

QUESTIONS

7 Explain how heating a protein may change its shape.

8 Explain why the primary structure of the protein will be unaffected by heating.

Cooking different foods

Potatoes

Potatoes must be cooked.

When a potato is cooked its taste and texture changes irreversibly. The texture of the potato becomes softer and more fluffy.

FIGURE 5: Suggest why potatoes cannot be eaten raw.

Baking

Bread and cakes are made from flour.

Flour is made from wheat and must be cooked.

Yeast is used in baking bread to make it rise.

Baking powder is added to flour to make cakes rise.

When heated in an oven, baking powder gives off carbon dioxide, which makes the cake mixture rise.

FIGURE 6: What is added to bread dough to make the mixture rise during baking?

FIGURE 7: What is added to cake mixture to make it rise during baking?

QUESTIONS

9 What changes take place when potatoes are cooked?

10 What gas makes cakes rise during baking?

11 What is the test for carbon dioxide?

...baking powder   ...carbohydrate   ...decompose   ...product

EXAM HINTS AND TIPS

Make sure you know the test for carbon dioxide.

It turns limewater from colourless to a milky white.

Baking powder

Potatoes and flour are good sources of **carbohydrate**.

To make a cake, baking powder is added to flour to make the cake rise. Baking powder is a chemical called **sodium hydrogencarbonate**. When it is heated it breaks down (**decomposes**) to give sodium carbonate, carbon dioxide and water.

The reactant is sodium hydrogencarbonate and the **products** of the reaction are sodium carbonate, carbon dioxide and water.

The word equation for the reaction is:

$$\text{sodium hydrogencarbonate} \xrightarrow{\text{heat}} \text{sodium carbonate} + \text{carbon dioxide} + \text{water}$$

To test for carbon dioxide the gas is passed through limewater.

The limewater changes from colourless to milky white if carbon dioxide is present.

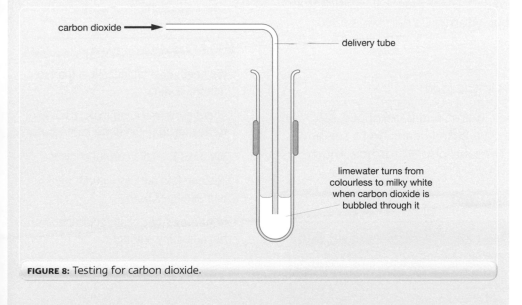

carbon dioxide

delivery tube

limewater turns from colourless to milky white when carbon dioxide is bubbled through it

FIGURE 8: Testing for carbon dioxide.

QUESTIONS

12 Potatoes are a good source of starch. What type of food is starch?

13 Draw the apparatus used to test a gas for carbon dioxide.

More on potatoes and baking powder

When a potato is cooked its cell walls break down and **starch grains** burst.

This makes the potato easier to digest.

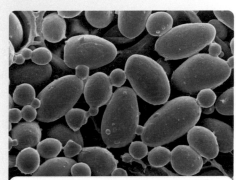

FIGURE 9: Electron micrograph of starch grains in a potato. Magnification x 700. Why does cooking make potatoes more digestible?

Starch in flour needs to be cooked in order to be digested. When baking powder is added to a mixture of flour the product rises.

The symbol equation for the decomposition reaction is:

$$2NaHCO_3 \longrightarrow Na_2CO_3 + H_2O + CO_2$$

QUESTIONS

14 What are the products of decomposition of baking powder?

15 Write a balanced symbol equation for the decomposition of baking powder.

Food additives

You will find out:

- that foods contain many different chemicals
- about the main types of food additive
- how to understand a food label
- how intelligent packaging is used to improve the quality of food

What's in a tomato?

Who would guess that a tomato contains all the chemicals listed below?

water   ascorbic acid   monosodium glutamate

cellulose   carotene   citric acid

malic acid   lycopene   riboflavin

sugar   oxalic acid   flavourings

When foods are processed, different chemicals are often added. These are called **additives**.

Food additives

The main types of food additive are:

- antioxidants
- emulsifiers
- colours
- flavour enhancers.

Antioxidants stop food from reacting with oxygen and turning bad.

An antioxidant is used to prevent apples from turning brown. It is also called **ascorbic acid** (its common name is vitamin C). Every chemical additive that is used a lot in food has a reference number. Vitamin C's number is E300.

FIGURE 1: Vitamin C (E300) is an antioxidant. Has it been used in this photograph?

Food labels

The label on a packet of food lists what is in the food.

A tin of baked beans has beans, tomatoes, water, sugar, cornflour, salt, vinegar, spices and herbs. Look at a label on a baked beans tin to see how much energy one average serving gives. The label also states how much fibre is in a 100 g serving.

WANT TO KNOW MORE?

We need most chemicals in food for healthy bodies.

There are some chemicals, such as tartrazine, that can harm individuals.

We need to make careful choices.

You can find out more about food and additives from:

http://news.bbc.co.uk/sportacadem/hi/sa/healthy_eating/

QUESTIONS

1. What does an antioxidant do?
2. What is the name of the antioxidant E300?
3. Look at the label from a tin of baked beans.

   How much protein does 100 g of baked beans give you?

Value	Per 100 g
energy	306 kJ
protein	4.6 g
carbohydrate	12.9 g
fat	0.2 g
fibre	3.7 g
sodium	0.3 g
salt	0.9 g

...active packaging ...additive ...antioxidant ...ascorbic acid ...catalyst ...enhance

Why are food additives used?

Food additives are added to **preserve** food so it can be distributed around the country or to other countries without **spoiling**.

Spoiling happens when a food reacts with oxygen, bacteria or mould.

Additives are also added to give a different sensory experience. They are used to **enhance** the colour or flavour of food.

Information about food additives is given on food packet labels.

Sanchez
MEXICAN
Crunch
Potato chips

Ingredients: dried potato, vegetable oil, potato starch, flavouring, flavour enhancer E621, E27

FIGURE 2: Which ingredient do these crisps contain the least of?

Ingredients are listed in descending order by mass.

Some ingredients, such as flavour enhancer E621, are given numbers instead of their chemical name. This is because they are used so often in food that they have had to be tested for **toxicity**. Some, such as tartrazine, may cause problems in some people but others, such as E500 (baking powder), have been used safely for years.

Antioxidants stop food from reacting with oxygen. Ascorbic acid (vitamin C) is used in tinned fruit and wine as an antioxidant.

Intelligent packaging

Intelligent packaging is another method used to stop food spoiling.

- **Active packaging:** actively changes the condition of packaged food to extend its life while maintaining the quality of the products.
- **Intelligent packaging:** monitors the condition of packaged food and gives information on the quality of the packaged food using sensors and indicators.

European governments are working towards a goal that at least 60 per cent of packaging waste is recovered and between 55 and 80 per cent is **recycled**.

Active packaging

Active packaging uses a **polymer** and a **catalyst** as a packaging film that scavenges for oxygen. The system works for up to 2 years and extends the shelf-life of foods such as cheese, fruit juice and mayonnaise. It prevents the need for additives, such as antioxidants, to be added to foods.

Intelligent packaging includes **indicators** on packages.

An indicator shows how fresh a food is on the outside of a package. A central circle darkens as the product loses its freshness.

fresh

still fresh –
consume immediately

no longer fresh

central circle darkens as
food loses its freshness

FIGURE 3: What does an indicator on packaging show?

Other intelligent packaging systems include self-heating packages so that foods such as soup can be eaten without the use of a heater.

QUESTIONS

4 Give **two** reasons why additives are added to foods.
5 Name **two** foods that contain antioxidants.
6 What is intelligent packaging?
7 What percentage of packaging waste should be recovered?

QUESTIONS

8 What is active packaging?
9 Describe the advantages of intelligent packaging.

Washing the dishes

Have you ever tried to wash up oily plates in hot water?

It is not easy!

This is because oil and water do not mix.

If washing-up liquid is added the plates are easily cleaned.

FIGURE 4: Adding washing-up liquid helps remove oil from plates.

You will find out:
- how emulsifiers help oil and water to mix
- how mayonnaises are made

Washing-up liquid

Oil does not attract water. Oil **repels** water.

A **detergent** in washing-up liquid provides 'hooks' between oil and water.

The oil is 'hooked' onto the water and pulled off a dirty plate.

This is an example of an **emulsion**.

FIGURE 5: What is it in washing-up liquid that helps to clean oil from plates?

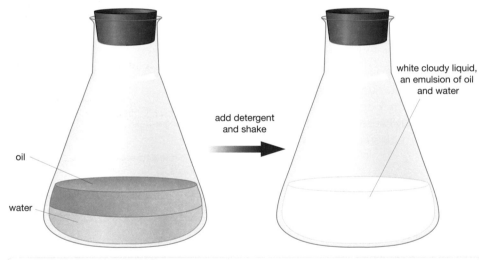

oil

water

add detergent and shake

white cloudy liquid, an emulsion of oil and water

FIGURE 6: Making an emulsion. Can you think of examples of emulsions in everyday use?

A detergent is an **emulsifier**.

=== QUESTIONS ===

10 Why does oil not mix with water?

11 How does detergent help oil and water mix?

...detergent   ...emulsifier   ...emulsion

Examples of emulsions

- If oil leaks into the sea it can harm sea birds and other sea life.

To disperse an oil slick, detergent is sprayed from light aircraft over the area of the slick.

The detergent 'hooks' the oil onto the water and it is then much easier to clean up. The detergent acts as an emulsifier.

- Some paints are emulsions.

- Milk is an emulsion.

- Mayonnaise is an emulsion of oil and vinegar with egg. Egg is the emulsifier.

FIGURE 7: Suggest why crude oil harms sea birds.

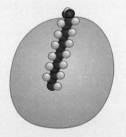

FIGURE 8: Examples of emulsions: **a** emulsion paint, **b** milk, **c** mayonnaise.

How does a detergent work?

Detergents are long molecules made up of two parts, a head and a tail.

The tail is a 'fat-loving' part and the head is a 'water-loving' part.

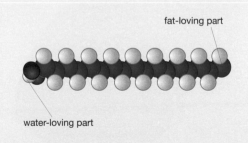
fat-loving part

water-loving part

FIGURE 9: In a detergent, which is the fat-loving part and which is the water-loving part?

████ QUESTIONS ████

12 Explain how a detergent works.

13 What is the emulsifier in mayonnaise?

More on mayonnaise

Mayonnaise is a food made using egg as an emulsifier.

The egg yolk binds the oil and vinegar together to make a smooth substance.

The mayonnaise does not separate because the egg yolk contains a molecule that has two parts.

One part is a water-loving part that attracts vinegar to it. This is called the **hydrophilic** head.

The other part is a water-hating part that attracts oil to it. This is called the **hydrophobic** tail.

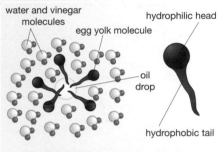

water and vinegar molecules
egg yolk molecule
hydrophilic head
oil drop
hydrophobic tail

an emulsion of oil and vinegar

emulsifying molecule

FIGURE 10: An emulsifying molecule showing the hydrophilic head and hydrophobic tail.

The hydrophobic tail is attracted into the lump of oil but the head is not. The hydrophilic head is attracted to water and 'pulls' the oil on the tail into the water.

████ QUESTIONS ████

14 Describe the **two** parts of the molecule in egg that act as an emulsifier.

15 How does this molecule help to keep oil and vinegar from separating?

16 Explain why the fat-loving part of an emulsifying molecule is called the hydrophobic end.

...hydrophilic ...hydrophobic ...repel

Smells

Face painting

Since Egyptian times, people have put coloured materials and creams on their bodies and faces to protect and attract.

What a pong!

Onions and garlic both have a very strong **smell**.

They are **pungent**.

Rose and honeysuckle flowers have very strong, pleasant smells.

They have sweet **scents**.

FIGURE 1: Onions and garlic smell very strongly. Can you name any other natural substances that have a strong smell?

FIGURE 2: Bougainvillea flowers have a sweet scent. Can you name any other plants that have scented flowers?

The natural substance found in pine trees is used to give a pleasant smell to disinfectant.

Perfumes and cosmetics can be made from natural sources.

Oil from roses can be **distilled** to make perfume. Lavender oil is made from lavender grown in Norfolk.

A similar perfume can be made **synthetically**. Chemicals are boiled to make an **ester**.

What makes a good perfume?

A good perfume has the properties shown in Figure 3.

DID YOU KNOW?

If you stand by a scented flower, a gas goes into your nose.

Sensors in the lining of your nose pick up the scent and send a signal to your brain.

People who taste wine are said to have 'a good nose' as they smell many different wines each day!

evaporates easily

is non-**toxic**

does not react with water

does not irritate the skin

is **insoluble** in water

FIGURE 3: Suggest why a good perfume needs to evaporate easily.

▮ QUESTIONS ▮

1. What is the word used to describe a material that has a strong smell?
2. What is the method used for taking the perfume substance out of a natural material?

...diffusion ...distilled ...ester ...evaporate ...insoluble

Making a perfume

To make a perfume a chemical called an ester is made. An alcohol mixed with an acid makes an ester.

alcohol + acid ⟶ ester + water

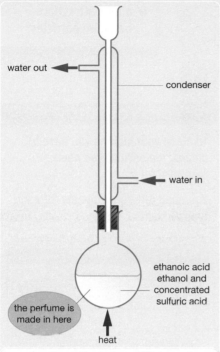

water out

condenser

water in

ethanoic acid ethanol and concentrated sulfuric acid

the perfume is made in here

heat

FIGURE 4: Suggest what would happen to the experiment if the flask was not heated.

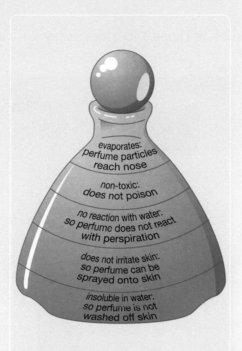

evaporates: perfume particles reach nose

non-toxic: does not poison

no reaction with water: so perfume does not react with perspiration

does not irritate skin: so perfume can be sprayed onto skin

insoluble in water: so perfume is not washed off skin

FIGURE 5: Suggest why perfumes are not coloured.

Nail varnish remover is also an ester.

The reasons why a good perfume needs certain properties are shown in Figure 5.

This table gives some esters and the alcohol and acid they are made from.

Alcohol	Acid	Ester
ethanol	ethanoic	ethyl ethanoate
butanol	ethanoic	butyl ethanoate
propanol	butanoic	propyl butanoate

Smelling

If a liquid evaporates easily then the substance is **volatile**.

Volatile perfumes are liquids that have energetic, fast-moving particles at room temperature. There is only a weak attraction between particles in the liquid perfume so the forces of attraction between the molecules are easy to overcome. This means that particles with lots of energy can escape from the surface of the liquid, becoming gas particles. These gaseous particles move through the air by **diffusion** until they reach the sensors of the nose.

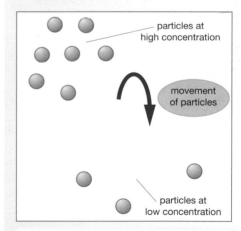

particles at high concentration

movement of particles

particles at low concentration

FIGURE 6: The movement of particles by diffusion.

QUESTIONS

6 Explain how the smell of an unopened bottle of perfume can be detected on the other side of the room. Use the word 'volatile' in your answer.

QUESTIONS

3 Name **two** uses of esters.

4 Describe how to make an ester.

5 Describe and explain **three** properties of perfumes.

...pungent   ...scent   ...smell   ...synthetic   ...toxic   ...volatile

Solubility

A substance that dissolves in a liquid is **soluble**. The substance is called the solute and the liquid that it dissolves in is called the **solvent**. A substance that does not dissolve in a liquid is insoluble.

Water does not dissolve in some substances. In Figure 7, oil does not mix with water.

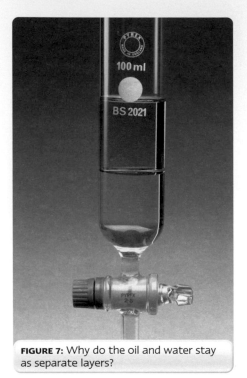

FIGURE 7: Why do the oil and water stay as separate layers?

FIGURE 8: Is nail varnish remover soluble in nail varnish?

DID YOU KNOW?

To clean your clothes you have to choose the solvent you need carefully.

You need different solvents for each type of stain.

Stain	Solvent
mud	water
blood	water
oil	methylated spirit
nail varnish	propanone
wine	salt water

Water does not dissolve in nail varnish so it cannot be used to remove varnish from nails.

Nail varnish remover does dissolve in nail varnish.

All cosmetics must be tested to make sure they are safe.

Some cosmetics are tested on animals. Some people do not agree with animals being used. What do you think?

QUESTIONS

7 What does insoluble mean?

8 Using the table above what solvent would you use to remove a bloodstain from a shirt?

9 Why do cosmetics need to be tested?

...colloid   ...dissolve   ...soluble

Solutions

> A **solution** is a solute and a solvent that do not separate.

Esters can be used as solvents.

Solvents can be used as cleaners as shown in the table.

Solvent	Solute that is cleaned
oil	grease
ester	nail varnish
thinners	paint

Cosmetics need to be thoroughly tested so that they do not harm humans.

- They must not cause rashes or itchiness.
- They must not cause skin damage or lead to cancer or other life-threatening conditions in long-term use.

Testing takes many years.

Some people object to cosmetics being tested on animals as the animals may be harmed. The animals have no control over what happens to them. These people say that there are other ways of testing products that are less damaging to living things.

Other people say they feel safer if the cosmetics have been tested on animals. They say that an animal's reaction to a chemical closely mimics the reaction in a human. If there is no danger to the animal then it is likely that the cosmetic or perfume will be safe for use by people.

Diffusion

If you stand behind a car you can see and smell exhaust fumes. They are collections of tiny molecules of different gases that diffuse through air molecules. This is called a **colloid**.

You can see the larger clumps of droplets diffusing through the air.

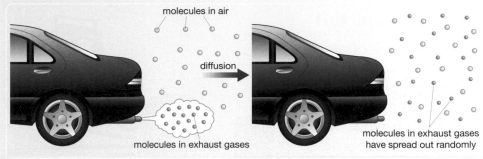

molecules in air

diffusion

molecules in exhaust gases

molecules in exhaust gases have spread out randomly

FIGURE 9: Suggest why in winter, when a car is started from cold, its exhaust fumes are more visible.

Gas particles have a high kinetic energy and move rapidly and randomly.

> Diffusion is the movement of particles from an area of high concentration to an area of low concentration.

Evaporation

Particles of a liquid have less kinetic energy and are weakly attracted to each other. When some particles of a liquid increase their kinetic energy the force of attraction between the particles is overcome and the particles escape through the surface of the liquid into the surroundings.

Attractions between particles are important

Water does not dissolve nail varnish. This is because the force of attraction between two water molecules is stronger than that between a water molecule and a molecule of nail varnish.

Also the force of attraction between two varnish molecules is stronger than between a varnish molecule and a water molecule.

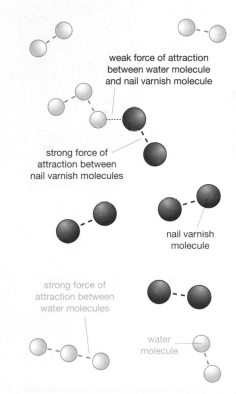

weak force of attraction between water molecule and nail varnish molecule

strong force of attraction between nail varnish molecules

nail varnish molecule

strong force of attraction between water molecules

water molecule

FIGURE 10: What would happen if nail varnish remover was used instead of water? What does this tell you about the strength of the force of attraction between a nail varnish remover molecule and a molecule of nail varnish?

Making crude oil useful

You will find out:

- how fossil fuels formed
- how and why fractional distillation works
- how the forces between molecules affect their boiling points

Precious oil

Crude oil is one of our most important natural resources. It is a finite resource and will eventually run out. It is non-renewable because it cannot be made again.

Different parts of crude oil are used to make transport fuels, plastics, medicines, fabrics and dyes.

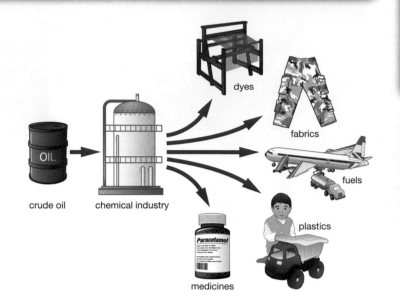

dyes

fabrics

fuels

plastics

medicines

crude oil   chemical industry

OIL

Paracetamol

How were fossil fuels formed?

Coal, gas and oil are **fossil fuels**.

Fossil fuels have formed from dead animals and plants trapped in the Earth millions of years ago.

These dead animals and plants were squashed together (compressed) over millions of years. Dead plants form coal. Dead animals form crude oil.

Drilling for crude oil

Crude oil has to be 'won' from the ground by drilling. It is then pumped to the surface.

Separating crude oil

Crude oil is separated by heating it up and then, when parts of it have boiled, cooling it down. This is called **fractional distillation**.

The crude oil is separated into different **fractions** (parts). The process works because each fraction has a different **boiling point**.

135 million years ago

remains of dead plants   remains of dead animals

oil or coal

How oil and coal form in layers under the surface

FIGURE 1: What is crude oil made from?

QUESTIONS

1 How was crude oil formed?
2 How is crude oil separated?
3 Look at Figure 5. How many fractions is crude oil separated into?

...boiling point   ...finite resource   ...force   ...fossil fuel   ...fraction

More on fossil fuels and the separation of crude oil

Fossil fuels are **finite resources** because they are no longer being made. The conditions on Earth are not the same as they were millions of years ago. When these fossil fuels are used up there will be no more. They are called a **non-renewable** source as they cannot be made again.

Crude oil was made from the compressed bodies of many animals over millions of years. It is made up of a mixture of many types of oils. All these oils are **hydrocarbons**. A hydrocarbon is made up of molecules containing carbon and hydrogen only.

The oils are separated by fractional distillation.

Crude oil is heated at the bottom of a tower.

Oil that does not boil sinks as a thick liquid to the bottom of the tower. This fraction is called bitumen. It is used to make tar for road surfaces.

Bitumen has a very high boiling point. It 'exits' at the bottom of the tower.

Other fractions boil and their gases rise up the tower.

The tower gets colder the higher up it is.

Fractions with lower boiling points such as petrol and LPG 'exit' at the top of the tower, where it is colder.

More on fractional distillation

Crude oil can be separated by fractional distillation because the molecules in different fractions have different length chains. This means that the **forces** between the molecules are different.

The forces between molecules are called **intermolecular** forces. These forces are broken during boiling. The molecules of a liquid separate from each other as molecules of gas.

Heavy molecules, such as those that make up bitumen and heavy oil, have very long chains so there are strong forces of attraction between the molecules. This means that they are difficult to separate. A lot of energy is needed to pull each molecule away from another. They have high boiling points.

Lighter molecules such as petrol have short chains. The molecules do not have very strong attractive forces between them and are easily separated. This means that less energy is needed to pull the molecules apart. They have very low boiling points.

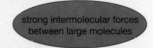
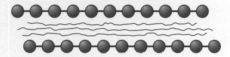

FIGURE 2: Heavy molecules such as bitumen have strong intermolecular forces of attraction. Where in the fractionating column do they exit?

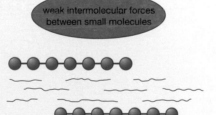

FIGURE 3: Lighter molecules such as petrol have weak intermolecular forces of attraction. Do they have high or low boiling points?

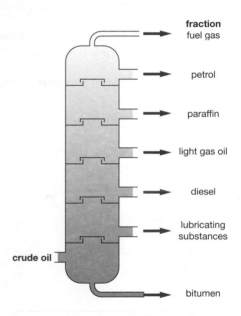

FIGURE 4: A fractional distillation column. What characteristic of the fractions in crude oil means that they can be separated using this method?

...*fractional distillation*   ...*hydrocarbon*   ...*intermolecular*   ...*non-renewable*

Problems in extracting crude oil

You will find out:

- about environmental problems in extracting crude oil
- about political problems associated with the distribution of crude oil
- how the supply of petrol keeps pace with demand

- When crude oil is found, a large area is taken over for drilling and pumping oil to the surface. This causes damage to the environment.
- Crude oil is also found under the sea. It has to be pumped using oil rigs. This is a dangerous activity.
- Crude oil has to be transported through pipelines or by tanker.
- If sea-going tankers run aground and are damaged, the oil spills and forms an **oil slick**. This can cause enormous harm to wildlife and habitats. Beaches have to be cleaned up which is expensive and can take years.

However, not many people want to give up their car, their heating or their plastic goods.

The need for petrol and other products from crude oil has to be balanced with the cost to the environment.

More petrol needed

More petrol is needed, but less paraffin is needed.

Paraffin can be broken down or '**cracked**' into petrol. This can be done on an industrial scale or in the laboratory.

To crack liquid paraffin a high temperature and a **catalyst** are used.

FIGURE 5: Cracking towers used to crack paraffin into petrol on an industrial scale.

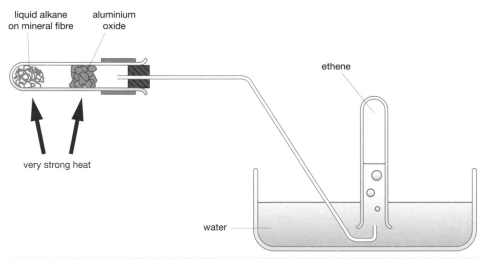

liquid alkane on mineral fibre

aluminium oxide

very strong heat

ethene

water

FIGURE 6: Large molecules are not so useful. Liquid paraffin is cracked into smaller, useful molecules.

DID YOU KNOW?

Petrol, diesel and paraffin are hydrocarbon molecules.

Diesel and paraffin are large hydrocarbon molecules.

Petrol is a small hydrocarbon molecule.

Cracking turns large hydrocarbon molecules into smaller, more useful hydrocarbon molecules.

QUESTIONS

11 Name **three** uses of petrol.

12 Name **one** disadvantage of getting petrol from crude oil.

13 How is petrol made from fractions that contain large molecules of oil?

...alkane   ...alkene   ...catalyst   ...cracking

Environmental damage

Extracting crude oil causes damage to the environment. Oil fields are usually found over very large areas, which then cannot be used for other purposes. Once extraction has ceased it is very expensive to return the landscape to its former state.

However, demand for oil and its products is enormous and increases each year. Not only is it used for fuels for transport and heating, but there is also a large demand for the fraction called **naphtha**. Medicines, plastics and dyes are made from this fraction.

Extracting oil from under the sea is a dangerous and skilled activity. Oil slicks caused by leaks from tankers can harm animals, pollute beaches and destroy unique habitats for long periods of time. Clean-up operations to save the animals and clean beaches are extremely expensive. The detergents and barrages used in clean-ups pose their own environmental problems.

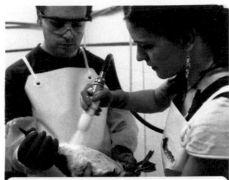

FIGURE 7: When a bird is covered with oil it is no longer buoyant and often ingests the oil. What do you suggest would be the best substance to clean oil off the bird's feathers?

Supply and demand

The supply of oil can never match the demand for petrol and other products.

There is over-supply of long-chain hydrocarbon fractions, such as heavy oil, and a shortage of short-chain hydrocarbons, such as petrol.

The solution to this problem of supply and demand is a process called cracking.

Cracking

Cracking involves heating long-chain molecules at high temperatures over a catalyst. The long-chain hydrocarbons are split into smaller, more useful molecules such as petrol.

The hydrocarbons from crude oil are called **alkanes**. They have a general formula of C_nH_{2n+2}.

example

Octane has eight carbon atoms. The number of hydrogen atoms is therefore $2n + 2 = 18$.

The formula for octane is C_8H_{18}.

When a large alkane is cracked it becomes a smaller alkane and an **alkene**. An alkene has a **double bond**. This makes it useful for making **polymers**.

Political problems

Extracting crude oil can cause political problems.

Oil-producing nations can set prices high and cause problems to non-oil producing nations.

It is difficult for industry to match supply with demand for petrol.

Expensive industrial cracking plants have to be built near to refineries so that large hydrocarbons can be cracked to make smaller, more useful molecules.

FIGURE 8: A cracking plant built beside an oil refinery. Why are cracking plants needed?

QUESTIONS

14 Name **three** products made from the naphtha fraction in crude oil.

15 What conditions are needed for cracking to take place?

16 What is the general formula for an alkane?

17 Explain the difference between the supply of heating oil and its demand, using the figures in the table on the right.

What could be done with the excess?

Product	Supply in tonnes	Demand in tonnes
petrol	100	300
diesel	200	100
heating oil	250	50

QUESTIONS

18 How does industry match the demand for petrol with the supply from crude oil?

...double bond   ...naphtha   ...oil slick   ...polymer

The Dartmoor challenge!

SELF-CHECK ACTIVITY

CONTEXT

Will, Sacha, Mike and Nisha are on their school summer camp in Dartmoor, in south-west England. They have spent a day in school at the start of the week with the rest of the group going over their plans. Now they are up on the moorland for 4 days. The group is planning to walk to 20 tors by the end of the week. A tor is a rocky outcrop, and some of them are quite high.

The weather on Dartmoor can change very quickly and in the summer it is often sunny and warm. However, clouds can gather quickly and rain can fall and make the unsuspecting walker very wet very quickly.

Staying dry is very important. If you get wet you soon start to feel cold and miserable and that makes it much harder to carry on walking. However, climbing the tors is hard work and you soon start to sweat on a warm day.

This is a problem when selecting suitable clothing. Outer clothes that are not waterproof would soon get wet through, but ordinary waterproofs like Nylon, though they keep rain out, keep perspiration in.

A special material called GORE-TEX® provides an answer, and many moorland walkers now use hats, coats, trousers and boots made from this material. GORE-TEX is a membrane made from a substance called PTFE, combined with Nylon. It keeps external moisture from rain out, but lets water vapour from the body escape.

GORE-TEX works because PTFE is hydrophobic ('hates' water) and causes water to gather in beads on its outer surface that are then too large to pass through to the inside. Water vapour (perspiration) from the body can still pass through to the outside as the molecules are around 700 times smaller than the pores in the membrane.

STEP 1

Why do Will and his friends need coats that are 'waterproof and breathable'?

STEP 2

Why is GORE-TEX successful at keeping them dry but not getting them sticky with sweat?

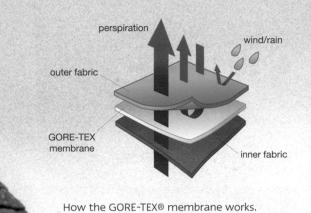

How the GORE-TEX® membrane works.

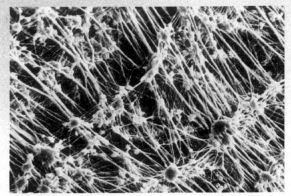

Expanded GORE-TEX® PTFE membrane in electron microscope view. One pore is 0.0002 mm in diameter.

STEP 3

Draw and label diagrams to show the difference between beads of rainwater and molecules of water vapour.

Maximise your grade

These sentences show what you need to be including in your work. Use these to improve your work and to be successful.

Grade	Answer includes...
F	State either why such clothing is better if it is waterproof or why it is better if it is breathable.
	State why such clothing is better if it is waterproof and also breathable.
	Draw a diagram to show beads of water on material or water vapour passing through.
	Draw a diagram to show beads of water on material and water vapour passing through.
C	Explain why GORE-TEX has particular advantages for active outdoor people with reference to rain and to perspiration.
	Explain how liquid water cannot pass or how water vapour can.
A	Explain how liquid water cannot pass and how water vapour can.
	As above, but with particular clarity and detail.

Making polymers

You will find out:

- that polymers are large molecules made up of many small molecules
- about polymerisation
- how to draw displayed formulae for polymers

Out with the old, in with the new

Compare the two pictures.

Our lifestyles are very different to those led by people in the Victorian age.

You can see how plastics have changed our lives.

Plastics are made from polymers.

What is a polymer?

A polymer is a:

- very big molecule
- very long chain molecule
- molecule made from many small molecules called **monomers**.

The polymer that this rope is made from is called poly(propene). It is made from lots (poly) of small propene monomers.

This shopping bag is made from a plastic polymer called poly(ethene). It is made from lots of small ethene monomers.

What do you think the monomer is called that makes poly(styrene), used to make this cup?

If a monomer called vinyl chloride is used, what is the name of the polymer used to make this apron?

When lots and lots of monomers are joined to make a polymer the **reaction** is called **polymerisation**.

QUESTIONS

1. What is a polymer?
2. Write down the name of **one** polymer.
3. Write down the name of the monomer that makes poly(ethene).
4. Name **one** use of a polymer.

...addition polymer   ...catalyst   ...displayed formula   ...double bond   ...monomer

Polymerisation

A polymer is made from many monomers joined together.

The letter '*n*' is used in science to mean 'lots of'.

So a polymer made from the monomer ▧ is written (▧)*n* and can be represented like this.

The dashed line means 'and longer'.

When a polymer is made from monomers that are the same type it is called an **addition polymer**.

A polymerisation reaction needs:

■ high pressure

■ a **catalyst**.

FIGURE 1: A polymerisation plant. What conditions does this plant need to provide in order for a polymerisation reaction to take place?

QUESTIONS

5   What is the process called where lots of monomers join to make long chain molecules?

6   What **two** conditions are needed for this process to take place?

Addition polymerisation

Addition polymerisation is the reaction of many monomers that have **double bonds** to form a polymer that has single bonds.

The **displayed formula** of an addition polymer can be constructed when the displayed formula of its monomer is known.

example

The displayed formula for the ethene monomer is:

During a polymerisation reaction, the high pressure and catalyst cause the double bond in the ethene monomer to break. Each of the two carbon atoms needs to form a new bond and joins with another ethene molecule, which also has two carbon atoms needing to form two new bonds, and so the reaction continues.

poly(ethene)

If the displayed formula of an addition polymer is known, the displayed formula of its monomer can be worked out by looking at its repeated units.

example

This addition polymer:

has a repeated unit of two carbon atoms, three hydrogen atoms and one chlorine atom. The bond between the two carbon atoms would have been a double bond originally.

Therefore the monomer's displayed formula is:

In addition polymerisation:

A monomer that makes a polymer contains at least one double bond between carbon atoms.	➡	A polymer contains only single bonds between carbon atoms.
When a molecule has one or more double bonds it is called an **unsaturated** compound.	➡	When a molecule has only single bonds it is called a **saturated** compound.

QUESTIONS

7   Copy the monomer. Draw **three** repeat units of its polymer.

8   Look at the polymer. Draw its monomer.

Alkanes and alkenes

You will find out:

- that hydrocarbons are molecules made from carbon and hydrogen only
- about the general formulae of alkanes and alkenes

One atom of carbon and four atoms of hydrogen chemically combine to make a **hydrocarbon** called methane.

CH_4

A hydrocarbon is named according to:

- the number of carbon atoms it has
- whether it has a double bond or single bonds.

Number of carbon atoms in hydrocarbon molecule	Alkane	Alkene
1	methane	—
2	ethane	ethene
3	propane	propene
4	butane	butene

Alkane	Molecular formula	Alkene	Molecular formula
methane	CH_4	—	—
ethane	C_2H_6	ethene	C_2H_4
propane	C_3H_8	propene	C_3H_6
butane	C_4H_{10}	butene	C_4H_8

Alkane	Displayed formula	Alkene	Displayed formula
methane	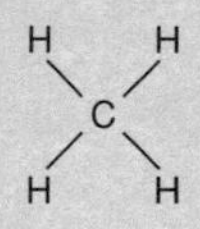	—	—
ethane	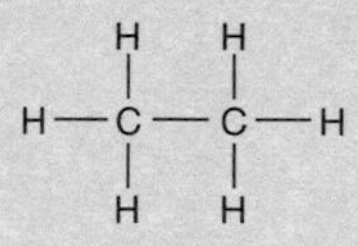	ethene	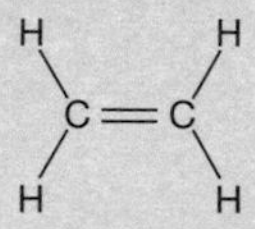
propane	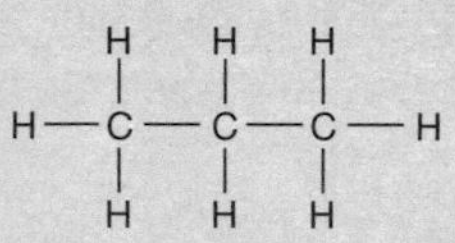	propene	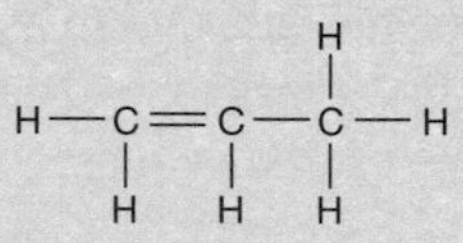
butane	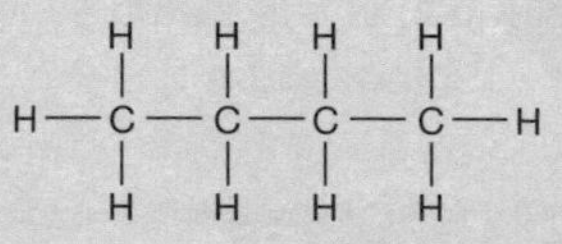	butene	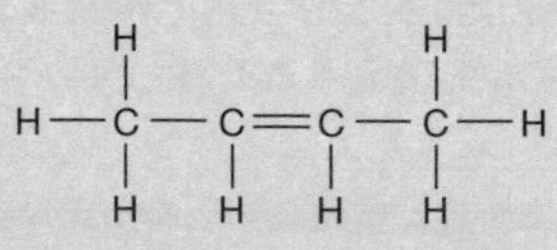

If the name of the **alkane** is known it is easy to predict the name of the **alkene**.

C_5H_{12} is pentane. The alkene with five carbon atoms is pentene.

▪▪ QUESTIONS ▪▪

9 What is the name of the alkane that has three carbon atoms?

10 Butene has the molecular formula C_4H_8. What is the formula of butane?

...alkane   ...alkene

Recognising hydrocarbons

Hydrocarbons are made from hydrogen and carbon only.

Propane, C_3H_8, is a hydrocarbon.

propane

Propanol, C_3H_7OH, is not a hydrocarbon. It contains an oxygen atom.

propanol

Hydrocarbons that contain single bonds only are called alkanes.

Hydrocarbons that have at least two carbon atoms joined together by a double bond are called alkenes.

propene

Propene is a monomer. Polypropene is the polymer made from propene.

More on hydrocarbons

The building blocks of many polymers are hydrocarbons.

Polymers are made from hydrocarbons that have at least one double bond between two carbon atoms.

ethene

These hydrocarbons are called alkenes and they are unsaturated.

The general formula of an alkene is C_nH_{2n}.

The general formula of an alkane is C_nH_{2n+2}.

Ethane is saturated. It has no double bonds.

ethane

Testing for saturation

Bromine solution is used to test for unsaturation. It is an orange solution. When an alkene is added the orange solution turns colourless. This is because the bromine solution has reacted with the alkene and has formed a new compound.

An alkane does not react with bromine solution and so the bromine remains orange.

FIGURE 2: Using bromine solution to test for unsaturation in hydrocarbons. Two test tubes of bromine solution were set up and labelled **a** and **b**. An alkane was added to one tube and an alkene to the other. Which tube, **a** or **b**, had the alkane added to it?

QUESTIONS

11 What is a hydrocarbon?

12 What is the difference between an alkane and an alkene?

13 What is the difference between a saturated molecule and an unsaturated molecule?

14 Explain why there is a difference between the general formulae for an alkane and an alkene.

Designer polymers

You will find out:
- about polymers used for packaging and clothing
- how nylon is useful but is not breathable
- how GORE-TEX® has all the properties of nylon and is breathable

Polymers all around

Modern cars, communication equipment and building materials are all made from polymers in some way.

Uses of polymers

Fabrics for clothes, paint for cars and cases for computers are all made from different **polymers**.

Polymers are chemicals such as nylon, PVC (which is also called poly(vinylchloride)) and polyester.

Each polymer is chosen carefully for the job that it does best.

One property of PVC is that it is waterproof. This is an advantage when it is used to make raincoats as the wearer is kept dry.

There is another material used to make raincoats that is 'breathable'. The advantage to wearers of raincoats made from this material is that they keep dry not only from the rain but also from their sweat.

I wish I'd bought the breathable one.

Polymer	Property 1	Property 2	Use
PVC poly(vinylchloride)	waterproof	flexible	raincoats
poly(ethene)	waterproof	flexible	plastic bags
poly(styrene)	insulates	absorbs shock	packaging
poly(propylene)	strong	flexible	ropes

QUESTIONS

1. Write down the names of **three** polymers.
2. What **two** properties make PVC a good polymer for raincoats?
3. What is the advantage of wearing material that is breathable?

...condense   ...hydrophobic   ...laminate

Breathable polymers

Nylon is tough, lightweight and keeps rainwater out. However, it also keeps water vapour from body sweat in. The water vapour from the sweat **condenses** and makes the wearer wet and cold inside their raincoat.

If nylon is **laminated** with a PTFE/polyurethane **membrane**, clothing can be made that is waterproof and breathable.

GORE-TEX® has all the properties of nylon and is breathable.

The discovery of GORE-TEX material has helped active outdoor people to cope with wetness from sweat. Water

FIGURE 1: Suggest what type of material this hiker's clothes are made from.

vapour from sweat can pass through the membrane but rainwater cannot.

This table compares the properties of nylon and GORE-TEX.

Nylon	GORE-TEX
waterproof	waterproof
flexible	flexible
non-breathable	breathable

More on breathable polymers

GORE-TEX material is used to make waterproof and breathable clothing.

The inner layer of the clothing is made from expanded PTFE (polytetrafluoroethene), which is **hydrophobic**.

water droplets from rainwater do not pass through

hydrophobic PTFE is expanded to form a microporous membrane

FIGURE 2: Why does water not soak through expanded PTFE?

wind

wind does not pass through membrane

FIGURE 3: Suggest what happens to wind as it meets the microporous membrane.

Scientist Bob Gore discovered a special way of processing PTFE. The PTFE is expanded to form a **microporous membrane**. Only small amounts of the polymer are needed to create this airy, lattice-like structure. Wind does not pass through the membrane.

In expanded PTFE a membrane pore is 700 times larger than a water vapour molecule and therefore moisture from sweat passes through.

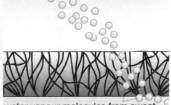

water vapour molecules from sweat pass through membrane to outside

FIGURE 4: Suggest why sweat can pass through the membrane.

DID YOU KNOW?

These boots are made for walking!

They have a GORE-TEX lining and are tested walking through water for 400 km on this simulator!

300 000 MOVEMENTS

QUESTIONS

4   What is the disadvantage of using nylon to make outdoor clothes?

5   What is the advantage of the membrane used in GORE-TEX material?

QUESTIONS

6   What is the property of expanded PTFE that makes it repel water?

7   Why does GORE-TEX not let wind through?

8   How big are the pores in an expanded PTFE membrane compared to the size of water vapour molecules?

Uses of polymers in healthcare

You will find out:
- about the uses of polymers in healthcare
- about problems with disposal of waste polymers
- about new polymers being developed that are easy to dispose of

Polymers have many uses in healthcare. They are used:

- in contact lenses
- to make white fillings to fill cavities in teeth
- to make wound-dressing materials

Polymers are better than other materials for some uses as the table shows.

Use	Polymer	Other material
contact lens	wet on the eye	dry on the eye
teeth filling	attractive	looks metallic
wound dressing	waterproof	gets wet

Most addition polymers are non-biodegradable. They do not decay and are not decomposed by bacteria.

Most **addition polymers** are **non-biodegradable**. They do not decay and are not decomposed by bacteria. This can cause problems.

Some ways that waste polymers can be disposed of are:
- in landfill sites
- by burning
- by **recycling**.

Some of the problems of using non-biodegradable polymers are:
- they are difficult to dispose of
- they can cause litter.

FIGURE 5: What are the three main ways that addition polymers can be disposed of?

▐▐ QUESTIONS ▐▐

9 Write down **two** uses of polymers in healthcare.

10 What is the advantage of a wound dressing made from a polymer over a different dressing material?

11 What does non-biodegradable mean?

12 Write down **one** way to dispose of polymers.

...addition polymer ...biodegradable ...dissolve

Stretchy polymers and rigid polymers

The atoms of the monomers in each of the chains in a polymer are held together by strong **intramolecular** bonds.

The chains of the polymer are held together by weak **intermolecular** forces of attraction.

Plastics that have weak intermolecular forces of attraction between polymer molecules have low melting points and can be stretched easily as the polymer molecules can slide over one another.

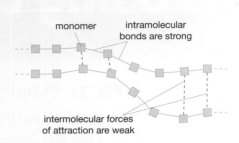

FIGURE 6: Which are stronger, intramolecular bonds or intermolecular forces of attraction?

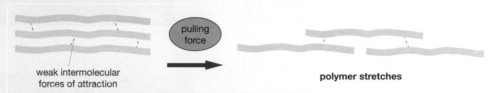

FIGURE 7: Why can polymers that have weak intermolecular forces of attraction stretch easily?

Some plastics form intermolecular chemical bonds or cross-linking bridges between polymer molecules. These are strong. The polymers have high melting points and cannot be stretched easily as the polymer molecules cannot slide over one another. They are rigid.

FIGURE 8: Different polymers form intermolecular chemical bonds or cross-links that are strong. Explain how this characteristic makes them rigid.

Biodegradable polymers

Scientists are developing addition polymers that are **biodegradable**. These are disposed of easily by **dissolving**.

Disposal problems for non-biodegradable polymers

- Landfill sites get filled quickly and waste valuable land.
- Burning waste plastics produces toxic gases.
- Disposal by burning or landfill sites wastes a valuable resource.
- Difficulty in sorting different polymers makes recycling difficult.

Type of polymer	Property 1	Property 2
weak intermolecular forces of attraction	stretches easily	low melting point
strong intermolecular chemical bonds or cross-links	rigid	high melting point

QUESTIONS

13 Why is disposing of plastics by burning a problem?

14 Explain how the two different types of bonds or forces affect the stucture of a polymer.

15 Some polymers stretch easily, some are rigid. Explain why.

Using carbon fuels

You will find out:
- what makes a good fuel
- how to use a word equation to describe a fuel burning

Choosing a fuel

Have you ever considered how suitable the fuel put into a car is?

It is important to choose the right fuel for the job.

Fuels are used for cooking, transport and heat.

Choosing a fuel

A good **fuel** for a motorbike or quadbike needs to be a liquid. It needs to flow round the engine easily. Coal is not a good fuel for a motor vehicle!

Petrol and diesel are good liquid fuels for cars.

Petrol is not a good fuel for an open fire in a thatched cottage!

Coal is used in most power stations. However, some power stations now use gas as the main fuel.

How fuels burn

When a fuel burns it gives off gases.

Waste gases can be seen in the exhaust of a car.

Water is given off in the form of steam. Other gases depend on how well the fuel burns and what else is in the fuel.

Oxygen is needed for fuels to burn.

The word equation for a fuel burning in air is:

fuel + oxygen ⟶ carbon dioxide + water

FIGURE 1: How can you tell petrol is being burnt by this car's engine?

EXAM HINTS AND TIPS

Remember:
- **oxygen is needed for burning**
- **burning is called combustion**
- **lots of oxygen is needed for complete combustion**
- **complete combustion of a hydrocarbon fuel produces carbon dioxide and water.**

QUESTIONS

1 What characteristic must a fuel used in a car have?
2 What gas is always given off when a fuel burns?

...energy ...fuel

Comparing fuels

A fuel is chosen because of its characteristics:

- energy value
- availability
- ease of use
- storage method
- cost
- toxicity
- pollution caused.

When coal and petrol are compared, coal produces more pollution than petrol. However, coal is not as dangerous to store as it does not catch light so readily. It is not **volatile** (able to turn into a gas easily). However, coal is dirty and takes up a lot of storage space.

Characteristic	Coal	Petrol
energy value	high	high
availability	good	good
storage	bulky and dirty	volatile
cost	high	high
toxicity	produces acid fumes	produces less acid fumes
pollution caused	acid rain carbon dioxide soot	carbon dioxide nitrous oxides
ease of use	easier to store as an energy source for power stations	flows easily around an engine so makes a good energy source for a car

Burning hydrocarbon fuels produces **energy**.

It also produces carbon dioxide and water.

fuel + oxygen $\longrightarrow$ carbon dioxide + water

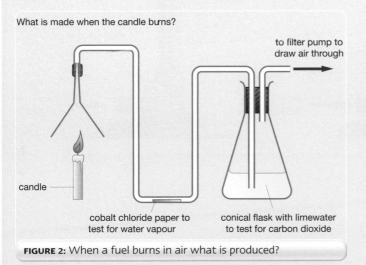

What is made when the candle burns?

to filter pump to draw air through

candle

cobalt chloride paper to test for water vapour

conical flask with limewater to test for carbon dioxide

FIGURE 2: When a fuel burns in air what is produced?

It can be shown in the laboratory that a fuel burns in oxygen to give carbon dioxide and water. Limewater is used to test for carbon dioxide. White copper sulfate powder is used to test for water, which is produced as steam.

More on choosing fuels

Coal would not be easy to use in an engine for a car as it does not ignite easily. It also produces pollution in the form of sulfur dioxide.

You would choose petrol or diesel as a fuel for a car. Petrol and diesel are liquids so they can circulate easily in the engine. They are also stored easily in petrol stations and garages along road networks.

These fuels are so easy to use and, as the population increases, more and more fossil fuels are being consumed.

Governments are concerned because of the increasing carbon dioxide emissions that result when fossil fuels are burnt. Many governments have pledged to try to cut carbon dioxide emissions over the next 15 to 20 years. It is a global problem that cannot be solved by one country alone.

QUESTIONS

5 What concerns governments about the increasing population?
6 Suggest what individuals could do to reduce carbon dioxide emissions.

QUESTIONS

3 Explain why you would use coal as the fuel for an open fire rather than petrol.
4 How can you test for the products of combustion of fuels?

Incomplete combustion

If a fuel burns in a shortage of oxygen it gives off unwanted gases. These gases contain soot and are **toxic**.

One of the toxic **fumes** is a gas called **carbon monoxide**.

Carbon monoxide is a poisonous gas and is very dangerous if it is breathed in.

FIGURE 3: Why should heaters in people's homes be checked regularly?

You will find out:

- about complete combustion and incomplete combustion
- about pollution caused by burning fossil fuels
- how to write a balanced symbol equation to describe a fuel burning

Sometimes a heater in a poorly ventilated room in a house becomes faulty and burns fuel in a shortage of oxygen. This causes it to give off carbon monoxide and the people who live in the house are in danger of being made ill or even dying from carbon monoxide poisoning.

A heater should be checked regularly to make sure it is burning properly.

Bunsen burner flame

A Bunsen burner flame produces energy from burning gas.

If the **air hole** is open the flame burns in plenty of oxygen. Combustion is complete and a blue flame is seen.

If the air hole is closed there is a shortage of oxygen. Combustion is incomplete and less energy is transferred.

When combustion is incomplete, an orange flame is seen. Carbon monoxide, soot and water vapour are produced.

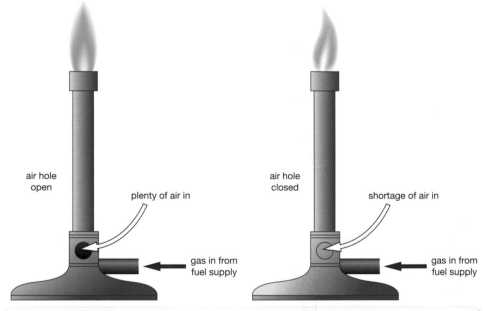

air hole open

plenty of air in

gas in from fuel supply

air hole closed

shortage of air in

gas in from fuel supply

FIGURE 4: What colour is the flame from a Bunsen burner when the air hole is open?

▪▪ QUESTIONS ▪▪

7 What is given off when fuels burn in a shortage of oxygen?

8 Why is this a problem?

9 Which Bunsen burner flame transfers the most energy?

10 What are the products of incomplete combustion?

...acid rain ...air hole ...balance ...carbon monoxide ...complete combustion ...fumes

Combustion

A fuel is burnt to release useful energy.

Complete combustion

Complete combustion occurs when a fuel burns completely in air.

A fuel, such as methane, uses oxygen in the air to produce products.

The products are carbon dioxide and water.

methane + oxygen ⟶ carbon dioxide + water

More energy is released during complete combustion than during incomplete combustion.

Incomplete combustion

Incomplete combustion occurs when a fuel burns in limited oxygen.

The products are carbon monoxide and water.

Complete combustion is better than incomplete combustion because:

- less soot is made
- more heat is released
- toxic carbon monoxide gas is not produced.

Pollution problems

A fossil fuel contributes to the **greenhouse effect** when it burns because it produces carbon dioxide. This is believed to contribute to **global warming**.

Fuels also cause other problems. Coal has sulfur in it. Burning coal gives off sulfur dioxide. Sulfur dioxide dissolves in rainwater to make **acid rain**, which damages stone buildings and statues and kills fish and trees.

FIGURE 5: What has caused this stone gargoyle to erode?

FIGURE 6: Trees killed by acid rain in Scandinavia. Suggest why forests are particularly badly hit in these countries.

Watch Out
Complete combustion gives carbon dioxide and water.

Incomplete combustion gives carbon monoxide and water.

More on complete combustion

Complete combustion releases useful energy.

The formulae for the products of complete combustion are:

carbon dioxide	CO_2
water	H_2O

Methane is a common hydrocarbon fuel. The formula for methane is CH_4.

Complete combustion can be shown by the equation:

$$CH_4 + O_2 \longrightarrow CO_2 + H_2O$$

The equation must be made to **balance**.

There are two oxygen atoms in the reactants and three oxygen atoms in the products.

The balanced equation is:

$$CH_4 + 2O_2 \longrightarrow CO_2 + 2H_2O$$

There are now four oxygen atoms in both reactants and products.

 Equations need to be balanced.

First count up the numbers of atoms in each molecule (shown by the subscript numbers).

Don't change these numbers.

Then, if necessary, add to the molecule number (large number in front of formula) in order to balance the numbers on either side of the arrow.

QUESTIONS

11 What are the products of complete combustion?

12 Which type of combustion releases more useful energy?

13 What effect does carbon dioxide contribute to?

14 What problems do fuels containing sulfur cause?

QUESTIONS

15 Write a balanced equation for the complete combustion of propane, C_3H_8.

Energy

You will find out:

- how energy can be given out or taken in during a chemical reaction

- about the difference between an endothermic and exothermic reaction

Using energy

Frying an egg needs energy. Energy is taken in by an egg as it changes during cooking.

Fireworks give off energy because of a chemical reaction.

The first recorded use of fireworks in England was at the wedding of Henry VII in 1486!

Almost all chemical reactions either give off or take in energy.

Chemical reactions can make:

- heat
- light
- sound
- electricity.

A chemical **reaction** happens when **reactants** change into **products**.

The first recorded use of fireworks in England was at the wedding of Henry VII in 1486!

If things get hotter or cooler, **energy** has been transferred.

 Energy is not a product.

It is not a chemical.

EXAM HINTS AND TIPS

Remember that energy is measured in joules (J).

Temperature is measured in degrees Celsius (°C).

▪▪ QUESTIONS ▪▪

1. Name **three** types of energy that can be made by chemical reactions.
2. What are reactants turned into in a chemical reaction?
3. How can an energy change be recognised?
4. What unit is temperature measured in?

...bond   ...endothermic   ...energy   ...exothermic

Types of reaction

Chemical reactions can be divided into two groups.

When energy is transferred to the surroundings in a chemical reaction it is an **exothermic** reaction (energy is released).

When energy is taken from the surroundings in a chemical reaction it is an **endothermic** reaction (absorbs energy).

- An exothermic reaction is shown by a **temperature** increase. An example of an exothermic reaction is a lit firework.

FIGURE 1: What happens during an exothermic reaction?

- An endothermic reaction is shown by a temperature decrease. An example of an endothermic reaction is photosynthesis – energy from the Sun is taken in.

FIGURE 2: What happens during an endothermic reaction?

5   What is an exothermic reaction?

6   What type of reaction takes in energy?

'Make or break'

- **Bond** breaking is an endothermic process.

- Bond making is an exothermic process.

If more energy is needed to break bonds than make new bonds then a reaction is endothermic overall.

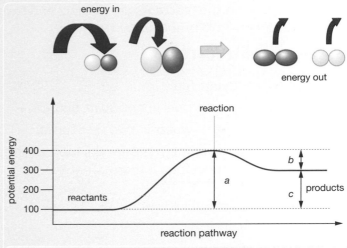

FIGURE 3: Is this reaction endothermic or exothermic overall?

If less energy is needed to break bonds than make new bonds then a reaction is exothermic overall.

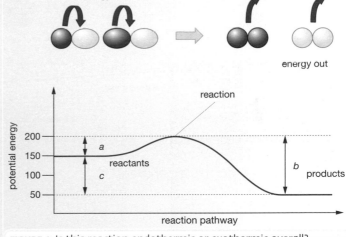

FIGURE 4: Is this reaction endothermic or exothermic overall?

7   In a reaction, during which process is energy taken in?

8   In a reaction, during which process is energy given out?

9   What type of reaction occurs when more energy is given out when the products are formed, than taken in to break the bonds of the reactants?

Fuels

Fuels need oxygen to burn.

Ethanol burns in oxygen to make carbon dioxide and water.

ethanol + oxygen ⟶ carbon dioxide + water

In this word equation the reactants are ethanol and oxygen and the products are carbon dioxide and water.

Choosing the best fuel

To compare two different fuels:

1 Place the same **mass** of fuel in two spirit burners.
2 Place the same mass of water in two test tubes.
3 When all the fuel has burnt, measure the increase in temperature of the water in each test tube using a thermometer.

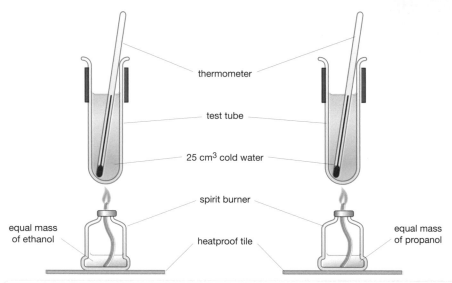

thermometer

test tube

25 cm³ cold water

spirit burner

equal mass of ethanol

heatproof tile

equal mass of propanol

FIGURE 5: Why is the same mass of water used in the experiments?

How else could you do this experiment?

WANT TO KNOW MORE?

Alcohols are fuels.

Ethanol is an alcohol. So is propanol.

There is a whole series of alcohols.

You can find out more about naming alcohols from an organic chemistry textbook.

DID YOU KNOW?

Carbon monoxide attaches to red blood cells four times quicker than oxygen does.

If you know anyone who smokes, tell them how much their brain is being starved of oxygen!

▦ QUESTIONS ▦

10 What does ethanol make when it burns in oxygen?
11 Name **three** things that must be kept constant (stay the same) to make it a fair test when you compare fuels by heating water.

...calorimeter ...combustion

Comparing the energy from different flames

The flame of a Bunsen burner changes colour depending on the amount of oxygen that it burns in.

- Blue flames are seen when the gas burns in plenty of oxygen (complete **combustion**).

- Yellow flames are seen when the gas burns in limited oxygen (incomplete combustion).

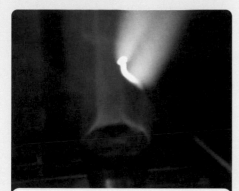

FIGURE 6: The gas is burning with a yellow flame. What does this tell you about the oxygen supply?

- - - - - - - - - - - - - - - - - - - -

Design your own experiment

Think how you could design an experiment to compare the energy transferred by the two different Bunsen flames.

Hints:

- Remember the apparatus used to compare fuels.

- The amount of gas used needs to be measured.

- Remember to make the tests fair.

- - - - - - - - - - - - - - - - - - - -

QUESTIONS

12 Jo and Rasa carry out an experiment to see if a blue flame or a yellow flame gives out more heat energy. Write down **three** measurements they should take.

Comparing fuels using calculations

The amount of energy transferred during a reaction can be calculated.

- A spirit burner or a bottled gas burner is used to heat water in a copper **calorimeter**.

- A temperature change is chosen and measured, for example 50 °C.

- The mass of fuel burnt is measured by finding the mass before and after burning.

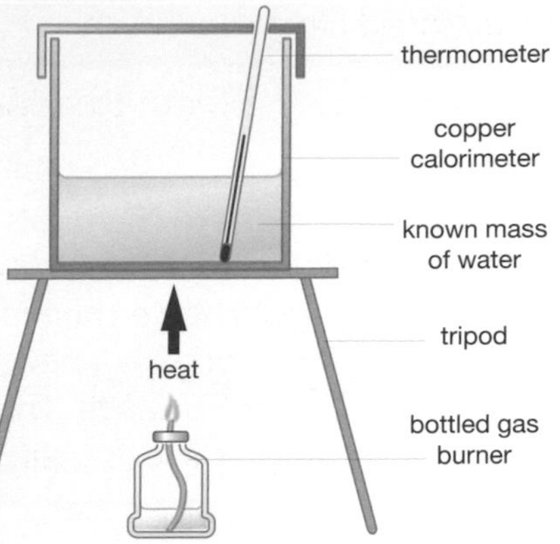

The tests are made fair by having the:

- same mass of water

- same temperature change

- same distance of the calorimeter from the flame.

The tests are made reliable by:

- repeating the experiment three times

- excluding as many draughts as possible.

The energy transferred is calculated using the formula:

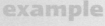

energy transferred = mass of water x 4.2 x temperature change

The unit is joules (J).

example

Calculate the energy transferred if 100 g of water is heated from 20 °C to 70 °C.

$$\text{energy transferred} = 100 \times 4.2 \times (70 - 20)$$
$$= 420 \times 50$$
$$= 21\,000 \text{ J}$$
$$= 21 \text{ kJ}$$

EXAM HINTS AND TIPS

Always set your working out clearly and show all the steps.

FIGURE 7: Suggest why a copper calorimeter is used in the experiment.

Diagram labels: thermometer, copper calorimeter, known mass of water, tripod, heat, bottled gas burner

The energy output of a fuel is calculated using the formula:

$$\text{energy per gram} = \frac{\text{energy supplied}}{\text{mass of fuel burnt}}$$

The unit is joules per gram (J/g).

example

If this water has been heated by 3.0 g of fuel then the energy output is:

$$\text{energy per gram} = \frac{21\,000}{3.0}$$
$$= 7000 \text{ J/g}$$

QUESTIONS

13 Calculate the energy per gram released by 5.0 g of fuel that raises the temperature of 100 g of water from 18 °C to 78 °C.

Module summary

Concept map

Food and additives

All foods are chemicals. Cooking is a chemical change. When a chemical change occurs, a new substance is made. This change is irreversible.

Some foods must be cooked. This kills microbes, improves the texture and flavour of the food, and makes it easier to digest.

Additives may be added as antioxidants, colours, emulsifiers or flavour enhancers. Intelligent packaging helps us to store food correctly.

Smells and crude oil

Perfumes are esters that can be made from acids and alcohols.

Nail varnish does not dissolve in water, but does dissolve in nail varnish remover.

Crude oil is a fossil fuel. It was formed from dead animals that were compressed over millions of years. Crude oil is non-renewable.

Crude oil is separated by fractional distillation. Fractions with lower boiling points exit at the top of the tower.

Polymers

Polymers are large, long chain molecules made from small monomers.

Nylon and GORE-TEX® can be used to make coats because they are waterproof. GORE-TEX has the advantage because it is also breathable.

Fossil fuels and energy

If a fossil fuel burns in a good supply of oxygen, complete combustion occurs. If not, incomplete combustion occurs.

An exothermic reaction transfers heat out to the surroundings. An endothermic reaction takes heat in.

When choosing a fuel for a particular purpose, several factors need to be considered:
- energy value and availability
- storage and cost
- toxicity and how much pollution they cause
- how easy they are to use.

Fuels can be compared by heating a fixed amount of water in a calorimeter and measuring the change in temperature. The energy transferred can be calculated by:

Energy transferred = mass of water × 4.2 × temperature change

Module quiz

1 What type of food are eggs and meat?

2 What gas is given off when baking powder breaks down as a cake is cooking?

3 What does an emulsifier do to oil and water?

4 What does an antioxidant do?

5 What **two** chemicals do you need to make an ester for a perfume?

6 What is a solute?

7 Why are fossil fuels non-renewable?

8 Why does bitumen have a high boiling point?

9 What is a hydrocarbon?

10 What are the conditions needed for polymerisation to take place?

11 What are nylon and polyester used for?

12 What properties should a plastic have to be used for a drain pipe?

13 What are the products of complete combustion?

14 What is the name of the toxic gas produced during incomplete combustion?

15 What is an exothermic reaction?

16 When fuels are compared by heating water, why is the same mass of water used?

17 What is the formula of water?

18 What is the formula of carbon dioxide?

19 What is CH_4?

20 How many atoms are there in the formula C_2H_5OH?

Citizenship activity

Your family owns a petrol car. You have a chance to buy a new hydrogen-powered car. Hydrogen only makes water when it is burned, and it is obtained from water. This makes it very environmentally friendly. However, the car is expensive to buy.

Your neighbour thinks you are wrong to even consider replacing your petrol car with a hydrogen-powered car, but you are concerned about global warming. You have heard about the Kyoto agreement and think that everyone should help reduce global warming where they can.

QUESTIONS
1 Explain your reasons for wanting to switch cars.
2 Now explain your neighbour's reasons for wanting to stick with a petrol car.

Exam practice

1 Baking powder, as its name suggests, is used in cooking.

  a **i** When baking powder is heated what gas does it release? [1]

      ii How would you test for this gas? [2]

  b **i** List two good sources of protein. [2]

      ii Name a good source of carbohydrate. [1]

      iii What happens to the shape of the molecules in meat when they are cooked? [1]

      iv Higher tier: Name the process described in **b iii**. [1]

      v Higher tier: What happens to the structure of the cells in potatoes when they are cooked? How does this explain why we cook potatoes before eating them? [2]

[Total 10 marks]

2 Copy and complete the following table to show information on the four main types of food additive.

Additive	What it does	Example of food containing it
antioxidant		
	makes oil and water mix	mayonnaise
	improves the flavour of the food	ready-made meals

[Total 4 marks]

3 Perfumes can be made from natural products or they can be synthetic.

  a **i** Name one natural perfume. [1]

      ii What type of chemical contained in many perfumes gives them their smell? [1]

      iii What two chemicals must be reacted in the laboratory in order to make this chemical? [2]

  b Copy and complete the following table to show the properties a perfume must have.

Property	Why it must have this property
	so it can reach your nose
non-toxic	so it does not poison you
does not react with water	
insoluble in water	

[3]

c Higher tier: Using kinetic theory, explain how the smell from a perfume bottle gets to your nose. [3]

[Total 10 marks]

4 **a** Name three fossil fuels. [2]

  b Explain why fossil fuels are said to be finite. [2]

[Total 4 marks]

5 The diagram below shows a fractionating tower.

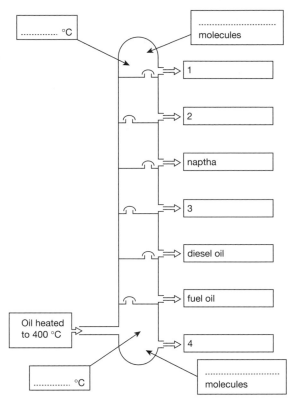

  a **i** Name the fractions collected at 1, 2, 3 and 4. [4]

      ii Copy the diagram and add the following labels to the correct place.

       -40 to 40   **300 to 350**
       large   **small** [4]

[Total 8 marks]

6 **a** Explain what you understand by the term 'cracking'. [1]

  b In terms of supply and demand, explain why cracking is carried out at the oil refinery. [2]

[Total 3 marks]

Worked example

a The apparatus opposite can be used to show that when a hydrocarbon fuel is burnt in a plentiful supply of air, it produces carbon dioxide.

  i Explain what will happen in such an experiment? [1]

  ii The experiment could be repeated but using dry cobalt chloride paper in the U tube. What result would you get and what would this show? [3]

b **i** Is combustion endothermic or exothermic? [1]

  ii Higher tier: Explain your answer to **b i** in terms of bonds broken and made. [3]

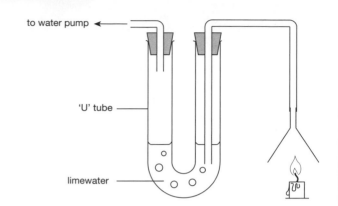

c Two fuels, A and B, are burnt and the energy used to heat 50 g of water. The data is shown in the table below.

Fuel	Mass burnt (g)	Temperature before (°C)	Temperature after (°C)	Temperature change (°C)
A	1.2	20.0	60.0	
B	1.2	20.0	74.6	

  i Calculate the temperature change for each fuel and add this to the table. [1]

  ii Which fuel gives out most energy? [1]

  iii Higher tier: Calculate the energy output of fuel A in J/g. [4]

---

a   *i*   *The limewater would turn milky.*
     ii   *The cobalt chloride paper would turn pink showing that water was made.*

Two marks out of three for a ii. For the extra mark, the student needed to state that the paper turned from *blue* to pink.

b   *i*   *Combustion is always exothermic.*
     ii   *More bonds are made than broken during combustion.*

The first answer is correct but no marks are awarded for the second answer. This is a common mistake. The correct answer is '*More energy is given out* during *bond-forming* than bond-breaking.'

c   *i*   *A = 40.0 °C, B = 54.6 °C.*
     ii   *Fuel B gives out most energy.*
     iii   *Energy transferred = 50 × 4.2 × 40.0 = 8400 J.*

The first two answers are correct, but the student has not completed the calculation in part iii, which asked for energy per gram of fuel burned. To finish off:
Energy per gram   = energy supplied ÷ mass burnt
                   = 8400 J ÷ 1.2 g = 7000 J/g.

Overall Grade: B

How to get an A

Remember the common mistake in b ii – over half of all candidates forget! In calculations, use the units as a check to see if you have arrived at the correct answer. The question asked for J/g, so your final step has to be dividing Joules by grams.

The movement of tectonic plates produces volcanoes.

Some of the rock on the Earth's surface has been formed by volcanic activity.

Lava is molten rock that erupts from a volcano.

Movements within the Earth are responsible for our landscape, our atmosphere and the raw materials that we use.

Volcanoes pump gases into the air – they produced the Earth's first atmosphere. The atmosphere is getting more polluted worldwide.

CONTENTS

133

Paints and pigments

You will find out:

- about pigments, binding agents, solvents and colloids
- how oil paints and emulsion paints are similar
- how paint dries

Ancient paintings

Some paintings in Egyptian tombs are 4000 years old, and they look as if they were painted last week!

The paintings shown in the photograph are in caves in France. They are the oldest cave paintings we know about. They are about 30 000 years old.

What is paint?

Painting a wall is simple. All you do is take coloured rock, grind it into a powder, add a glue and stick it to the wall!

The coloured rock is a **pigment**.

The glue is called the **binding medium**.

FIGURE 1: Pigments are solid powders.

In oil paint the binding medium is oil. It is specially chosen to stick the pigment to surfaces. The tiny particles of pigment powder are dispersed (spread) through the oil.

If the oil is too thick it is dissolved in a **solvent**. The solvent thins the paint making it easier to use.

A mixture of solid pigment powder dispersed in a liquid is called a **colloid**.

Why do we use paint?

- For protection. Woodwork outside is painted to protect the wood against rain. The oil sticks to the wood and forms a skin.
- To look attractive. When pictures or walls inside a house are painted, it is the pigment part of the paint we enjoy. The binder is used to stick pigment to the canvas or walls.

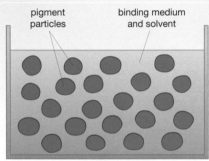

pigment particles   binding medium and solvent

paint in the can

FIGURE 2: What is a mixture of pigment and oil dissolved in to make it easier to use?

DID YOU KNOW?

A good glue for sticking pigment on to walls is egg white.

It takes a lot of eggs to paint a wall!

WANT TO KNOW MORE?

To find out more about emulsions, read pages 100–101.

QUESTIONS

1   White paint is made of a white powder mixed into oil.
    a Which is the pigment?
    b Which is the binding medium?
2   What is a mixture of a solid powder in a liquid called?

...binding medium   ...colloid   ...emulsion   ...emulsion paint

Pigments

In the past the range of different coloured rocks was limited. Chemists now make more solids that are good pigments.

A good pigment does not fade. It hides the colour of whatever is underneath the paint and stays mixed throughout the binding medium.

A pigment is not dissolved in the binding medium and solvent. It forms a colloid of small solid particles dispersed through the whole liquid.

Watching paint dry

An **oil paint** contains a pigment, a binding medium and a solvent.

Once the oil paint has been painted onto a surface, the solvent **evaporates** into the air leaving the binding medium to dry and form a skin, which sticks the pigment to the surface.

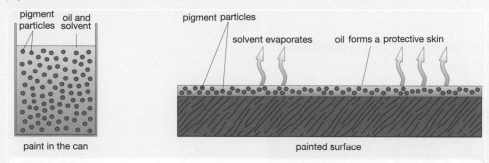

FIGURE 3: What evaporates when an oil paint dries?

The evaporating solvent is a pollutant. Paint manufacturers try to reduce the pollution in their paints. One way is to use **emulsion paint** which contains less solvent.

Emulsion paint is a type of oil paint. The oil is still the binding medium with pigment particles dispersed through it.

The oil is in the form of small droplets spread through water. This is because oil does not mix in water. Tiny droplets of one liquid in another is called an **emulsion**.

When an emulsion paint has been painted onto a surface, the water evaporates leaving droplets of oil behind. The drops of oil join together to make a continuous film.

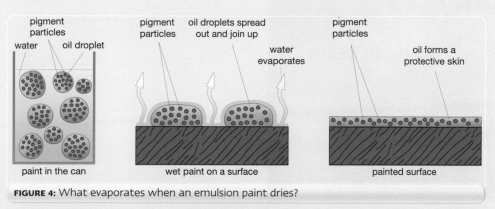

FIGURE 4: What evaporates when an emulsion paint dries?

Colloids

Colloids are mixtures of tiny particles of one thing in another. Oil paint is a colloid because it is a mixture of solid particles in a liquid.

Emulsion paint is a colloid in two ways. It is a mixture of one liquid inside another – oil droplets in water. Each oil droplet also has solid particles dispersed through it.

Particles, or droplets, that are very small stay mixed in the liquid, they do not settle out. Particles in paint are small enough to stay dispersed through the liquid while it is in use, though some paints need stirring if they are left in the tin for a long time.

Drying oil paint

The oil in oil paint is very sticky and takes a long time to harden. Normal oil paints 'dry' by chemical reaction.

Once the solvent has evaporated the oil slowly reacts with oxygen in the air to form a tough, flexible film over the wood. The oil binding medium is oxidised by the air.

You will find out:

- about thermochromic and phosphorescent pigments
- about synthetic dyes

Special pigments

Paints made with **thermochromic** pigments are very unusual. When they get hot they change colour. When they cool down they change back to their original colour.

When you were small, did you have stickers over your bed that glowed in the dark? The paint on a sticker contains a **phosphorescent** pigment. A phosphorescent pigment takes in light energy during the day and gives out light at night.

Clothing

We can buy clothes in a much wider range of colours than our grandparents could. The first cloth dyes were natural dyes such as juice from coloured berries.

Over the last 150 years chemists have been making man-made (**synthetic**) dyes. A synthetic dye gives a brighter colour that does not fade as much as a natural dye.

FIGURE 5: Why do we use synthetic dyes?

▌▌ QUESTIONS ▌▌

6 What do we call a dye that is man-made?

7 What type of pigment changes colour when it is heated?

8 What do phosphorescent pigments do?

...luminous   ...phosphorescent

Thermochromic paints

Thermochromic pigments used in some paints are chosen for their colour and also for the temperature at which their colour changes.

Many people find that anything over 60 °C is too hot to hold.

■ A thermochromic pigment that changes colour at 45 °C can be used to paint cups or kettles to act as a warning.

■ A pigment that changes colour just above 0 °C makes a good warning paint for road signs to show if it might freeze.

FIGURE 6: What type of paint has been used to make these mugs?

Phosphorescent paints

Phosphorescent pigments absorb energy from daylight. They slowly release the energy as light.

FIGURE 7: What type of pigment gives out light?

QUESTIONS

9 Give **one** use of a thermochromic pigment.

10 Suggest why phosphorescent stickers do not glow for the whole night.

Thermochromic paints

Most thermochromic pigments change from a colour to colourless.

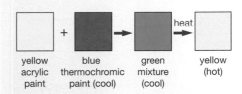

cool   hot

Thermochromic paints come in a limited range of colours. To get a larger range of colours they are mixed with different colours of normal acrylic paints, in the same way that you mix any coloured paints.

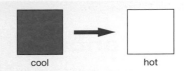

| yellow acrylic paint | blue thermochromic paint (cool) | green mixture (cool) | yellow (hot) |

When the mixture gets hot the blue thermochromic paint becomes colourless, so all that is seen is the yellow of the acrylic paint.

Phosphorescent paints

Phosphorescent pigments are sometimes used in **luminous** watch dials.

They are not the only type of pigment that has been used in this way. Some radioactive chemicals glow in the dark. The people who painted the watch dials with radioactive paint used to lick their brushes to get them to a fine tip. Many of them developed cancer as a result.

Phosphorescent paints are much safer than radioactive paints.

QUESTIONS

11 Jonathan mixes yellow thermochromic paint with red acrylic paint.

 a What colour paint does he produce?

 b What colour does Jonathan see when the paint is hot?

...synthetic ...thermochromic

Construction materials

You will find out:

- the names of some construction materials
- where the materials come from
- some differences between limestone, marble and granite

'Just another brick in the wall'

The buildings in your local town started as raw materials beneath or on the surface of the Earth.

Think about what the buildings around you are made from.

Brick is a traditional building material.

The Taj Mahal Tomb in Agra, India is inlaid with marble.

St Paul's Cathedral in London is built from limestone.

These steel frames will be hidden inside the walls.

Here, steel is a feature on the outside of a building.

Aluminium panels can go on the outside.

Glass is a construction material.

EXAM HINTS AND TIPS

Make sure you know the names of these construction materials:

- granite, marble, limestone
- aluminium, iron (steel)
- brick, cement, concrete, glass.

QUESTIONS

1. Name **five** construction materials.
2. Make a list of the materials used to build your school.
3. Find out if your school has a steel frame.

...igneous   ...metamorphic   ...reinforced concrete

The raw materials

Most modern buildings are made from materials dug out of the Earth.

Stone such as limestone, marble and granite is cut out of the ground and used in buildings. Blocks of stone are expensive to quarry and are only used for special buildings.

Stone buildings, such as cathedrals, are normally made from limestone. Limestone is easier to cut into blocks than marble or granite. Marble is much harder than limestone. Granite is harder still and is very difficult to shape.

Some buildings look as if they are built completely from stone but they aren't. They are only lined on the outside with stone and have a different material on the inside. The stone is used as an attractive 'front'.

Smaller buildings such as houses are normally built from brick.

Larger structures are made from a steel frame or **reinforced concrete**. The walls are then built inside the frame. These walls can be made of brick, concrete, aluminium or glass.

Brick, concrete, steel, aluminium and glass also come from the ground, but they need to be manufactured from raw materials.

FIGURE 1: What building material is made from the clay in this pit?

Raw material	clay	limestone and clay	sand	iron ore	aluminium ore
	⬇	⬇	⬇	⬇	⬇
Building material	brick	cement	glass	iron	aluminium

▒▒▒ QUESTIONS ▒▒▒

4 Look at the headstones in your local cemetery. They all have dates on them. How well have the different types of materials used for the headstones weathered?

5 List granite, limestone and marble in order of hardness, starting with the softest.

Rock hardnesses

Igneous and **metamorphic** rocks are normally harder than **sedimentary** rocks.

- Granite is an igneous rock and is very hard.
- Marble is a metamorphic rock. It is not as hard as granite but harder than limestone.
- Limestone is a sedimentary rock and is the softest.

Igneous rock is formed out of liquid rock that cools slowly and forms interlocking crystals as it **solidifies**. It is this interlocking structure that gives the rock its hardness.

Metamorphic rock is rock that has been changed. Marble is metamorphic, it is a form of limestone that has been subjected to heat and pressure in the Earth's crust, making it harder than original limestone.

Sedimentary rock is made of fragments that have settled into layers. Limestone is a sedimentary rock made from the shells of dead sea-creatures that have slowly stuck together.

▒▒▒ QUESTIONS ▒▒▒

6 Explain why granite is harder than marble and marble is harder than limestone. Include how each rock is formed in your answer.

Cement and concrete

Cement is made from limestone.

Limestone is a form of calcium carbonate. When calcium carbonate is heated it **thermally decomposes** to form calcium oxide and carbon dioxide.

To make **cement** the limestone is heated and clay is added.

Cement, sand and gravel are mixed with water and left to set to make **concrete**, which is an artificial rock.

Reinforced concrete has steel rods inside it and is much stronger than normal concrete. The concrete is poured around steel rods and left to set.

Getting building materials out of the ground

Every year millions of tonnes of limestone and other rocks are mined from quarries.

Without these quarries there would not be any buildings or roads. But quarries are often in areas of outstanding natural beauty and this can create environmental problems.

In the photograph look for:

- dust pollution
- damaged landscape (compare the quarry with the fields beyond)
- the space that the buildings take up.

Think about other problems:

- noise from explosives and machinery
- more lorries on country lanes
- what happens to the quarry after the stone has been taken out.

When a quarry closes the owners have to landscape the area.

The land can be:

- covered with soil and planted with grass
- used as a rubbish tip and then covered with soil
- left to fill with water and used for fishing and sailing.

FIGURE 2: Limestone quarry in the Peak District, Derbyshire.

You will find out:

- how cement is made
- about thermal decomposition
- about the difference between cement and concrete
- how reinforced concrete works
- about some of the environmental problems of quarries

EXAM HINTS AND TIPS

Remember that steel is a form of iron.

QUESTIONS

7 What is the chemical name for limestone?

8 Suggest **two** ways of dealing with a quarry once it is disused.

...cement   ...composite   ...compression   ...concrete

Cement and concrete

Calcium carbonate thermally decomposes at a very high temperature.

The word equation for the reaction is:

calcium carbonate ⟶ calcium oxide + carbon dioxide

> Thermal decomposition is the chemical breakdown of a compound into at least two other compounds under the effect of heat.

Cement mixed with sand and water is called **mortar**. It is very good for sticking bricks together, but it is not strong enough to use on its own. If gravel is added to the mixture it makes concrete, which is much stronger.

Reinforced concrete has steel rods or steel meshes running through it and is even stronger. It is a **composite** material.

FIGURE 3: a Steel rods and **b** steel meshes are used to reinforce concrete. Steel is flexible so the rods and meshes can be bent into different shapes.

FIGURE 4: Why do you think this road bridge is made from reinforced concrete and not ordinary concrete?

DID YOU KNOW?

The Romans invented concrete.

They could even make a concrete that set under water!

The symbol equation for the thermal decomposition of calcium carbonate is:

$$CaCO_3 \longrightarrow CaO + CO_2$$

More on reinforced concrete

Concrete is very strong under **compression** (squashing force). It is much weaker under **tension** (pulling force).

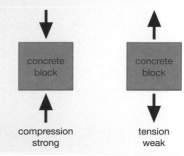

FIGURE 5: Is concrete stronger under compression or tension?

If a heavy load is put on a concrete beam it will bend very slightly. When a beam bends its underside starts to stretch. This puts it under tension and cracks start to form.

Steel is strong under tension. Steel rods in reinforced concrete stop it stretching.

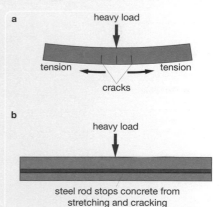

FIGURE 6: Why does putting steel rods or mesh in concrete stop cracks appearing in it?

QUESTIONS

10 Concrete is hard, but this is not enough to make it a really useful building material. Explain why.

QUESTIONS

9 Explain why the first reaction below is an example of thermal decomposition and the other two are not.

- When limestone is heated it forms calcium oxide and carbon dioxide.
- When magnesium is heated in air it forms magnesium oxide.
- When salt is heated it melts.

...mortar ...tension ...thermal decomposition

Does the Earth move?

You will find out:
- about the structure of the Earth
- about plate tectonics
- what happens when two plates collide

Yes, it does!

This can make life very dangerous.

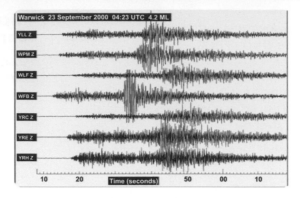

What is the Earth made from?

The Earth has an iron **core** surrounded by a **mantle**.

On the outside is a thin rocky **crust**.

The outer layer of the Earth is made from **tectonic plates**. Tectonic plates move very slowly. Their movement causes earthquakes and volcanoes at the plate boundaries.

DID YOU KNOW?

The trip from Europe to Disneyworld in Florida, America is getting longer.

America and Europe are moving apart by about 2 cm a year.

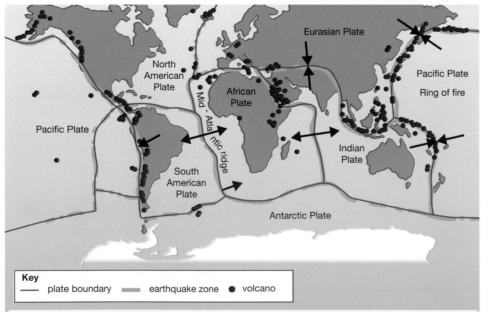

Key
— plate boundary ▬ earthquake zone ● volcano

FIGURE 2: What do you notice about the positions of the plate boundaries and the volcanoes and earthquake zones?

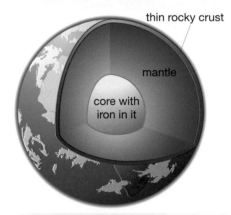

FIGURE 1: What part of the Earth has iron in it?

⚏ QUESTIONS ⚏

1 Where on the Earth's crust do most volcanoes and earthquakes happen?

...continental plate ...convection current ...core ...crust ...lithosphere

Structure of the Earth

The outer layer of the Earth is called the **lithosphere**. It is relatively cold and rigid. It is made of the crust and the part of the mantle that lies just underneath.

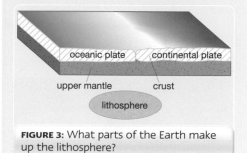

FIGURE 3: What parts of the Earth make up the lithosphere?

The tectonic plates that make up the Earth's crust are less dense than the mantle and they 'float' on it.

There are two kinds of plate:

- **continental plates** that carry the continents
- **oceanic plates** that lie underneath the oceans.

The crust is far too thick for anyone to be able to drill through it – yet. Most of our knowledge comes from measuring seismic waves produced by earthquakes. (See Stable Earth on pages 204–5 for more on measuring seismic waves.)

The measurement of seismic waves improved in the 1960s when scientists were developing ways of detecting nuclear explosions.

▦▦ QUESTIONS ▦▦

2   Name the **two** types of tectonic plate.

3   Explain why tectonic plates do not sink into the Earth's mantle.

More on the Earth's structure

Tectonic plates move very slowly and can move in different ways:

- apart
- collide
- scrape sideways past each other.

The mantle is hard and rigid near to the surface of the Earth and hotter and non-rigid near to the Earth's core.

The mantle is solid at all times, but at greater depths it is more like Plasticine, which can 'flow' despite being solid.

Energy from the hot core is transferred to the surface by slow **convection currents** in the mantle.

An early explanation for the movement of tectonic plates was that they were dragged by the convecting mantle like a conveyor belt. Geologists now think that the explanation is much more complicated.

The two types of tectonic plates have different densities.

- Oceanic plates are more dense than continental plates and sink low down into the mantle. Oceans accumulate on top of them.
- Continental plates float high up in the mantle.

When two plates collide the more dense oceanic plate sinks below the less dense continental plate. This is known as **subduction**.

The oceanic plate partially re-melts and is reabsorbed into the mantle. Some of the molten rock works its way back up to the surface and creates a chain of volcanoes.

The subducting oceanic plate does not move smoothly; it slips at intervals. When it slips the vibration causes earthquakes.

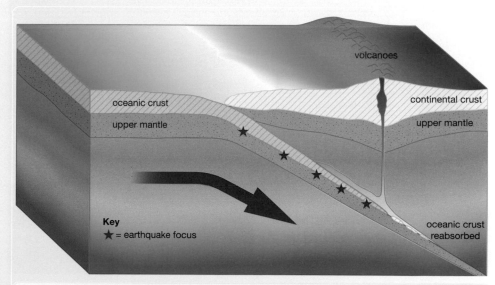

FIGURE 4: What is subduction?

▦▦▦ QUESTIONS ▦▦▦

4   Suggest what would happen to the oceans if oceanic and continental plates were the same density.

You will find out:

- what happens to molten rock
- how to tell how fast a rock cooled
- about evidence for moving plates

What happens to molten rock?

Underneath the surface of the Earth most of the rock is solid.

But some of the rock does melt and is called **magma**. It slowly moves up to the surface of the Earth. Eventually it cools down and **solidifies** to make **igneous** rock.

Molten rock that reaches the surface of the Earth is called **lava** and it comes out in a volcano.

Volcanoes that produce runny lava are often fairly safe.

If the lava is thick and sticky then an eruption can be explosive and the volcano is much more dangerous.

Why do people live near dangerous volcanoes?

In 79 AD the Roman town of Pompeii was destroyed when Vesuvius erupted.

People moved back and built a modern town even nearer to the volcano. Vesuvius erupts fairly often but usually not so violently.

The ash from volcanoes makes a rich soil that is good for growing things. Most volcanic eruptions are not that dangerous, so people think it is worth moving back.

FIGURE 6: Why do some people choose to live near to active volcanoes?

FIGURE 5: Moving magma.

▥ QUESTIONS ▥

5 What is the difference between magma and lava?

6 Some volcanoes produce runny lava and some produce thick sticky lava. Which is the safest type of lava?

...igneous   ...graded bedding   ...lava   ...magma

Magma and rocks

Magma rises through the Earth's crust because it is less dense than the crust.

Magma cools and solidifies into igneous rock either after it comes out of a volcano as lava, or before it even gets to the surface.

We can tell how an igneous rock cooled by looking at its crystals.

- Igneous rock that cools rapidly (close to the surface) has small crystals.
- Igneous rock that cools slowly (further from the surface and better insulated) has large crystals.

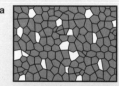
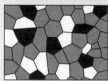

FIGURE 7: The structure of igneous rock crystals **a** rapidly cooled and **b** slowly cooled away from the surface of the Earth. What is the main difference in the crystals?

Example of rock type	Small crystal	Large crystal
iron-rich magma	basalt	gabbro
silica-rich magma	rhyolite	granite

Geologists study volcanic rocks to decide what previous eruptions were like.

They also use seismic measurements to help them predict future eruptions and learn more about the structure of the Earth.

Evidence for plate tectonics

A bit of history

People noticed how well the coastline of Africa matches that of South America.

It was then suggested that the continents were formed from one 'supercontinent' that was splitting apart at the time of the dinosaurs. This was called the continental drift theory.

However, nobody could explain how the continents were able to move through the rocks of the ocean floor. The first real evidence came when geologists found a huge ridge in the middle of the Atlantic Ocean. The rocks around the ridge are very young.

The further the rocks are from the ridge the older they are. The sea floor moves outwards and new rock forms in the gap. This is where plates are actually being formed.

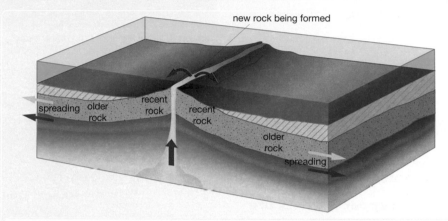

FIGURE 8: Does rock get older or younger as the distance from the central ocean ridge increases?

Subduction zones are where plates are being destroyed.

Magma and volcanoes

Differences in the composition of magma do not just lead to different types of rock. If magma reaches the surface of the Earth, then different types of magma can cause different types of eruption.

- Iron-rich magma (called basaltic magma) tends to be runny. Volcanoes with lava made from this sort of magma are often fairly 'safe'. The lava tends to spill over the edges of a volcano and people who live nearby can get out of the way.
- Silica-rich magma is less runny. It produces volcanoes that may erupt quietly or explosively. This happens when dissolved gases in the magma have no time to escape from the stiff liquid. The magma erupts like spray from a shaken can of fizzy drink. It shoots out as clouds of searingly hot ash and pumice. The falling ash buries houses and people before they have time to escape. Rain turns the ash into mudslides which can trap and kill. The falling ash often includes large lumps of rock over a metre across called **volcanic bombs**.

Geologists investigate past eruptions by looking at the ash layers. In each eruption, coarse ash falls first, followed by fine ash, producing **graded bedding**.

Future eruptions can sometimes be predicted with the help of seismometers. This method is not precise and disasters still occur.

QUESTIONS

7 Why does lava from volcanoes not form large crystals?

QUESTIONS

8 Explain why silica-rich magma is more dangerous than iron-rich magma.

...solidify   ...subduction zone   ...volcanic bomb

Metals and alloys

You will find out:
- that copper can be extracted using carbon
- about purifying copper by electrolysis
- about recycling copper

The Bronze Age

About 6000 years ago man learnt how to extract copper from its ore.

This discovery marked the start of the Bronze Age.

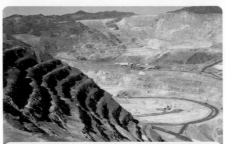

FIGURE 1: Huge amounts of rock are dug from copper mines to get enough ore for modern needs.

DID YOU KNOW?

We need tiny amounts of copper in our diet to stay healthy.

Bananas give us copper in our diet — but not enough to smelt!

Making copper

Digging copper

All the best ores were used up long ago. Now, only low grade ore is left.

Extracting copper from its ore

Copper is a metal **element**. Ores are **compounds**.

In the lab we get copper from its ore by heating it with **carbon**.

Industrial smelters work slightly differently but the ore still has to be heated in a furnace.

Making copper pure

Smelted copper is not very **pure**. We use **electrolysis** to purify it.

Millions of tonnes of copper are produced each year, so the electrolysis is done on a large scale.

Recycling

More than a third of all copper is **recycled**. Some of the copper in the pipes in your home may have been mined a long time ago!

Recycling copper saves resources and money. It is cheaper to recycle copper than to extract new copper from the ground.

Recycling also saves energy needed to crush rock and to operate smelters and electrolysis cells.

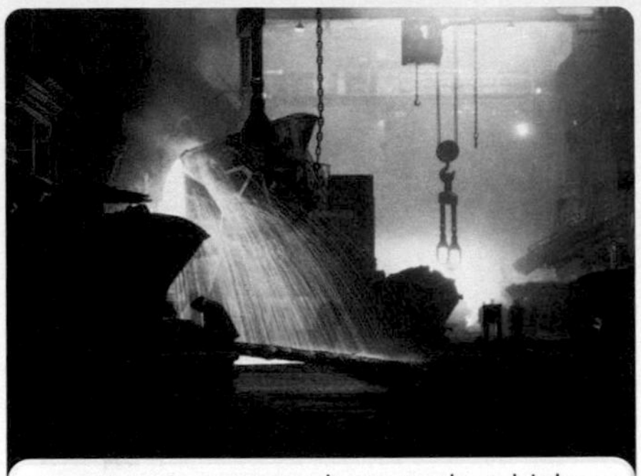

FIGURE 2: Copper smelters work at high temperatures. This needs an enormous amount of energy.

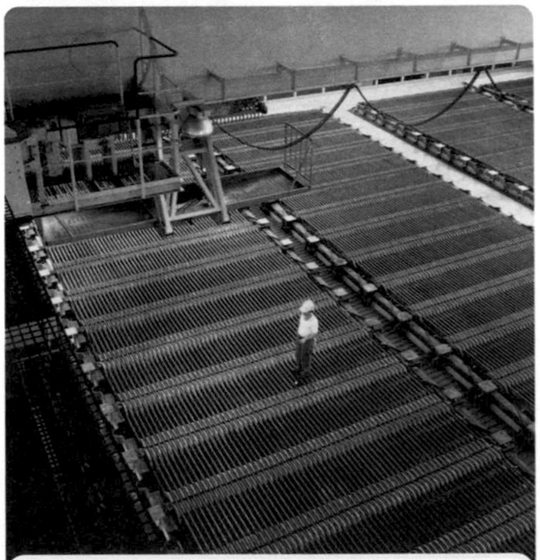

FIGURE 3: Electrolysis of smelted copper. The size of the men gives you an idea of scale.

QUESTIONS

1 What can you heat with copper ore to get the copper out?

2 Why can smelted copper not be used?

...anode ...brass ...bronze ...carbon ...cathode ...compound

Purifying copper using electrolysis

Impure copper can be purified in the laboratory using an **electrolysis cell**.

In an electrolysis cell the **anode** is impure copper. The anode dissolves into the **electrolyte** and pure copper coats the **cathode**. The cathode is 'plated' with new copper.

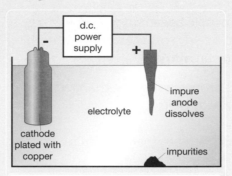

FIGURE 4: What is the anode made from in this electrolysis cell?

Recycling copper

Copper has a fairly low melting point. This makes it easy to melt down and recycle.

However, copper that has been used to make something may be contaminated with other elements, such as solder. This means that it can't then be used for purposes where the copper must be very pure, such as electric wiring.

FIGURE 5: Copper used in electric wires must be very pure.

FIGURE 6: Impure copper can be used in alloys such as brass.

Contaminated copper can be used to make copper alloys such as **brass** or **bronze**.

Copper for recycling has to be sorted carefully so that valuable 'pure' copper scrap is not mixed with less pure scrap.

When impure copper is used to make alloys it must first be analysed to find out how much of each element is present. If the scrap copper is very impure it has to be electrolysed again before it can be used.

More on purifying copper

> Normally, electrolysis is the break-up of a chemical compound (the electrolyte) when you use an electric current.

To purify copper we use an electrolyte of copper(II) sulfate solution and copper electrodes.

In this case, something special happens. Instead of the electrolyte breaking apart, the anode dissolves and the cathode is plated in pure copper.

A sheet of pure copper is used as a cathode. This sheet gets thicker as more pure copper is plated onto it.

The impure copper anode is called blister copper. Sometimes it is also called boulder copper.

The impurities from the copper anode sink to the bottom of the cell.

FIGURE 7: Industrial scale purification of copper by electrolysis. Copper cathodes are being lifted from electrolysis cells. What is unusual about this process compared to normal electrolysis?

QUESTIONS

3 Draw a labelled diagram of the apparatus needed to purify copper by electrolysis.

4 Suggest **one** problem linked to recycling copper.

QUESTIONS

5 During the electrolytic purification of copper, what happens at:

a the cathode

b the anode?

Tweaking metals

The Bronze Age only really started when people added tin to copper. They discovered that this changed copper from a fairly soft metal into something much harder called bronze. They had made an **alloy**.

By adding another element to a metal its properties can be changed to make it more useful. Steel is a very useful alloy of iron.

An alloy is a mixture of a metal element with another element.

Different alloys have different uses. To learn more about alloys see Cars for scrap on pages 152–155.

see Cars for scrap on pages 152–155.

You will find out:
- what alloys are
- why alloys are useful
- about 'smart' alloys

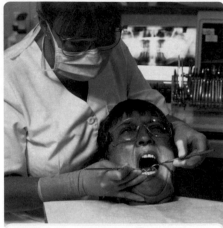

FIGURE 8: Amalgam is an alloy used by dentists to fill cavities in teeth.

FIGURE 9: Brass is an alloy used to make taps and door handles.

FIGURE 10: Solder is an alloy used to join metals.

EXAM HINTS AND TIPS

You need to know the names of these five alloys:

- brass
- bronze
- steel
- amalgam
- solder

DID YOU KNOW?

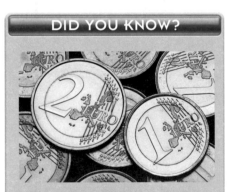

Copper alloys are used in coins.

In 2002 Europe introduced the new Euro coin.

184 000 tonnes of copper were needed to make them.

QUESTIONS

6 Look at the descriptions of alloys below.

alloy A — strong, cheap

alloy B — low melting point

alloy C — soft when made, hardens quickly

Which alloy would be good for:

a sticking two metals together

b making car bodies

c filling teeth?

...alloy   ...cast   ...nitinol

Alloys and their uses

Most metals form alloys. Here are just a few:

- bronze contains copper and tin
- brass contains copper and zinc
- solder contains lead and tin
- steel contains iron
- amalgam contains mercury.

Different alloys have different uses.

Bronze

Bronze is harder than copper, hard enough to make ploughshares, for ploughing fields, and swords! Bronze is one of the few metals that shrinks very slightly when it solidifies. This makes it easy to **cast**, which is one reason why statues are often made of bronze.

Steel

Steel is much stronger than iron, and **stainless steels** do not rust.

Solder

Alloys have lower melting points than the pure metal. This property is very useful. An alloy of lead and tin melts so readily that it can be used to join metals together. This alloy is called solder.

Alloys are often more useful than the original metals, though nowadays pure copper is more important than bronze or brass. Pure copper conducts electricity so well that vast amounts are turned into electric wire.

FIGURE 11: Suggest what properties make an alloy of aluminium and copper suitable for making aeroplanes.

Smart alloys

Do you wear glasses? Can you bend the frames without breaking them? (Do not try this!) If so, the frames are probably made from a **smart alloy**.

Nitinol is a smart alloy made from nickel and titanium.

Smart alloys are more bendy than steel so are harder to damage.

However, this is not why metal alloys are called 'smart'. Smart alloys can change shape at different temperatures. This is called '**shape memory**'. Surgeons can put a small piece of metal into a person's blocked artery and then warm it slightly. As it warms up it changes shape into a much larger tube that holds the artery open and reduces the risk of the person suffering a heart attack. Smart metal alloys are also used in shower heads to reduce the water supply if the temperature gets so hot that it might scald.

Smart alloys are becoming more important as new ways of using them are discovered.

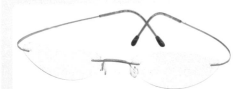

FIGURE 12: What property does the smart alloy used to make the frames of these glasses have?

QUESTIONS

7   Heavy lorries take cargo to a port where it is loaded onto ships. The lorries are driven onto a jetty. The legs of the jetty are made of an alloy and stretch down into the seawater.

Suggest **two** properties of the alloy.

8   What **one** property of solder makes it a useful alloy for sticking metals together?

QUESTIONS

9   The alloy filament in an electric light is designed to get hot when an electric current passes through it.

Suggest **two** properties of the alloy.

Vorsprung durch Technik – progress through technology

SELF-CHECK ACTIVITY

CONTEXT

Since 1994 Audi have been building cars with aluminium bodies. It is used not only in the panels but also in the frame below, called the ASF, or Audi Space Frame. First Audi built the luxury A8 saloon and more recently the smaller A3.

By 2001 over 150 000 aluminium Audis had been constructed and the number is still rising.

Two major factors that influence car design are fuel economy and passenger safety. With fuel becoming more expensive and pollution more of a problem, car designers have to find ways of making cars travel further for each litre of fuel used.

Cars also have to be safer and each design is thoroughly crash-tested before it is put on sale.

Cars have to be light and strong and Audi have found that a good way of achieving this is to make both the frame structure and the body panels from aluminium. Aluminium does not rust and so does not need the protection that steel does.

STEP 1

A more common material used to make car bodies is steel (mainly made up of iron). Discuss and decide in your group whether steel or aluminium, or both, would satisfy the following design features.

- Car bodies should conduct electricity as this can then form part of the electrical circuits such as to light bulbs.
- Car bodies should not corrode as it weakens them and spoils their appearance.
- Car bodies have to be shaped from flat sheets so they have to be workable (this is called malleability).

STEP 2

A car designer considers both materials and tests them. He comes to the conclusion that the aluminium-bodied car would be lighter, corrosion free and more expensive. Discuss and explain why each of these factors is significant.

These sentences show what you need to be including in your work. Use these to improve your work and to be successful.

Grade	Answer includes...
F	Describe **one** similarity or difference between steel and aluminium.
	Describe similarities and differences between steel and aluminium.
	Suggest which material would be better to build a car body from.
	Describe **one** advantage or disadvantage of building car bodies from aluminium or from steel.
C	Describe advantages and disadvantages of building car bodies from aluminium or from steel.
	Explain **one** advantage or disadvantage of building car bodies from aluminium or from steel.
A	Explain advantages and disadvantages of building car bodies from aluminium or from steel.
	As above, but with particular clarity and detail.

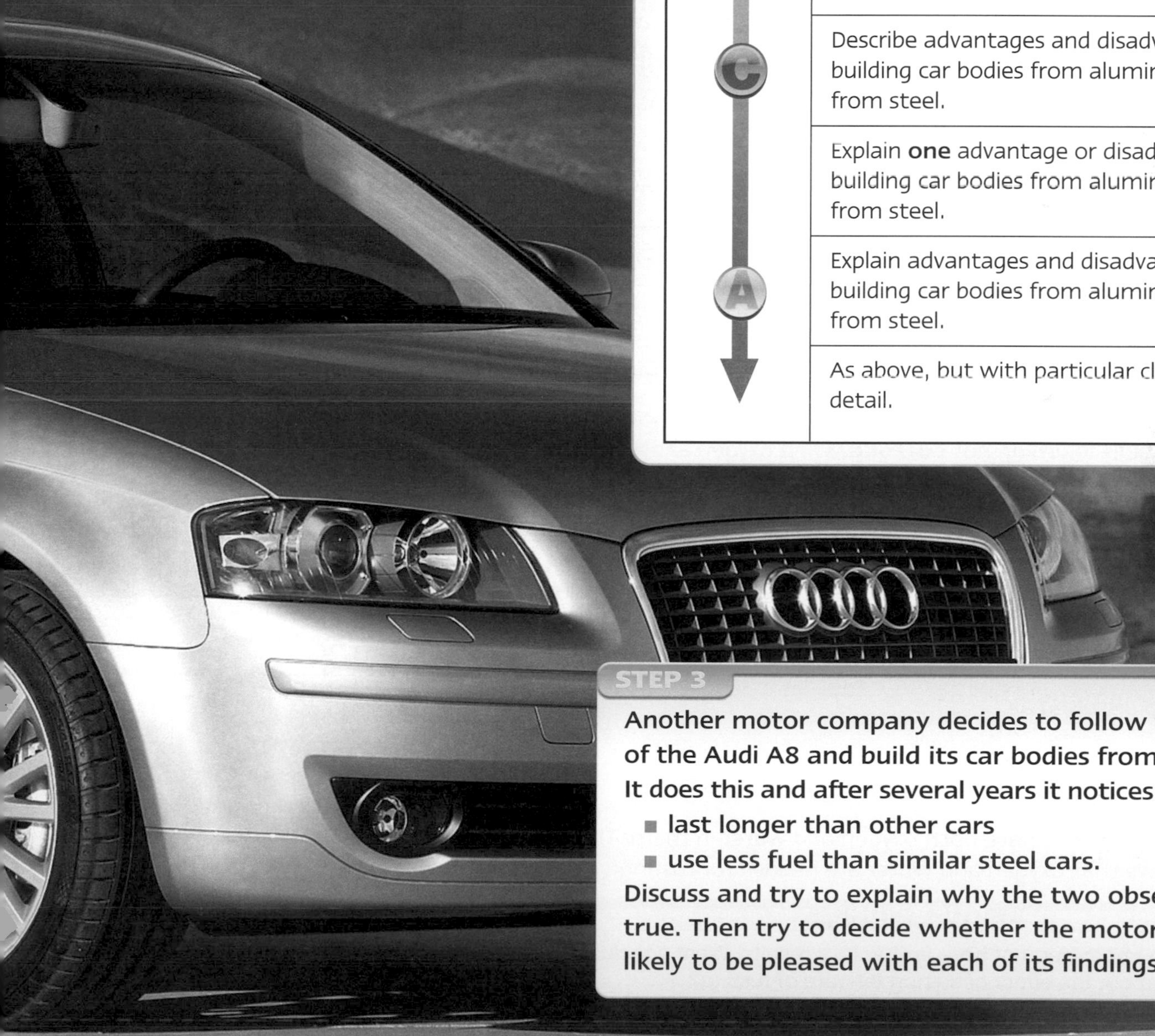

STEP 3

Another motor company decides to follow the example of the Audi A8 and build its car bodies from aluminium. It does this and after several years it notices that its cars:
- last longer than other cars
- use less fuel than similar steel cars.

Discuss and try to explain why the two observations are true. Then try to decide whether the motor company is likely to be pleased with each of its findings.

Cars for scrap

You will find out:
- about materials used in manufacturing motor vehicles
- about rusting and corrosion of metals

What happens to cars?

A car is mostly made from iron. Iron is a very valuable resource.

Today a lot of aluminium is also used to make cars. Aluminium is an even more valuable resource.

Plastics, glass and other metals are also used to make cars.

There are millions of cars in this country. Some people replace their cars after a few years. What happens to them?

Many cars are sold and millions are scrapped each year.

The scrap metal merchants keep the valuable metals and dispose of all the other materials.

Almost all of these materials could be recycled.

Rusting and corrosion

Most cars have a metal body. Steel or aluminium is normally used to make a car body. Steel is an **alloy** that contains mostly iron.

All cars made with steel **rust**. Rust is a brownish solid that forms when iron is in contact with **oxygen** and **water**. Rust flakes off the surface of the iron. This allows more rusting to take place.

Cars made with aluminium do not **corrode** when oxygen and water are present.

Kate and Anita investigate the rusting of iron. They put two iron nails into four numbered test tubes and put a bung in each tube. They then leave their experiment for two weeks. Each test tube has different conditions:

1 distilled water

2 dry air

3 water with no dissolved air

4 salt water.

After two weeks only the nails in test tubes 1 and 4 have rusted.

Test tubes 2 and 3 did not have both oxygen and water in them. This experiment shows that oxygen and water are needed for rusting.

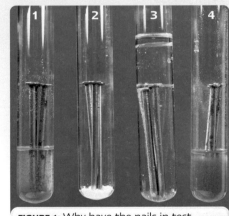

FIGURE 1: Why have the nails in test tubes 2 and 3 not rusted?

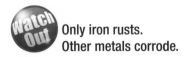
Watch Out Only iron rusts. Other metals corrode.

▓ QUESTIONS ▓

1 Look at the photograph of Kate and Anita's results. What conclusion can you make about the effect of salt on the rate of rusting?

2 Car bodies made of iron are painted. How does this help to prevent a car body from rusting?

...alloy ...corrode ...hydrated iron(III) oxide

More on rusting and corrosion

Rate of rusting

Salt water makes the rusting reaction much faster. In winter icy roads are treated with salt. This means that car bodies rust quicker. Acid rain also increases the rate of rusting.

FIGURE 2: Why do vehicles rust more quickly in winter?

Aluminium is useful because it does not corrode very much in moist air. So car bodies made from aluminium do not need much protection against corrosion. In air, a protective oxide layer forms on the surface of aluminium. Rust is also an oxide layer but it does not protect the rest of the iron. It flakes off leaving more exposed iron to rust.

Corrosion of metals other than iron

Today there is far more atmospheric pollution. Acid rain can have a pH value as low as 3. This means that many metals corrode quickly in moist air. Kate and Anita investigate the effect of different atmospheric conditions on metals. They leave strips of metal for two weeks and then look at the appearance of the metal. They show their results in a table.

Condition Metal	At start	Dry air	Moist clean air	Moist acidic air	Moist nitrogen	Moist alkaline air
Aluminium	shiny silver	shiny silver	shiny silver	dull silver	shiny silver	dull silver
Copper	shiny salmon-pink	shiny salmon-pink	small patches of green on surface	green layer on surface	shiny salmon-pink	small patches of green on surface
Iron	shiny silver	shiny silver	small patches of brown on surface	lots of brown flakes on surface	shiny silver	small patches of brown on surface
Magnesium	silver	silver	dull silver	greyish layer on surface	silver	dull silver
Lead	shiny silver	shiny silver	dull silver	dark, almost black layer on surface	shiny silver	dull silver
Silver	shiny silver	shiny silver	shiny silver	dull silver	shiny silver	shiny silver
Zinc	shiny silver	shiny silver	dull silver	greyish layer on surface	shiny silver	dull silver

Kate and Anita conclude that more corrosion happens in moist acidic air than in any other conditions. They also find that oxygen is needed for corrosion.

The chemistry of rusting

Rusting is a chemical reaction between iron, oxygen and water. The chemical name for rust is **hydrated iron(III) oxide**.

iron
+
oxygen $\longrightarrow$ hydrated iron(III) oxide
+
water

Rusting is an example of a type of reaction called **oxidation**. This is because iron reacts with oxygen to make an oxide.

QUESTIONS

3 Which metal tested by Kate and Anita corroded the least?

4 Explain how Kate and Anita were able to conclude that water was needed for corrosion.

QUESTIONS

5 Explain how Kate and Anita were able to conclude that oxygen is needed for corrosion.

...oxidation ...oxygen ...rust ...water

Materials in a car

A car is made from lots of different **materials**. A material is chosen because of its **properties**. Glass is transparent. Imagine a car with copper windows!

Some of the materials used are:

- metals and alloys – copper, iron, steel, lead and aluminium
- plastics
- glass
- fibres.

Iron and aluminium

Aluminium and iron are good conductors of electricity. They are both **malleable**. This means the metals can be easily beaten into a thin sheet.

The table shows some other properties of aluminium and iron.

Property	Aluminium	Iron
Corrosion in moist air	no obvious corrosion	rusts rapidly
Density in g/cm^3	2.7	7.9
Melting point in °C	660	1527
Boiling point in °C	2467	2750
Magnetism	not attracted to a magnet	attracted to a magnet

Pure aluminium and pure iron are not very strong. They become strong when they are made into alloys. An alloy is a **mixture** of a metal with another element. Often this is also a metal. Steel is a mixture that contains iron and carbon.

Old cars are often dumped and taken to a scrap metal yard. Here their parts are recycled.

It is easy to separate iron from aluminium. Iron is magnetic and aluminium is not.

The car body is cut into smaller pieces and an **electromagnet** is used to attract iron or steel parts.

Recycling makes sense because:

- aluminium and iron are **finite resources** (they will eventually run out)
- it avoids environmental damage due to mining and quarrying
- it reduces the amount of rubbish that goes into landfill sites.

FIGURE 3: Iron filings are attracted to a magnet.

FIGURE 4: What scrap metal does this electromagnet collect?

QUESTIONS

6 Describe how you would separate a mixture of iron filings and aluminium powder.

...electromagnet   ...finite resources   ...malleable   ...material

Materials used in cars

Different materials are used in a car for different reasons.

Material and its use	Reasons material is used
aluminium in car bodies and wheel hubs	does not corrode, low density, malleable, quite strong
iron or steel in car bodies	malleable, strong
copper in electrical wires	ductile, good electrical conductor
lead in lead-acid batteries	conducts electricity
plastic in dashboards, dials, bumpers	rigid, does not corrode, cheap
pvc in metal wire coverings	flexible, does not react with water, electrical insulator
glass and plastic/glass composite in windscreens	transparent, shatterproof (may crack)
fibre in seats	can be woven into textiles, can be dyed, hard-wearing

Steel or aluminium car bodies?

An alloy has different properties from those of the pure metals that are used to make it. Alloys are used when they have better or more appropriate properties than the pure metal. Steel is stronger and harder than iron. It does not rust as easily as pure iron.

Steel and aluminium can both be used to make car bodies. Each material has its particular advantages.

- Iron is stronger and harder than aluminium.
- Aluminium is more malleable than iron.
- Aluminium does not corrode as easily as iron.
- Aluminium is less dense than iron. This means that the mass of a car body is much less than the same car body made from iron.
- Aluminium needed for a car body is more expensive than iron.

Recycling

European Union law requires 85% of a car to be recyclable. This percentage will increase to 95% in the future. These figures include all parts of a car, including the batteries. Technology has to be developed to separate all the different materials used in making a car. This is a challenge to the motor industry but recycling makes sense for everybody.

- More recycling of metals means that less metal ore needs to be mined. This saves finite resources and reduces environmental damage.
- Recycling of iron and aluminium saves money and energy compared with making them from their ores.
- The benefits of recycling plastics include less crude oil being used to make plastics and less non-biodegradeable waste being dumped.
- Recycling of glass has been happening for many years so the technology is well established.
- Recycling batteries reduces the dumping of toxic materials into the environment.

▥▥▥ QUESTIONS ▥▥▥

7   Compare and contrast the properties of aluminium and iron.

More on steel versus aluminium in car bodies

Today more car bodies are made from aluminium than from iron. The advantages of aluminium are beginning to outweigh those of iron.

- Iron is stronger and harder than aluminium. This is important in the event of a crash but additional safety features, such as air bags, have reduced the risk to car passengers.
- A car with an aluminium body has a better fuel economy than a similar car made from iron.
- Aluminium does not corrode as easily as iron so the car body has a much longer lifetime.

FIGURE 5: An aluminium car body. What are the advantages of aluminium over steel when making car bodies?

▥▥▥ QUESTIONS ▥▥▥

8   The cost of making 1 kg of aluminium is more than for making 1 kg of iron. Explain why this is not a tremendous disadvantage for using aluminium in making car bodies.

Clean air

You will find out:
- about the composition of air and how it remains constant
- about a possible theory on the evolution of the atmosphere

Pollution of our air

Photochemical smog happens more often in large cities than it did 30 years ago. This is because of the increases in population and use of motor vehicles. The gases from the vehicles react together in bright sunlight to produce smog. Photochemical smog irritates the eyes and the lungs.

Athens in Greece has a particular photochemical smog problem. The 2004 Olympic Games took place in Athens. Athletes were worried that photochemical smog would mean their performances may be below their best.

In the United Kingdom the number of people suffering from asthma is steadily increasing. Many people think this is because of an increase in the amount of pollution in the atmosphere.

Clean air

Air is a mixture of different gases. Clean air is air that has no **pollutants** caused by human activity. The main gases in clean air are:

- nitrogen
- oxygen
- carbon dioxide
- water vapour
- noble gases (argon, neon, krypton, xenon).

The amount of water vapour in the air changes. The amounts of the other gases in the air remain almost constant.

The levels of gases in the air depend on:

- **combustion** of fossil fuels, which increases the level of carbon dioxide and decreases the level of oxygen

- **respiration** by plants and animals, which increases the level of carbon dioxide and decreases the level of oxygen.

- **photosynthesis** by plants, which decreases the level of carbon dioxide and increases the level of oxygen

 Do not confuse breathing and respiration.

Breathing describes the way air enters and leaves the lungs.

Respiration takes place in cells.

■■ QUESTIONS ■■

1. Suggest why the amount of water vapour in the atmosphere can change.
2. Respiration uses up oxygen and makes carbon dioxide. Write down the name of **one** other process that uses up oxygen and makes carbon dioxide.

FIGURE 1: In what way does photosynthesis alter the levels of gases in air?

...carbon cycle ...combustion ...degassing

What is in clean air?

About 78% of clean air is nitrogen and about 21% is oxygen. Of the remaining 1%, only 0.035% is carbon dioxide.

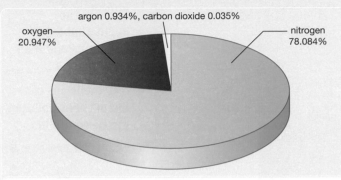

argon 0.934%, carbon dioxide 0.035%

oxygen 20.947%

nitrogen 78.084%

FIGURE 2: Why do the proportions of gases in clean air stay almost constant?

These percentages do not change very much. This is because there is a balance between processes that use up carbon dioxide and make oxygen and processes that use up oxygen and make carbon dioxide. Some of these processes are shown in a **carbon cycle**.

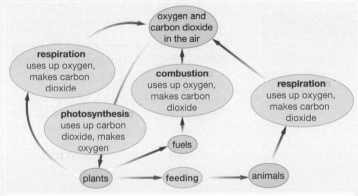

oxygen and carbon dioxide in the air

respiration uses up oxygen, makes carbon dioxide

combustion uses up oxygen, makes carbon dioxide

respiration uses up oxygen, makes carbon dioxide

photosynthesis uses up carbon dioxide, makes oxygen

fuels

plants → feeding → animals

FIGURE 3: Carbon cycle. The arrows show the direction of movement of carbon compounds. What is the only process that produces oxygen?

Evolution of the atmosphere

Scientists know that gases trapped in liquid rock under the surface of the Earth are always escaping. This happens in volcanoes.

Scientists speculate about the original atmosphere of the Earth. It is known that at some point in the Earth's history, microbes developed that could photosynthesise. These organisms could remove carbon dioxide from the atmosphere and add oxygen. Eventually the level of oxygen reached what it is today and it now stays fairly constant.

QUESTIONS

3 Write the word equation for respiration.
4 Write the word equation for photosynthesis.

WANT TO KNOW MORE?

To find out more about photosynthesis, read 'The food factory' on pages 62–65.
To find out more about respiration, read 'Fit for life', pages 14–15.

Changing atmospheric composition

Although the composition of the air remains fairly constant there are changes in the percentages of some gases.

Over the last few centuries the percentage of carbon dioxide in air has increased slightly. This is due to a number of factors.

- Increased energy usage – more fossil fuels are being burnt in power stations.
- Increased population – as the population increases, the world's energy requirements increase.
- Deforestation – as more rainforests are cut down less photosynthesis takes place.

Origin of the Earth's atmosphere

The Earth is over four and a half thousand million years old. During this time the Earth's atmosphere has evolved into its present day composition. Scientists can only guess about this evolution. One thing they do know is that the gases came from the centre of the Earth in a process called **degassing**.

One theory is as follows:

- The original atmosphere contained ammonia and later carbon dioxide.
- Chemical reaction between ammonia and rocks produced nitrogen and water.
- The percentage of nitrogen slowly increased. Since nitrogen is very unreactive, very little nitrogen was removed from the atmosphere.
- Much later organisms that could photosynthesise evolved. These organisms converted carbon dioxide and water into oxygen.
- As the percentage of oxygen in the atmosphere increased the percentage of carbon dioxide decreased until today's levels were reached.

QUESTIONS

5 Explain why it is impossible for scientists to be certain of the answer to the question, 'How did the Earth's atmosphere evolve?'.
6 Describe how an increase in the use of motor vehicles may affect the composition of the atmosphere.

Atmospheric pollutants

Pollutants are substances made by human activity that harm the environment.

Acid rain erodes stone in buildings and statues and kills plants and fish.

FIGURE 4: This statue of a lion is made from limestone. Suggest why its features are eroded.

FIGURE 5: These trees in the Czech Republic have died from the effects of acid rain.

The atmosphere contains a large number of pollutants. The main ones are shown in the table.

Pollutant	Where it comes from	Environmental effects
carbon monoxide	incomplete combustion of petrol- or diesel-powered motor vehicles	poisonous gas
oxides of nitrogen	reaction of nitrogen and oxygen at very high temperatures such as in an internal combustion engine	photochemical smog, acid rain
sulfur dioxide	combustion of fossil fuels that contain sulfur impurities	acid rain

Reducing pollution

Scientists are finding ways to reduce the amount of these pollutants.

Most cars are now fitted with **catalytic converters**.

Effect catalytic converters have on the emissions from a 1.8 litre petrol engine			
Catalytic converter	Emissions in grams/kilometre		
	of carbon monoxide	of hydrocarbons	of oxides of nitrogen
not fitted	5.59	1.67	1.04
fitted	0.61	0.07	0.04

A catalytic converter reduces the levels of carbon monoxide and oxides of nitrogen.

WOW FACTOR!

The pH of acid rain in some parts of Central Europe is so low that it's able to attack church roofs that contain gold.

WANT TO KNOW MORE?

To find out more about pollution, read 'Population out of control?' on pages 80–83.

QUESTIONS

7   Look at the table above. How does a catalytic converter help to reduce atmospheric pollution?

...acid rain   ...catalytic converter

Pollution control

Atmospheric pollution affects the environment and people's health. These effects will get worse unless atmospheric pollution is controlled. The European Union and the United Kingdom government have introduced many laws regarding pollution control. These have had some effect but still more controls are needed.

Catalytic converters

Exhaust gases from a car contain several pollutants including nitric oxide (an oxide of nitrogen) and carbon monoxide. A car fitted with a catalytic converter produces exhaust fumes that contain only a very small amount of these two pollutants.

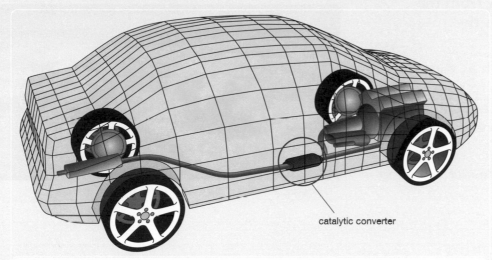

catalytic converter

FIGURE 6: Why are catalytic converters in motor cars good for the atmosphere?

A catalytic converter changes carbon monoxide into carbon dioxide. At the same time oxides of nitrogen are converted into nitrogen.

Carbon dioxide is a **greenhouse gas**. But it is less dangerous to the environment than carbon monoxide.

More on catalytic converters

Catalytic converters contain a **rhodium catalyst**.

A reaction between nitric oxide and carbon monoxide takes place on the surface of the catalyst. The reaction forms nitrogen and carbon dioxide.

carbon + nitric ⟶ nitrogen + carbon
monoxide oxide dioxide

$$2CO + 2NO \longrightarrow N_2 + 2CO_2$$

QUESTIONS

9 Cars that use a hydrogen-oxygen fuel cell instead of petrol are being developed.

In these cars hydrogen and oxygen react to make water.

a Write the balanced equation for the reaction between hydrogen and oxygen.

b Suggest why a car using a hydrogen-oxygen fuel cell produces very little atmospheric pollutants.

QUESTIONS

8 In a catalytic converter nitric oxide reacts with carbon monoxide to make carbon dioxide and nitrogen.

Write the word equation for this reaction.

Faster or slower (1)

You will find out:
- how the rate of a reaction can be changed
- about the relationship between the number of collisions between reacting particles and the rate of a reaction

Explosions

Some of the most impressive chemical reactions that you can see are explosions. An explosion is a very fast reaction that makes lots of gas. It is the gas molecules moving away from the centre of an explosion that produces the 'explosive force'.

Some explosions are very useful such as those that use dynamite, TNT or nitroglycerine to help in the mining of metals. The explosive forces split large sections of rock so that the metal ores can be extracted.

Other uses of explosives can cause devastation and destruction.

Explosions are used to help extract metal ores from rocks.

Speed of reaction

In a chemical reaction **reactants** are made into **products**.

reactants ⟶ products

A chemical reaction takes place when reactant **particles** hit or collide with each other.

The **rate of reaction** measures how much product is made each second. Some reactions are very fast and others are very slow. Rusting is a very slow reaction and burning is a very fast reaction.

In factories it is important to be able to control the speed of a reaction. If a reaction is too fast there could be a dangerous explosion. If a reaction is too slow then the factory may not be able to make a material efficiently and will lose money.

The speed of a reaction can be controlled by changing the:

- **concentration** of the reactants
- temperature of the reactants
- **pressure** of reactants that are gases
- **surface area** of the reactants.

If the concentration of reactants or the temperature of a reaction is increased, the rate of the reaction increases. If the pressure of gases in a reaction is increased the rate of reaction increases.

QUESTIONS

1 Look at the word equation to show how ammonia can be made.

hydrogen + nitrogen ⟶ ammonia

a List the reactants needed to make ammonia.

b The reaction is very slow at room temperature.

Suggest ways in which the reaction could be made to go faster.

...collision frequency ...concentration ...kinetic energy ...particle

Simple collision theory

A reaction takes place when reactant particles collide. The more collisions there are the faster the reaction. The particles must be moving very fast and have lots of **kinetic energy** for collisions to occur.

Concentration and collision theory

As the concentration increases the particles become more crowded. Instead of four particles of **A** there are ten particles of **A** in the same volume.

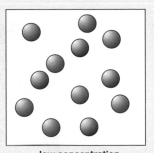
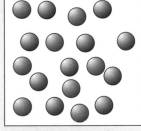

low concentration   high concentration

🔴 reacting particle of substance **A**

🔴 reacting particle of substance **B**

FIGURE 1: Why does the rate of reaction increase when the concentration of reactants increases?

The particles are more crowded so there are more collisions and the rate of reaction increases.

Temperature and collision theory

Particles move faster as the temperature increases. The reacting particles have more kinetic energy and so the number of collisions increases and the rate of reaction increases.

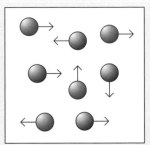
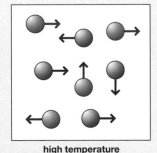

low temperature   high temperature

🔴 reacting particle of substance **A**

🔴 reacting particle of substance **B**

FIGURE 2: The thickness of the arrows indicates the amount of kinetic energy that the particles have. Explain why an increase in temperature makes a reaction go faster.

QUESTIONS

2 a Draw diagrams to show the particles in a gas at low pressure and the particles in a gas at high pressure.

   b Use your diagram to explain why a reaction between two gases at high pressure happens faster than when the gases are at low pressure.

More on collision theory

It is not the number of collisions that determines the rate of a reaction, it is the **collision frequency**.

Collision frequency describes the number of successful collisions between reactant particles that happen each second. The more successful collisions per second, the faster the reaction.

For a successful collision to occur each particle must have lots of kinetic energy.

As the concentration increases the number of collisions per second increases and so the rate of reaction increases.

As the temperature increases the reactant particles have more kinetic energy so there are more energetic collisions. These more energetic collisions are more successful.

QUESTIONS

3 Explain why reactions between gases happen faster at high temperature than at low temperature.

4 Suggest why increasing the pressure has little effect on the rate of a reaction between two solids.

Measuring the rate of reaction

It is very difficult to measure the rate at which many reactions happen.

However, the rate of reaction between magnesium and dilute hydrochloric acid can easily be measured in the laboratory.

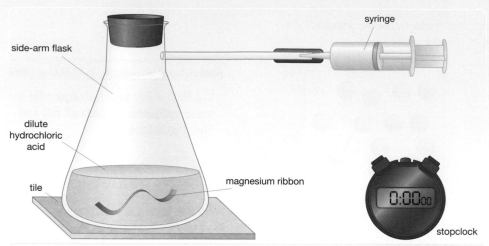

syringe

side-arm flask

dilute hydrochloric acid

tile

magnesium ribbon

stopclock

FIGURE 3: Measuring the rate of reaction between magnesium and dilute hydrochloric acid.

During the reaction magnesium ribbon fizzes in dilute hydrochloric acid and colourless bubbles of hydrogen are given off. The volume of hydrogen collected in the gas syringe is measured every 10 seconds.

magnesium + hydrochloric acid ⟶ magnesium chloride + hydrogen

The **reaction time** is the time taken for all the magnesium to react. The shorter the reaction time the faster the reaction.

The results of the experiment can be plotted on a graph as shown in Figure 4.

The graph shows the results of two different masses of magnesium ribbon added to 50 cm³ of hydrochloric acid. The **gradients** (slopes) of the lines show how fast the reaction is. So the reaction with 0.066 g of magnesium is faster than that with 0.033 g of magnesium.

When the reaction stops no more gas is made. The lines on the graph become horizontal. The reaction stops when one of the reactants is used up.

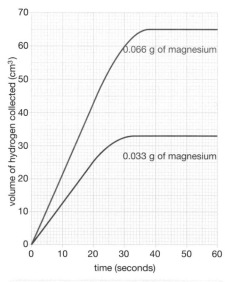

FIGURE 4: Graph to show volume of hydrogen produced over time when magnesium ribbon is added to dilute hydrochloric acid. Why do the lines on the graph flatten out?

■■ QUESTIONS ■■

5 Look at the line on the graph for 0.066 g of magnesium.

   a What is the volume of gas given off after 10 seconds?

   b How can you tell from the graph when the reaction has finished?

   c What is the total volume of hydrogen made when the reaction has finished?

...*gradient*

Rate of reaction and concentration

Figure 5 shows the results from two different experiments. In both experiments a 3 cm length of magnesium ribbon and 50 cm³ of hydrochloric acid were used. The blue line shows the results with concentrated hydrochloric acid. The red line shows the results of the experiment with dilute acid.

The gradient of the blue line is greater than that of the red line. This shows that the rate of reaction is faster when concentrated acid is used.

The total volume of hydrogen produced during both experiments is the same. This is because excess acid and the same mass of magnesium are used.

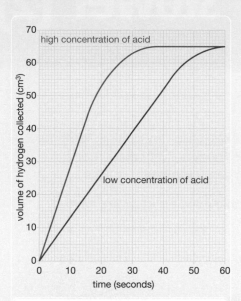

FIGURE 5: Graph to show how rate of reaction changes with a change in concentration of the reactants. How can you tell that one of these reactions proceeded faster than the other?

Rate of reaction and temperature

Figure 6 shows the results from two different experiments. In both experiments a 3 cm length of magnesium and 50 cm³ of hydrochloric acid were used.

The blue line shows the results with the acid at a temperature of 30 °C. Its gradient is greater than that for the red line, which describes the experiment where the acid is at a temperature of 20 °C.

The total volume of hydrogen produced during both experiments is the same. This is because excess acid and the same mass of magnesium are used.

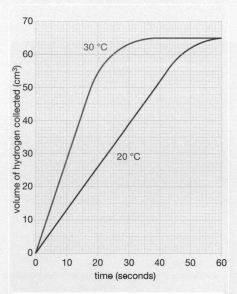

FIGURE 6: Graph to show how rate of reaction changes with a change in temperature. After what time have the reactants been used up?

Calculating the rate of reaction

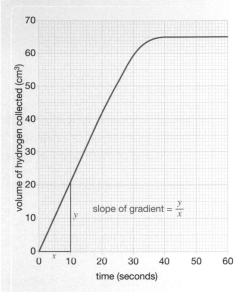

FIGURE 7: Calculating the gradient of a graph.

The rate of reaction can be worked out from the gradient of a graph.

The gradient is found by drawing construction lines. Choose a part of the graph where there is a straight line (not a curve). Measure the value of y and x and remember to use the scale of the graph carefully. Then divide y by x.

example

$$\text{gradient} = \frac{y}{x} = \frac{21.5}{10} = 2.15 \text{ cm}^3/\text{sec}$$

Sometimes it is easier to measure the mass of a product formed. The rate of reaction is then measured in g/sec.

QUESTIONS

6 Explain why the reaction between magnesium and dilute acid is slower than the reaction with concentrated acid.

7 Explain why the reaction between magnesium and dilute hydrochloric acid becomes faster as the temperature of the acid increases.

QUESTIONS

8 Magnesium ribbon and hydrochloric acid are put into a beaker. Hydrogen escapes from the reaction mixture.

Describe an experiment to find out the total mass of hydrogen given off every 10 seconds.

...reaction time

Faster or slower (2)

You will find out:

● how changing the surface area of a solid reactant affects the rate of a reaction

● about explosions

● how to analyse experimental data on rates of reaction

Explosions

An explosion happens when a reaction takes place very quickly. Remember the 'squeaky pop' test for hydrogen gas? There is a very quick reaction when a mixture of hydrogen and oxygen gas is **ignited**.

Other explosions happen when combustible powders in air are ignited.

Powder or lump?

Figure 1 shows two beakers.

Each beaker contains 1.0 g of calcium carbonate reacting with 40 cm^3 of dilute hydrochloric acid.

The temperature of the acid is the same in both beakers. The only difference is that one beaker contains powdered calcium carbonate and the other contains a lump of calcium carbonate. Powdered reactants always react faster than lumps.

FIGURE 1: Experiment to see if a reaction is faster if the solid reactant is a powder. How can you tell that the reaction on the left is faster?

■ QUESTIONS ■

1   In an experiment 1 g of calcium carbonate powder reacts with 50 cm^3 of concentrated hydrochloric acid at a temperature of 30 °C.

The mass of calcium carbonate and the volume of hydrochloric acid cannot be changed.

Write down **three** ways that the reaction can be made to go slower.

More on explosions

An explosion is an extremely fast reaction that releases a large volume of gaseous products. The gases move outwards from the reaction at great speed causing the explosive effect.

Combustible powders often cause explosions. A powder reacts with oxygen to make large volumes of carbon dioxide and water vapour. A factory using combustible powders such as sulfur, flour, custard powder or even wood dust, must be very careful. The factory owners must try to make certain that the powders cannot reach the open atmosphere. They must also make certain that the chance of producing a spark is very small.

Surface area and collision theory

A powdered reactant has a much larger **surface area** than the same mass of a block of reactant. As the surface area of a solid reactant increases so does the rate of reaction.

Look at Figure 2. When substance B is in a large lump, fewer reacting particles can be in contact with reacting particles of **A**. As the surface area increases there are more collisions between reacting particles. This means the rate of reaction increases.

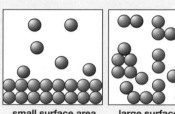

small surface area   large surface area

 reacting particle of substance **A**
 reacting particle of substance **B**

FIGURE 2: Explain why when a solid is made into a powder it reacts faster.

Measuring the rate of reaction

Figure 3 shows how the rate of reaction between calcium carbonate and dilute hydrochloric acid is measured. As the reaction takes place the mass on the balance decreases. This is because carbon dioxide gas is escaping.

$$CaCO_3 + 2HCl \longrightarrow CaCl_2 + H_2O + CO_2$$

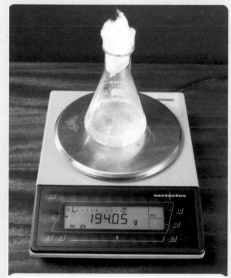

FIGURE 3: Measuring the rate of reaction between calcium carbonate and dilute hydrochloric acid.

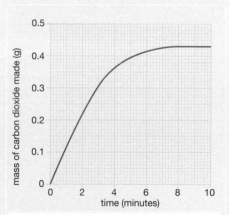

FIGURE 4: Graph to show how rate of reaction changes when calcium carbonate reacts with dilute hydrochloric acid.

More on surface area and collision theory

It is the collision frequency between reactant particles that is important in determining how fast a reaction takes place. The more successful collisions there are each second the faster a reaction.

When the surface area of a solid reactant is increased there will be more collisions each second. This means the rate of reaction increases.

The gradient of the graph in Figure 4 is a measure of the rate of reaction. Notice that as the reaction takes place, the rate of reaction becomes less and less. This is because the concentration of acid and the mass of calcium carbonate decrease. As the reaction proceeds there are fewer collisions between reactants.

▥▥▥ QUESTIONS ▥▥▥

2   A factory uses the combustible powder sulfur. One of the safety rules in the factory is that workers should report all spillages of sulfur powder.

     Suggest, with reasons, some other safety rules.

▥▥▥ QUESTIONS ▥▥▥

3   Use Figure 4 to calculate the rate of reaction during the first 2 minutes.

4   Explain how the mass of carbon dioxide produced in the reaction can be calculated using the readings from the top-pan balance.

Catalysts

> A **catalyst** is a substance added to a chemical reaction to make the reaction go faster. A catalyst does not change how much of a product is made.

A catalyst is very useful when making chemicals. When a catalyst is added to a reaction the same amount of product is produced but in a much shorter time.

Analysis of experimental results

Paul and Meghali investigate the reaction between zinc and sulfuric acid. Zinc sulfate solution and hydrogen gas are formed. They want to find a catalyst for this reaction.

They use a side-arm flask attached to a gas syringe.

In each experiment they use 1.5 g of zinc powder and 50 cm³ of dilute sulfuric acid. They also add 0.1 g of another substance.

Paul and Meghali measure the time it takes to collect 100 cm³ of hydrogen in the gas syringe. Their results are shown in the table.

Experiment number	Substance	Time to collect 100 cm³ of gas (in seconds)	Colour of substance at start of experiment	Colour of substance at end of experiment
1	no substance	150	—	—
2	magnesium chloride	150	white	white
3	copper chloride	15	green	pink
4	copper powder	25	pink	pink
5	iron(II) sulfate	20	green	grey

The slowest reactions are experiments 1 and 2 because the time taken to collect 100 cm³ of hydrogen is the longest.

The fastest reaction is experiment 3 because the time taken to collect 100 cm³ of hydrogen is the shortest.

⊞ QUESTIONS ⊞

5 Use the information about the reaction between zinc and sulfuric acid to answer the following.

   a What is the name of the gas collected in the gas syringe?

   b Paul and Meghali repeat the experiment using lumps of zinc instead of zinc powder. Predict what will happen to the time taken to collect 100 cm³ of gas.

Watch Out The time taken for a reaction to finish can be longer or shorter but not faster or slower.

...catalyst

Catalysts and rate of reaction

A catalyst increases the rate of a reaction. Some other properties of a catalyst are:

■ it is unchanged at the end of a reaction

■ only a small mass of catalyst is needed to catalyse a large mass of reactants.

Analysis of experimental results

Look at Paul and Meghali's results on the facing page. It is possible to conclude that only copper powder is a catalyst for the reaction between zinc and sulfuric acid.

The results show that when copper powder is added, the reaction is faster than when zinc and sulfuric acid alone are used. There was no change in the appearance of the copper during the reaction.

In another experiment, Paul and Meghali use 0.27 g of zinc powder, 0.1 g of copper powder and 50 cm³ of sulfuric acid. The acid is in excess so that at the end of the reaction all the zinc is used up. This time they measure the total volume of gas collected in the gas syringe every 10 seconds.

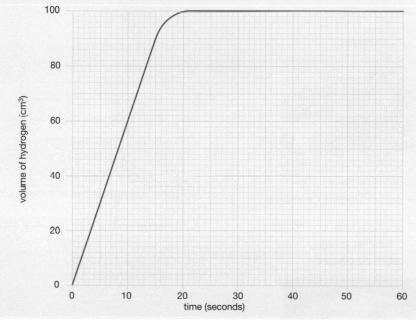

FIGURE 5: Graph to show the volume of gas collected when zinc powder and sulfuric acid react in the presence of copper powder. What volume of gas is produced after 10 seconds?

In the graph in Figure 5, the reaction has stopped when the volume of hydrogen remains constant. This occurs after 20 seconds.

If a 0.27 g lump of zinc is used instead of zinc powder, the graph obtained is different. The initial gradient of the line is less, but at the end of the reaction the same volume of gas (100 cm³) is produced.

If a 0.135 g lump of zinc is used, the final volume of gas produced is 50 cm³.

QUESTIONS

6   Using information from the table on the facing page, explain why copper chloride is not a catalyst for the reaction between zinc and sulfuric acid.

7   The experiment on this page is repeated using a block of copper not powder.
    Describe and explain what happens to the rate of reaction.

Catalysts and collision theory

Most catalysts only make a **specific** reaction faster. They do not make all reactions faster. Although copper catalyses the reaction between zinc and dilute sulfuric acid it will not catalyse other reactions. This means that scientists have had to discover many different catalysts. Examples are:

■ zeolites or aluminium oxide in the cracking of long-chain hydrocarbons

■ rhodium-based catalysts in a catalytic converter.

A catalyst does not increase the number of collisions per second. Instead it works by making the collisions that take place more successful.

■ It helps reacting particles collide with the correct orientation.

■ It allows collisions between particles with less kinetic energy than normal to be successful.

QUESTIONS

8   Paul and Meghali repeat the experiment with the gas syringe. This time they use a 0.27 g lump of zinc and 100 cm³ of sulfuric acid.
    Describe and explain how the rate of reaction and the total volume of hydrogen gas formed will change.

9   Write a balanced symbol equation for the reaction between zinc and sulfuric acid.

Module summary

Concept map

Paints

Paints are made from coloured rock (pigment) particles suspended in a glue.

Why do we paint houses?

Paint is a colloid. It 'dries' by oxidation.

Building materials

Building materials come from the ground. We use them directly or turn the rock into something else, such as concrete, glass or brick.

We heat limestone to make cement.

Metals from cars are easy to recycle. Plastics need legislation.

Metals

Metals are extracted from metal ores.

Iron and aluminium are used in cars. Iron rusts, but aluminium doesn't.

Pure metals can be mixed with other elements to make alloys. Some metals even form 'smart' alloys.

Rusting is the chemical reaction between iron, oxygen and water.

The Earth is made of tectonic plates that float on the mantle. The plates are moving all the time.

Earth and atmosphere

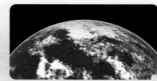

Air is corrosive stuff. It makes iron rust.

Moving tectonic plates trigger volcanic eruptions.

Volcanic eruptions produced the Earth's first atmosphere.

The size of the crystals tells us how a molten rock cooled.

Explosions are chemical reactions which happen very quickly.

Fast or slow?

Rates of reaction are affected by:
- temperature
- surface area
- concentration
- catalysts

We can explain rates of reaction in terms of:
- collision frequency
- collision energy

Module quiz

1 How does paint stick to a wall?

2 What is the difference between oil paint and emulsion paint?

3 What does a thermochromic pigment do?

4 What is the link between bricks and rocks?

5 What is thermal decomposition?

6 Why is reinforced concrete so strong?

7 Where do continents disappear?

8 Where are continents made?

9 What are the **two** main types of magma?

10 How do you extract copper?

11 How do you purify copper?

12 What is the alloy brass made of?

13 What is rust?

14 Why doesn't aluminium seem to corrode?

15 What is the composition of the air?

16 Name **three** common polluting gases produced by cars.

17 Why do reactions go faster if the solutions are more concentrated?

18 Why do reactions go faster if the temperature is higher?

19 What does a catalyst do?

20 How can you tell when a reaction is finished?

Citizenship activity

Imagine what the world would be like if we didn't quarry any stone.

QUESTIONS
1 Describe what your typical day would be like.
2 List some of the problems that can be caused by stone quarries.
3 What can we do with quarries after they have been exhausted?

Exam practice

1 Copy and complete the following sentences using the words below.

A coloured substance used in paints is a .... In paints, solid particles are dispersed in a liquid and we call this a .... Oil paints often have the particles dispersed in oil and a .... that dissolves the oil, making the paint easy to apply. Some pigments change colour with temperature; these are called .... pigments. .... are used to colour fabrics.

solvent   **colloid**   **dyes**
thermochromic   **pigment**

[Total 5 marks]

2 **a** List three problems associated with the quarrying of rocks such as marble, limestone and granite. [3]

b Higher tier: Copy the statements below and draw lines to connect each description with the correct rock type.

Limestone is softer than granite or marble.		It is an igneous rock.
Marble is harder than limestone.		It is a sedimentary rock.
Granite is harder than marble.		It is a metamorphic rock.

[3]

[Total 6 marks]

3 **a** Copy and complete the following table to show information about various igneous rock types.

Rock	Crystal size	Iron or silica rich	From fast or slow cooling magma
Basalt		iron	
Granite	large		
Gabbro			
Rhyolite			fast

[4]

b **i** Why does magma rise up through the Earth's crust? [1]

ii Suggest one reason why some people live close to volcanoes despite the danger? [1]

iii Why do geologists study volcanoes? [1]

iv Higher tier: Explain why a volcano that erupts rhyolite is more dangerous than a basalt eruption. [2]

[Total 9 marks]

4 Copy and complete the following sentences, which describe the Earth's internal structure.

The Earth is a sphere consisting of a thin rocky crust, ... and core. The core contains the metal .... The .... is the rigid outer part of the Earth composed of the .... and upper mantle. The lithosphere is cracked into a number of .... plates.

[Total 5 marks]

5 **a** Copy and complete the following table. (Copper and solder have already been done for you.)

	Metal	Alloy	Main metals (present if an alloy)
Copper	✓		–
Brass			
Solder		✓	lead and tin
Lead			
Amalgam			

[5]

b Higher tier:
i Nitinol is a 'smart alloy'. What two metals does it contain? [2]
ii What is smart about nitinol? [1]
iii Name one use for nitinol that uses its special property. [1]

[Total 9 marks]

6 Both steel (an alloy of iron) and aluminium are used to make the bodies of cars.

a **i** Suggest two reasons why steel is used rather than iron. [2]
ii One advantage of using aluminium is that it does not corrode. Explain why. [2]
iii State another advantage and one disadvantage of using aluminium rather than steel for making car bodies. [2]

b What is the word equation for the rusting of iron? [2]

[Total 8 marks]

A student carried out an experiment to compare the reaction of magnesium ribbon with two different concentrations of hydrochloric acid (0.5 and 1.0 mol/dm³). The magnesium was in excess. The results are shown in the table on the right.

Time (min)	Volume gas collected (cm³)	
	Experiment 1	Experiment 2
0	0	0
0.5	29	13
1.0	48	30
1.5	59	29
2.0	67	48
2.5	71	55
3.0	72	59
3.5	72	62

a i   Plot a graph to show the results. Label the two concentrations on the lines. [5]
   ii What is the total volume of gas formed in Experiment 1? [1]
   iii Is the reaction complete in Experiment 2? Explain your answer. [2]
   iv State two things that must have been done to ensure the experiment was a fair test. [2]
   v   Suggest two more ways of speeding up the reaction. [2]
   vi When is the reaction the fastest in both experiments? [1]
   vii Sketch another line on your graph for hydrochloric acid of 2.0 mol/dm³. [2]

b   Use collision theory to explain your graph. [3]

c   Higher tier: Calculate the rate of reaction in Experiment 1 by finding the slope of the graph. [4]

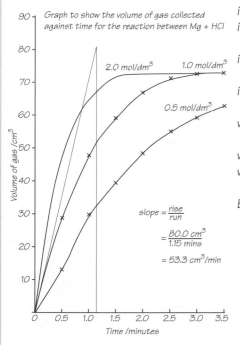

i   On the graph.
ii The total volume of gas in Experiment 1 is 72.
iii Yes, the reaction is complete.
iv Same mass of magnesium and same temperature.
v   Make the temperature higher and use magnesium powder.
vi At the beginning.
vii On the graph.

b   The graph shows that as the concentration increases, the rate of reaction also increases. This is because in order to react, the particles must collide and there are twice as many particles in 1.0 mol/dm³ acid as there are in 0.5 mol/dm³.

c On the graph.

a i   Good answer – points are plotted correctly; scales are sensible; lines are both labelled correctly, and the axes are also labelled. The 0.5 mol/dm³ line is a bit wobbly but gets the mark.
  ii The student should have given the units as well – 72 cm³.
  iii This is *incorrect*. The volume is still increasing and the reaction will not be complete until 72 cm³ of gas have been collected.
  iv–vii have all been answered well.

Only two of the three marks are awarded here. The student needed to say there are 'twice as many particles *in the same volume*' for full marks.

Good answer. The student has drawn a gradient for the initial rate of reaction (starting from the origin) and has correctly calculated the rate of reaction.

Overall Grade: B

How to get an A

This answer only has a few errors and is almost an A. The most important point to remember here is about explaining the rate of reaction using collision theory, as this is often given as the wrong answer.

Energy cannot be created or destroyed. It can only be changed from one form to another. The energy in the Earth and within the Earth's atmosphere can have catastrophic results when it is released.

Tornadoes are formed when warm air is trapped beneath layers of cold, dry air. When a tornado hits land, the devastation can be extreme!

Wind speeds in a tornado can reach 300 mph!

The energy in a tornado can easily throw a car through the air or rip a house apart.

CONTENTS

Heating houses

You will find out:
- about the difference between heat and temperature
- how energy flows
- how to read a thermogram

If you can manage to keep a piece of chocolate on your tongue long enough for it to melt, your tongue gets colder.

You may want to repeat this experiment just to make sure!

 Energy always flows from a warmer body to a cooler body.

Hot and cold

Hot objects have a high **temperature** and usually cool down.

The hotter the object, the quicker it cools down.

Cold objects have a low temperature and usually warm up.

Colder objects sometimes melt!

In the laboratory, temperature is normally measured with a **thermometer.**

About heat

- The unit of temperature is the **degree Celsius** (°C).
- **Heat** is a form of **energy**.
- The unit of energy is the **joule** (J).

FIGURE 1: Even cold objects sometimes melt.

EXAM HINTS AND TIPS

Remember to always give the units.

'°C' for temperature.

'J' for heat.

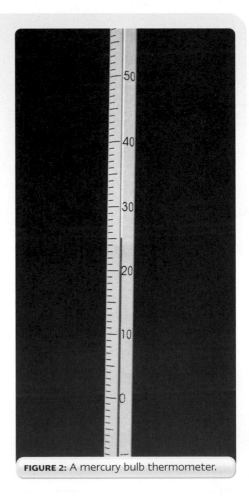

FIGURE 2: A mercury bulb thermometer.

QUESTIONS

1. What is the unit of temperature?
2. What is the unit of heat?
3. What temperature is recorded on the thermometer shown in Figure 2?
4. Mrs Collins takes a loaf of bread out of the freezer an hour before tea. Why does she take the bread out so early?

...absolute scale   ...arbitrary scale   ...degree Celsius   ...energy   ...heat

Energy flow

If you leave the front door open on a cold winter's day, the house gets colder.

FIGURE 3: What happens to the temperature of a house when the front door is left open on a cold day?

If you put an ice cube on your hand, your hand gets colder.

Energy, in the form of heat, flows from a warmer to a colder body.

Inside the house is warmer than outside, and your hand is warmer than the ice cube. Energy flows from the inside of the house to the outside and from your hand to the ice cube.

When energy flows away from a warm object, the temperature of that object decreases. The house and your hand become colder.

Temperature is a measure of 'hotness'. It allows one object to be compared with another.

QUESTIONS

5 When you blow warm air onto a wet patch of skin, your skin cools down. Suggest why.

6 Nitrogen freezes at −210 °C and boils at −196 °C. When a lump of ice at −5 °C is dropped into liquid nitrogen, the nitrogen boils. Explain why.

Temperature pictures

Thermograms are pictures which represent temperature instead of true colour.

FIGURE 4: White represents the hottest areas and blue represents the coolest. What is the coolest thing in the picture?

Temperature does not have to be measured on the degree Celsius scale. It can be measured on any chosen scale. Temperature in a thermogram is measured using colour as the scale.

On a cold winter's day you do not use a thermometer to help you decide what to wear.

Temperature is measured on an **arbitrary scale**.

A	B
20 °C	40 °C

B is not twice as hot as **A**.

Heat is a measure of internal energy. It is measured on an **absolute scale**.

Twice as much energy is transferred from **C** to **D** as from **A** to **B**.

QUESTIONS

7 How does the thermogram above show that one of the upstairs rooms is not heated?

8 The house has a glass front door not a solid wooden one. How does the thermogram show this?

9 The bonnet of one car is yellow in the thermogram. Suggest why.

Does heating mean hotter?

A liquid in a beaker is heated to a certain temperature. The amount of energy needed depends on:

- how much liquid there is in the beaker (its mass)
- what the liquid is
- the rise in temperature.

Changes of state

If you heat a solid such as a lump of ice, its temperature rises until it changes to a liquid. The temperature stays the same until all of the solid has changed to a liquid.

The temperature of the liquid then rises until it changes into a gas. The temperature stays the same until all of the liquid has changed to a gas.

The temperature of the gas then rises.

Heat is needed to **melt** a solid at its **melting point**.

Heat is needed to **boil** a liquid at its **boiling point**.

You will find out:

- about factors that affect the amount of energy needed to change the temperature of a substance
- about factors that affect the amount of energy needed to change the state of a substance

FIGURE 5: In a second experiment more water was added to the beaker and the liquid was heated to the same temperature. Would the amount of energy needed to heat the water be different from that needed in the first experiment?

DID YOU KNOW?

The syrup in a steamed syrup pudding appears to be hotter than the sponge even though they have been cooked at the same temperature.

This is because the specific heat capacity of the syrup is greater than the specific heat capacity of the sponge.

 Heat and temperature are different.

Energy transfer does not always involve a rise or fall in temperature.

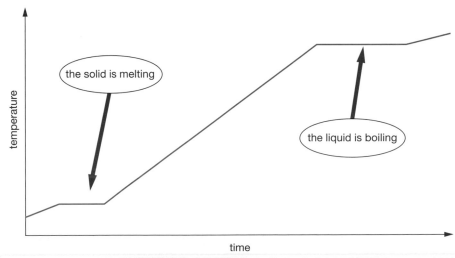

the solid is melting

the liquid is boiling

temperature

time

FIGURE 6: Why does the line on the graph flatten out during changes of state?

Latent heat is the heat needed to change a state without a change in temperature.

QUESTIONS

10 What is the melting point of ice?

11 What is the boiling point of water?

...*boil* ...*boiling point* ...*latent heat* ...*melt*

Specific heat capacity

The amount of energy needed to change the temperature of an object depends on the material the object is made from. All substances have a property called **specific heat capacity**.

The specific heat capacity is:

> the amount of energy needed to change the temperature of one kilogram of a substance by one degree Celsius
>
> specific heat capacity unit is joule per kilogram degree Celsius (J/kg °C)

When an object is heated and its temperature rises, energy is transferred.

Specific latent heat

The amount of energy needed to change the state of an object without a change in temperature depends on the material the object is made from. All substances have a property called **specific latent heat**.

The specific latent heat is:

> the amount of energy needed to change the state of one kilogram of a substance without a change in temperature
>
> specific latent heat unit is joule per kilogram (J/kg)

When an object is heated and it changes state, energy is transferred.

QUESTIONS

12 Mohammed says that when you heat an object it gets hotter. Anne says it does not. Who is correct? Explain your answer.

13 The specific heat capacity of oxygen is 913 J/kg °C. How much energy is needed to raise the temperature of 1 kg of oxygen by 1 °C?

Calculations

Specific heat capacity

energy transferred = mass × specific heat capacity × temperature change

example

Calculate the energy transferred when the 80 kg of water in a tropical freshwater fish tank is heated from 10 °C to 25 °C.

energy transferred = mass × specific heat capacity × temperature change

energy transferred = 80 × 4200 × (25 – 10)

energy transferred = 80 × 4200 × 15

energy transferred = 5 040 000 J   =   5040 kJ

The tables show some specific heat capacities and specific latent heat capacities.

Substance	Specific heat capacity in J/kg °C
copper	390
mercury	140
rubber	1600
seawater	3900
water	4200

Change of state	Specific latent heat in J/kg
ice to water	340 000
water to steam	2 260 000

Specific latent heat

energy transferred = mass × specific latent heat

example

Calculate the energy transferred when the 1.5 kg of water in a kettle changes from liquid to gas at 100 °C.

energy transferred = mass × specific latent heat

energy transferred = 1.5 × 2 260 000

energy transferred = 3 390 000 J = 3390 kJ

When a substance changes state from solid to liquid or liquid to gas, energy is needed to break the bonds that hold the molecules together. This is why there is no change in temperature.

QUESTIONS

14 Calculate the energy transferred from a glass of coke to melt 100 g of ice cubes at 0 °C.

15 A copper saucepan has a mass of 1.5 kg. It is used to cook potatoes. Calculate how much extra energy is needed to raise the temperature of the saucepan from 15 °C to 100 °C.

16 190 MJ of energy are needed to melt 500 kg of aluminium at 660 °C. Calculate the specific latent heat of aluminium.

Keeping homes warm

You will find out:
- how energy is lost from uninsulated homes
- about payback time
- how to compare costs of energy sources and fuels

Saving energy

Save 10% on energy bills!

Just by turning the thermostat down by 1 °C you can save 10% of your household energy costs.

Turn it down and keep the costs down!

Keeping warm

The lights are on and the people in this log cabin are comfortably warm, despite the snow.

The roof of the cabin contains **insulation**.

Insulation in a loft reduces energy loss from the roof. **Fibreglass**, or a similar material, is placed between the joists. Fibreglass contains a lot of gaps in its structure. Air is trapped in these gaps. Air is a good **insulator**.

FIGURE 1: How can you tell that this cabin is well insulated?

Snow takes longer to melt on a well insulated roof.

FIGURE 2: Why is fibreglass a good insulator?

The house in Figure 3 does not have a well insulated roof.

FIGURE 3: How can you tell that this house does not have loft insulation?

QUESTIONS

1   Why do people have their lofts insulated?

...fibreglass   ...insulation

Energy loss

Homes lose energy from the roof, walls, doors, floors and windows. There is a saying, 'Don't heat the street'!

To reduce energy loss, uninsulated homes need to be insulated. This can be quite expensive.

The savings, in terms of energy resources and money, depend on what type of insulation is fitted.

Insulation	Typical cost in £	Typical annual fuel saving in £
cavity wall	400	80
double glazing	3000	50
draught-proofing	80	20
loft	250	100

To work out which is the most cost-effective type of insulation, the **payback time** is calculated.

$$\text{payback time} = \frac{\text{cost of insulation}}{\text{annual saving}}$$

The unit of payback time is years.

This means that after five years, the homeowner has recovered in fuel saving the cost of the cavity wall insulation.

After that they are £80 a year better off.

The homeowner can also choose between different energy sources to heat their home. Each source has its advantages and disadvantages. One factor is cost. How do you compare oil price per litre, with gas cost per cubic metre, with coal price per tonne, or with electricity cost per kilowatt-hour?

Energy suppliers now provide tables so that the homeowner can make an informed decision.

Energy source	Energy unit	Typical energy equivalent in kWh
coal	tonne	8000
electricity	kWh	1
gas	m³	11
oil	litre	10

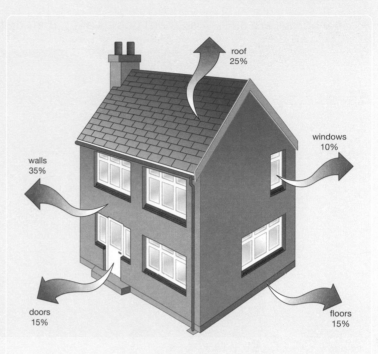

FIGURE 4: Where is most energy lost from this house?

roof 25%
windows 10%
walls 35%
doors 15%
floors 15%

WOW FACTOR!

An average home emits about 7 tonnes of carbon dioxide each year.

QUESTIONS

Use the tables to help you answer the following questions.

2   Which insulation saves the most money per year?

3   Calculate the payback time for loft insulation.

4   Calculate the payback time for draught-proofing.

5   Double glazing saves more money each year than draught–proofing. Explain why it is not sensible to have double glazing fitted unless windows need to be replaced.

6   Electricity costs 9p per kWh. Heating oil costs 30p per litre. Suggest why some people prefer to have oil-fired central heating.

Saving energy

As new homes are built, solid foam boards are put inside the cavity walls.

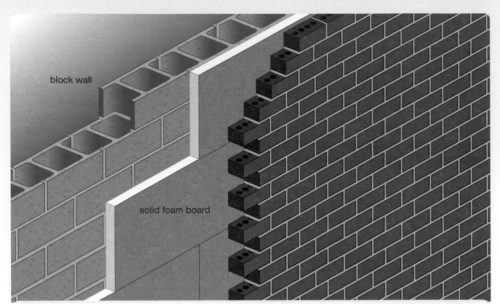

block wall

solid foam board

FIGURE 5: Why is foam a good insulator?

Older homes can have foam injected.

Loft insulation and cavity wall insulation contain air. Air is a poor **conductor**. Poor conductors are good insulators.

Closing the curtains and fitting double glazing cut down energy loss through windows.

Some people put aluminium foil behind their radiators.

Draught strips around doors and windows are cheap and effective.

FIGURE 6: Injecting foam into a wall cavity.

DID YOU KNOW?

A staggering 25% of all carbon dioxide emissions in the UK are as a result of heating and lighting our homes.

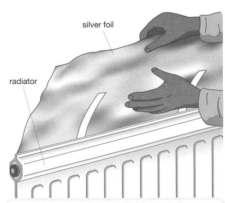

FIGURE 7: Why does closing the curtains reduce energy loss from windows?

silver foil

radiator

FIGURE 8: Would energy be saved if aluminium foil was fixed to the front of radiators?

QUESTIONS

7   What property of aluminium foil makes it suitable to use behind radiators to reduce energy loss? Choose **one** word from this list.

   cuts easily   light   metal   shiny

...conduction   ...conductor   ...convection

Efficiency

A traditional coal fire set in a wall of a room is not the most efficient way to heat a room.

For every 100 J of energy stored in coal and released as heat, about 25 J are transferred to the room.

The remaining 75 J are lost to the surroundings.

The fire has an **efficiency** of 0.25 (or 25%).

Not all fires are so inefficient.

A fire in the centre of a room can be more than 50% efficient.

$$\text{efficiency} = \frac{\text{useful energy output}}{\text{total energy input}}$$

FIGURE 9: Where does most of the energy produced by this fire go?

FIGURE 10: This fire is in the middle of the room and is much more efficient than a traditional fire.

Energy transfer processes

Energy from a coal fire warms the room by **radiation**.

The hot air rises up the chimney by **convection**.

Energy is transferred through the surrounding bricks by **conduction**.

Buildings that are energy efficient are well insulated and make sure that as little energy as possible is lost to the surroundings.

Designers and architects have to consider the best way to heat a home and the best way to make sure that energy is not wasted.

Energy efficiency is not just about heating homes. Everything that transfers energy wastes some of the energy as heat to the surroundings.

Designers of household appliances have to consider where energy may be lost and how they can reduce the loss.

QUESTIONS

8 Explain why a coal fire in the centre of a room is more efficient than one against an outside wall.

9 Mr Collins sees an advertisement for a gas fire.

Energy Efficient Gas Fire!
| Input | 7000 J/s |
| Output | 5600 J/s |

Calculate the efficiency of the gas fire.

QUESTIONS

10 Mrs Collins' coal fire is 20% efficient. It burns 10 kg of coal each day.

The energy output to the room is 57.6 MJ.

Calculate the energy in 1 kg of coal.

How insulation works

You will find out:

- about the insulating properties of air
- how energy is transferred by conduction
- how insulation reduces energy loss by conduction

These spacesuits are made for walking...

When astronauts go outside for a spacewalk they need to wear a special spacesuit.

The surface of the suit facing the Sun might reach 120 °C. The other side of the suit may be as cold as –160 °C!

The spacesuit keeps the astronaut's body at normal Earth temperature.

Insulators

It is very cold in the Arctic. Explorers and polar bears keep warm because they have fur coats.

FIGURE 1: How do their fur coats keep them warm?

There is a lot of air inside the coat.

Air is a good **insulator**. It does not allow **energy** to transfer from a warm body to cold surroundings.

WOW FACTOR!

British polar explorer Tom Avery has announced that he will carry the Olympic Torch on his forthcoming expedition to the North Pole. On the 483-mile trip to the Pole the team will face constant dangers of thin ice, attack from polar bears and temperatures as low as –45 °C.

QUESTION

1   In winter it is better to wear several layers of thin loose-fitting clothes rather than one thick tight-fitting layer. Suggest why.

...argon   ...conduction   ...conductor   ...energy

Double glazing

Double glazing reduces energy loss.

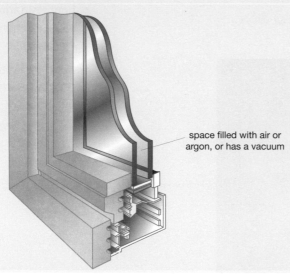

space filled with air or argon, or has a vacuum

FIGURE 2: Suggest another advantage of double glazing for a family living in a house close to a busy road.

A double-glazed window has a space between two panes of glass. The space is filled with air or **argon** or has a **vacuum**.

- Air and argon are good insulators. The particles in a gas are far apart, so energy cannot be transferred easily. This means that energy loss by **conduction** is reduced.

- A solid is a good **conductor** of heat. The particles in a solid are close together so energy is easily transferred.

- A vacuum is the best insulator. There are no particles to transfer energy.

Conduction

Conduction in a solid is due to the transfer of **kinetic energy** from one particle to another.

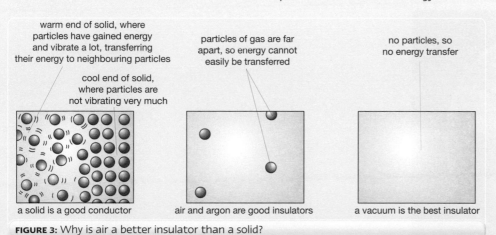

warm end of solid, where particles have gained energy and vibrate a lot, transferring their energy to neighbouring particles

cool end of solid, where particles are not vibrating very much

particles of gas are far apart, so energy cannot easily be transferred

no particles, so no energy transfer

a solid is a good conductor

air and argon are good insulators

a vacuum is the best insulator

FIGURE 3: Why is air a better insulator than a solid?

QUESTIONS

2 Name the process that reduces energy transfer in double glazing.

3 Why is glass a better conductor of heat than argon?

4 Explain why a vacuum does not transfer energy by conduction.

...insulator ...kinetic energy ...vacuum

Convection

Hot air balloons work because hot air rises.

Colder air falls and takes the place of the hot air. This movement of air is called a **convection current**.

FIGURE 4: Why does a hot air balloon operator have to turn on the flame during a flight?

Radiation

In some countries, **infrared radiation** from the Sun is reflected from a shiny reflector. The heat is used for cooking or generating electricity.

FIGURE 5: This reflector in Australia is at a power station that generates electricity. An electronic device at the **focus** of the reflector converts heat energy into electricity.

QUESTIONS

5. Explain what is meant by a convection current.
6. Suggest why there is little demand for solar power stations in the UK.

...convection   ...convection current   ...expand

Practical insulation in the home

Loft insulation

The distribution of warm air in a loft is as follows.

- Warm air in a room below the loft is in contact with the ceiling.
- The solid ceiling is a conductor so some energy is transferred through the ceiling.
- Air in the loft is warmed by the top surface of the ceiling.

The energy is transferred through the ceiling to the air in the loft.

If there is no insulation in a loft:

- warm air rises by **convection**
- cooler air takes its place
- the warm air heats the roof tiles
- the tiles are conductors and transfer energy to the outside
- a convection current continues to remove energy from the ceiling.

If there is insulation in a loft:

- warm air is trapped in the insulation
- warm air cannot rise by convection
- there is little temperature difference between the top and bottom surface of the ceiling
- little energy is removed from the ceiling.

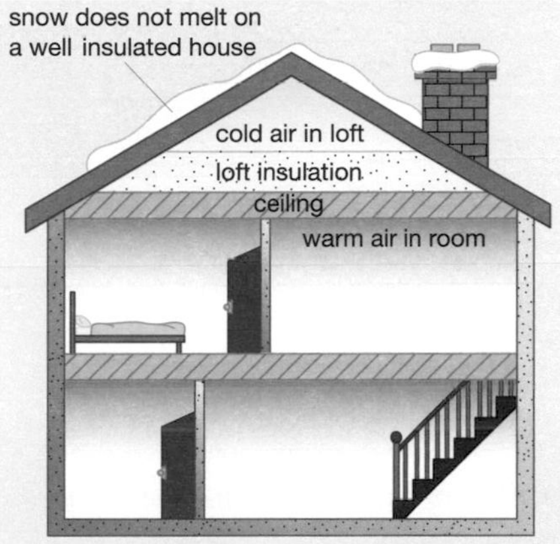

Cavity wall insulation

- Foam in a cavity contains a lot of trapped air. Air is a good insulator. The foam reduces energy loss by conduction.
- The blocks that are used when building new homes have shiny foil on both sides. This means that energy transfer by **radiation** is reduced.
- In winter, the energy in the home is reflected keeping it warmer.
- In summer, the energy from the Sun is reflected keeping the home cooler.

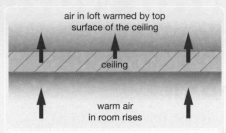

FIGURE 6: Why is the ceiling a conductor?

Watch Out Hot air does not rise into the loft — unless you leave the trap-door open.

FIGURE 7: Why does snow not melt on the roof of a well insulated house?

Why convection?

When a gas is heated it **expands**. The same mass of gas occupies a greater volume.

As the volume increases, the density decreases. This is why hot air rises.

$$\text{density} = \frac{\text{mass}}{\text{volume}}$$

The unit of density is g/cm^3 or g/m^3.

If air is such a good insulator, why do we need cavity wall insulation? Why is the air in the cavity not good enough?

Air is a very good convector.

- As air in the cavity is warmed it rises through the cavity into the loft.
- Colder air from the loft falls and a convection current is formed.
- The air trapped in the foam stops convection from taking place.

Radiation and space

Energy transfer by radiation does not need a material. Energy can be transferred through a vacuum as in space.

QUESTIONS

7 Describe how loft insulation helps to keep a house cool in summer.

8 Why do the foam blocks used for cavity wall insulation have shiny foil on both sides?

QUESTIONS

9 Explain how cavity wall insulation reduces energy transfer by conduction, convection and radiation.

...focus ...infrared radiation ...radiation

Cooking with waves

You will find out:

- about bodies that give out infrared radiation
- about heating effects of microwaves
- how wavelength affects the energy transferred

Don't try this at home!

There are some things that you should not try to cook in a microwave oven, and a light bulb is one of them — the gas inside (glowing pink in the photograph) will make it explode!

Microwaves are part of a range of different waves. Radio waves are used to transmit signals to your radio and X-rays are used to make an image of your bone in case doctors think that you have broken it.

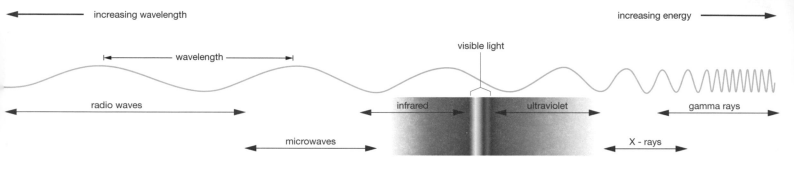

← increasing wavelength

increasing energy →

wavelength

visible light

radio waves

infrared

ultraviolet

gamma rays

microwaves

X - rays

Infrared radiation

It is not just the flames that are emitting **infrared** (heat) radiation in Figure 1.

The cat and the newborn kitten are also emitting infrared radiation. All warm and hot objects emit infrared radiation.

- Hotter objects give out more radiation.
- Dull, black objects give out more radiation than shiny, bright objects at the same temperature.
- Infrared radiation is absorbed by the surface of any object. The object warms up. Black surfaces are very good absorbers of radiation.

FIGURE 1: What do objects have to be to emit infrared radiation?

Microwaves

Microwaves are also used for heating. Microwaves in a microwave oven are absorbed by water molecules in food.

Infrared radiation and microwaves are part of a family of waves called the **electromagnetic spectrum**.

QUESTIONS

1 What colour of the visible spectrum is next to infrared radiation?
2 What part of the electromagnetic spectrum has waves with wavelengths longer than microwaves?

FIGURE 2: How does a microwave oven cook food?

...conduction ...convection ...electromagnetic spectrum ...energy ...frequency

Microwaves can cook human meat as well as the evening meal!

Infrared cookery

- Infrared radiation does not penetrate very far into food.
- It only heats the surface of food.
- Meat that appears to be cooked is often still quite rare on the inside.

FIGURE 3: Why can steak still be pink inside when it appears well done on the outside?

Microwave cookery

- Microwaves penetrate about 1 cm into the outer layers of food.
- Microwaves pass through glass and plastic but are reflected from shiny metal surfaces.
- The door of a microwave oven is made from special glass that reflects microwave radiation.
- Microwaves can cook human meat as well as the evening meal!

QUESTIONS

3 You can warm rolls or defrost a loaf in a microwave oven but you cannot make good toast. Why?

4 Suggest **two** advantages of using a microwave oven instead of an infrared oven.

Electromagnetic spectrum

Energy is transferred by waves in the electromagnetic spectrum.

The amount of energy transferred depends on the **wavelength** or **frequency** of the wave.

The shorter the wavelength (or higher the frequency), the more energy is transferred.

Gamma rays transfer the most energy and **radio waves** the least.

Microwaves have a longer wavelength than infrared radiation and transfer less energy.

Infrared cookery

- Energy from infrared radiation is absorbed by the particles on the surface of the food.
- This increases the **kinetic energy** of the particles.
- The energy is transferred to the rest of the food by **conduction**.

Microwave cookery

- The water molecules in the outer layers vibrate more and their kinetic energy increases.
- The energy is transferred to the rest of the food by conduction and **convection**.

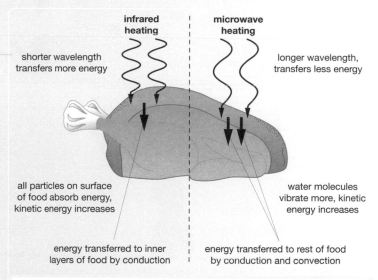

FIGURE 4: What happens to the kinetic energy of food particles in infrared and microwave cookery?

QUESTIONS

5 The door of a microwave oven is made from special glass that does not allow microwaves to pass through. Suggest why.

6 Sacha is sitting near to a glowing coal fire. How does the wavelength of infrared radiation from the fire compare to the wavelength of radiation from Sacha?

...gamma ray   ...infrared   ...kinetic energy   ...microwave   ...radio wave   ...wavelength

Microwave communication

You will find out:

- about other uses of microwaves
- about possible dangers associated with mobile phones and phone masts

Microwaves are used for **communication** as well as for cooking.

Recently there have been many reports about the dangers of mobile phones.

Newspaper headlines have read 'Mobiles don't fry the brain, they just warm it!'

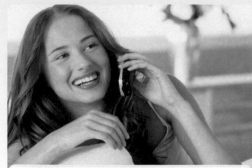

FIGURE 5: Should young people use their mobiles for non-essential calls?

Mobiles don't fry the brain, they just warm it!

As yet there is no scientific proof one way or the other. There is some evidence of warming and rats show signs of stress near mobile phones.

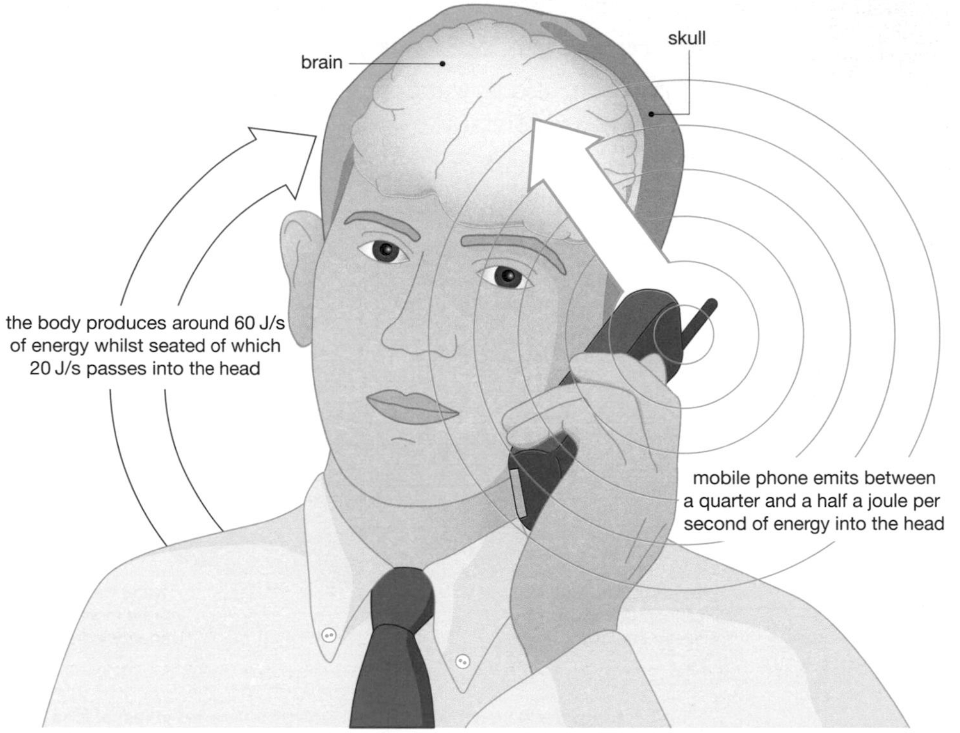
brain
skull
the body produces around 60 J/s of energy whilst seated of which 20 J/s passes into the head
mobile phone emits between a quarter and a half a joule per second of energy into the head

FIGURE 6: The science of mobile phones.

Young people use mobile phones a lot and their brains are still developing.

The government advises that young people should not use mobile phones for 'non-essential' calls.

WOW FACTOR!

Goonhilly Earth Station, in Cornwall, is the largest satellite station in the world.

It can handle 600 000 telephone calls at the same time!

QUESTIONS

7 How much energy enters the head from a typical mobile phone?

8 Why is texting a better way to communicate than speech?

9 Why does the government advise young people to use mobile phones for essential calls only?

...aerial ...communication ...diffraction ...interference

Microwave communication

Microwaves are not just used for mobile phones and fast food. Long-distance communication also uses microwave signals.

The **transmitter** and **receiver** have to be in '**line of sight**'. That is why microwave **aerials** for sending telephone signals are on high buildings or towers. The Telecom Tower in London dwarfs surrounding tower blocks and the Eye. It has microwave aerials pointing in every direction.

Some areas of the country do not have good reception. This is because they are not in line of sight with a transmitter.

A satellite orbiting Earth is in line of sight with a giant aerial on the ground. The aerial can handle thousands of telephone calls and television pictures at once.

On a smaller scale, a satellite dish on the roof of a house receives microwave signals that deliver satellite television channels.

FIGURE 7: The Telecom Tower. Why are microwave aerials on high buildings?

FIGURE 8: What is sending microwaves to this giant aerial?

FIGURE 9: Why would it not be a good idea to fix a satellite dish to the side of a house?

FIGURE 10: Should parents worry about letting their children play in this playground?

Many people are worried about where mobile phone masts are situated. There are concerns about the possible risk of cancer due to microwave radiation. Masts should not be sited near schools or playgrounds.

QUESTIONS

10　Why are microwave aerials placed on very tall buildings?

11　Suggest why mobile phone masts should not be sited near to a children's play area.

Microwave properties

Even within the band of waves called microwaves, the wavelength can be different.

The shortest wavelength for microwaves is 1 mm and the longest is 30 cm.

Microwaves used for communication have a longer wavelength than those used for cooking.

This means that there is less energy transferred by mobile phones than by microwave ovens.

Diffraction

Microwaves do not exhibit very much **diffraction** around natural obstacles, such as hills.

This is why sometimes the reception on a mobile changes from maximum to zero in a very short distance.

For more information on diffraction see page 197.

Interference

Mobile phones are banned in most hospitals because there is evidence that the microwave signals can **interfere** with sensitive medical equipment. However, many doctors feel that the benefits of having mobile phones outweigh the risks.

QUESTIONS

12　Suggest why aerials used for mobile phone signals are placed close together, particularly in towns.

13　Suggest why mobile phones should not be used on aeroplanes.

Keeping warm

SELF-CHECK ACTIVITY

STEP 1

Look at the picture and imagine that you are in the building. Discuss the ways in which energy is being transferred from the fire and how the inhabitants are getting warm.

STEP 2

Describe and explain using words and diagrams how energy is being transferred and where it is being transferred to.

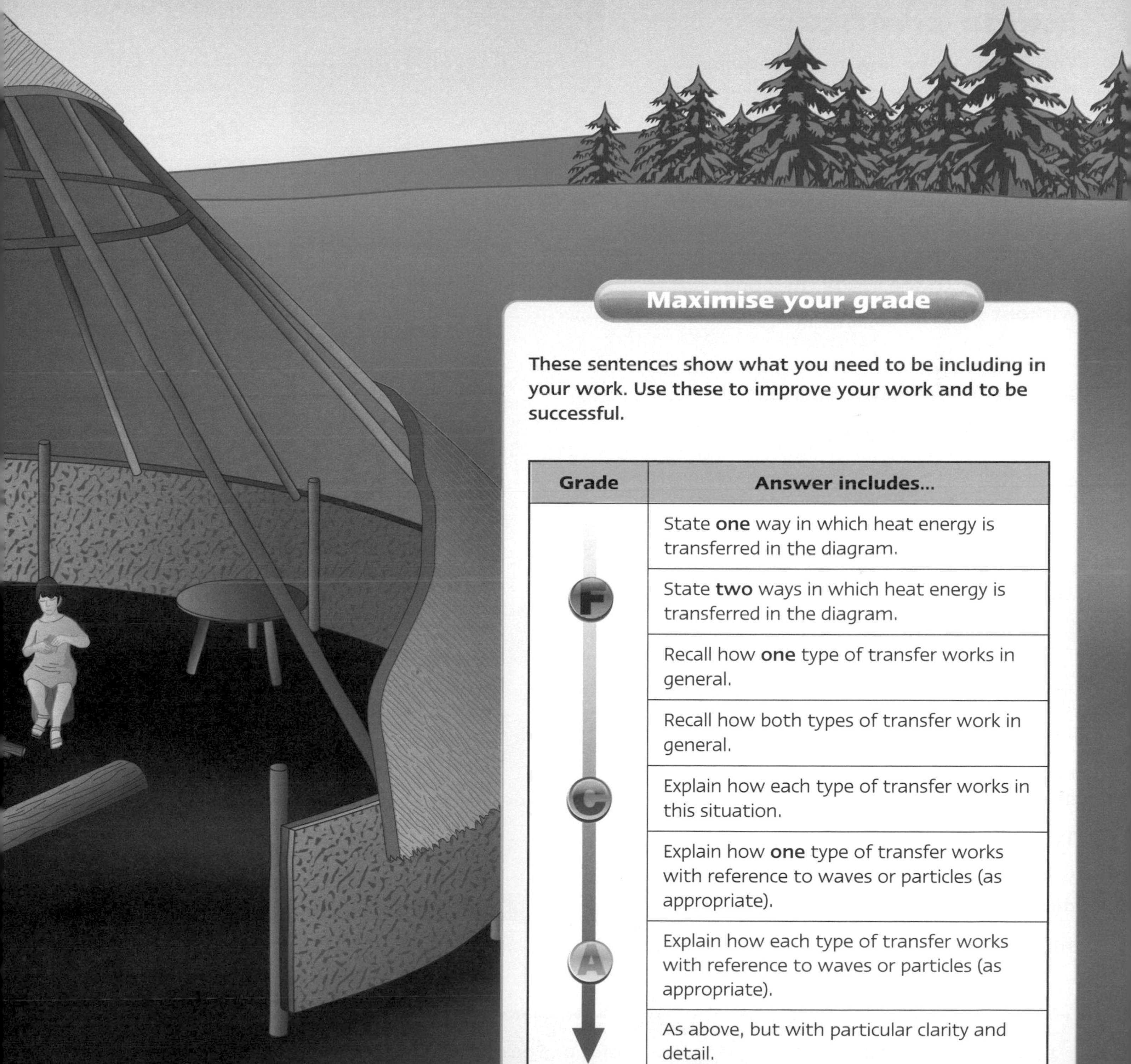

Explain why some of the occupants are warmer than others.

Maximise your grade

These sentences show what you need to be including in your work. Use these to improve your work and to be successful.

Grade	Answer includes...
F	State **one** way in which heat energy is transferred in the diagram.
	State **two** ways in which heat energy is transferred in the diagram.
	Recall how **one** type of transfer works in general.
	Recall how both types of transfer work in general.
C	Explain how each type of transfer works in this situation.
	Explain how **one** type of transfer works with reference to waves or particles (as appropriate).
A	Explain how each type of transfer works with reference to waves or particles (as appropriate).
	As above, but with particular clarity and detail.

Infrared signals

You will find out:

- how infrared radiation is used
- about analogue and digital signals
- about interference in signals

'Heroin pouch bursts inside trafficker'

This is a likely by-line in a newspaper. Heroin is an illegal drug. Drug traffickers often put themselves in great danger to import the drug. They wrap the heroin in black plastic tape and swallow it. Sometimes a packet bursts inside them. The trafficker can stop breathing and may die. Doctors can use a special instrument to see inside the body without surgery.

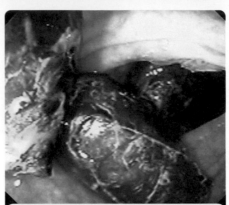

This is what a doctor using an endoscope sees inside a person who has swallowed packets of drugs.

'Heroin pouch bursts inside trafficker'

Invisible infrared waves

Uses of infrared waves

A remote control lets you change the channel on your television from (or behind!) your armchair.

A motorist can open the garage door when they arrive home on a cold wet night. They use a remote control from inside their car.

Remote controls work by emitting an **infrared** signal.

Some computers have a cordless mouse that emits infrared radiation. The signal is received by a passive infrared **sensor**.

Infrared sensors are used for security alarms. They detect low levels of infrared radiation.

Types of signals

The signal emitted by a remote control is called a **digital** signal.

There are other types of signals called **analogue** signals.

Thank goodness for remote controls!

QUESTIONS

1 What is the source of the infrared radiation detected by a passive infrared sensor during a burglary?

...analogue ...carrier wave ...combined signal ...continuously variable ...demultiplexer ...digital

Signal values

Analogue signals

When a person speaks into a microphone connected to an oscilloscope an analogue wave pattern is seen on the screen. The pattern represents what was said.

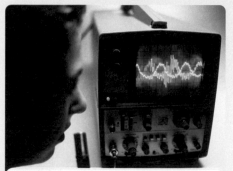

FIGURE 1: An analogue wave pattern on the screen represents speech.

Even humming a note produces a complicated wave pattern. The wave pattern is interpreted as follows.

- Height of a wave indicates **loudness**.
- Distance between waves indicates **pitch**. High-pitched sounds have waves close together.

An analogue signal can have any value. It is **continuously variable**.

Digital signals

A digital signal can only have two values, on or off.

On is represented by 1 (or high) and off by 0 (or low).

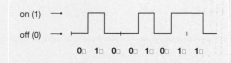

FIGURE 2: A digital signal can only have two values, on or off.

QUESTIONS

2 A wristwatch face has hands and numbers 1 to 12.
   a Explain why it is described as an analogue watch.
   b Make a sketch of a digital watch.

Interference

Analogue signals

An analogue signal is to be transmitted. A typical frequency for a person speaking is 200 Hz. A typical frequency for a **carrier wave** is 200 000 Hz.

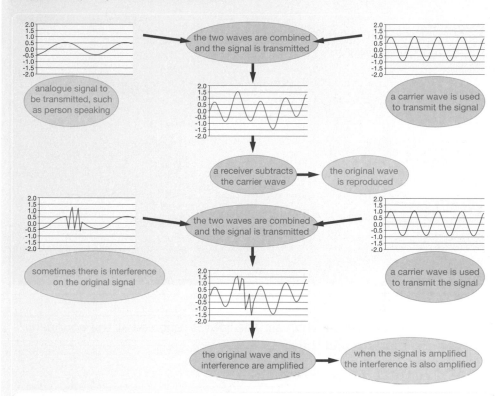

FIGURE 3: What happens to the interference on an analogue signal when it is amplified?

Digital signals

When a digital signal is transmitted it too can have **interference**. Because the digital signal is either high or low the interference is not apparent in the final output.

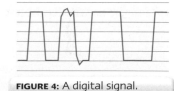

FIGURE 4: A digital signal.

Multiplexing

Multiplexing allows many different digital signals to be transmitted simultaneously. Each digital signal is divided into segments of very short duration. A **combined signal** takes each segment in turn and transmits it. A multiplexer combines the individual signals to be sent and a **demultiplexer** separates them at the receiving end of the transmission.

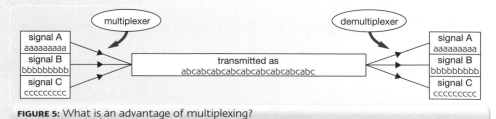

FIGURE 5: What is an advantage of multiplexing?

QUESTIONS

3 Give **two** advantages of transmitting a digital signal rather than an analogue signal.

You will find out:

- about total internal reflection
- about the uses of optical fibres in communication and medicine

Trapped light

Light can stay inside materials such as glass, Perspex or water.

FIGURE 6: How is light trapped in this fibre optic lamp?

Watch Out An optical fibre is solid, not a hollow tube.

These materials are denser than air. The light is reflected at the boundary between the material and the air.

This is called **total internal reflection**.

Light, infrared radiation or a laser beam can travel along a very thin piece of solid glass called an **optical fibre**. Every time the light meets the boundary with air, it is reflected back into the fibre.

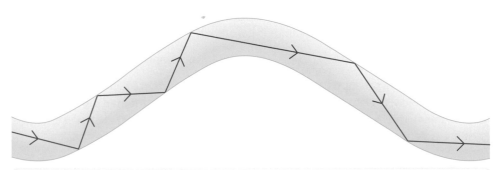

FIGURE 7: What happens to light when it meets the boundary with air in this optical fibre?

Optical fibres are very flexible.

▪ QUESTIONS ▪

4　What is the relationship between the angle of incidence and the angle of reflection?

5　Using total internal reflection in your answer suggest how a small fish in the sea can see a large fish behind it. You may find it helpful to draw a diagram.

...angle of incidence   ...angle of refraction   ...critical angle

Critical angle

When light is passing from a more dense material such as glass into a less dense material such as air, the **angle of refraction** is greater than the **angle of incidence**.

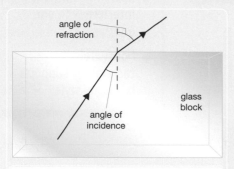

FIGURE 8: Is the angle of incidence more or less than the angle of refraction in this diagram?

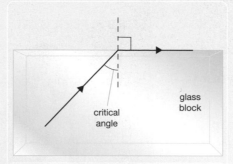

FIGURE 9: When is the angle of incidence called the critical angle?

If the angle of incidence increases, it is possible for the angle of refraction to be a right angle (90°). When this happens, the angle of incidence is called the **critical angle**.

Total internal reflection

If the angle of incidence is increased even more, the light is reflected back inside the more dense material. This is total internal reflection.

Optical fibres are used to transmit data at 300 000 km/s which is the speed of light. Telephone conversations and computer data can be transmitted very long distances with little energy loss. The optical fibres have a coating around them to improve reflection.

The signals are coded and sent digitally using **laser light**.

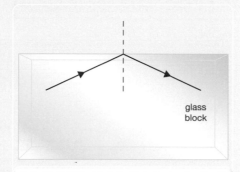

FIGURE 10: What is total internal reflection?

Endoscopy

One very important use of optical fibres is in an **endoscope**. This is an instrument used by doctors that allows them to see inside the body without surgery. It also allows some operations to be performed by keyhole surgery.

Light passes along the outer fibres and lights up the inside of the patient. The reflected light passes back along the inner fibres and the image is viewed through an eyepiece.

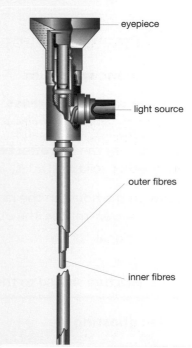

FIGURE 11: How does an endoscope help doctors?

QUESTIONS

6 The diagram shows two 45°, 45°, 90° prisms in a periscope.

The critical angle for glass to air is 41°.

Explain how total internal reflection is used in the telescope.

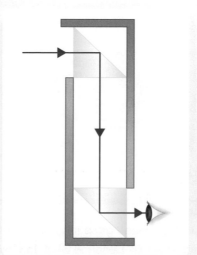

QUESTIONS

7 In an endoscope the inner fibres must be arranged in the same pattern at both ends, but the outer fibres need not. Suggest why.

Wireless signals

You will find out:
- about the reflection, refraction and diffraction of radio signals
- how radio stations interfere with one another
- how wireless technology supports a busy life-style

'Let the office be with you...'

It does not matter where you are, your office can be with you.

The mobile phone and wireless laptop mean that you are available 24 hours a day, seven days a week.

You can talk to people on the other side of the world. You can access the Internet and use e-mail to send and receive documents.

Wireless technology

Wireless technology uses **radio waves** and **microwaves**. These waves are part of the **electromagnetic spectrum**.

Getting the message across

Radio waves behave in the same way as light. They can be **reflected** off a hill or other solid obstacles.

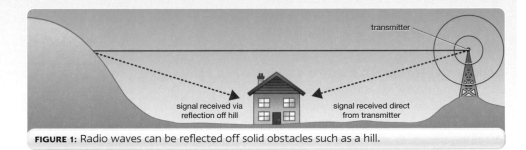

FIGURE 1: Radio waves can be reflected off solid obstacles such as a hill.

The **aerial** on the house in the picture receives two signals. One comes directly from a transmitter. The other is reflected from an obstacle.

The reflected signal
- travels further
- produces a picture shifted to the right.

This is called **ghosting**.

Sometimes reflected signals allow places in shadow to receive radio signals.

FIGURE 2: What causes ghosting?

FIGURE 3: Why can radio waves sometimes be received by places in shadow?

▪▪ QUESTIONS ▪▪

1 Suggest **two** obstacles, other than a hill, that cause ghosting.
2 A radio receives a direct signal and a reflected signal. Describe what you hear.

...*aerial*   ...*diffraction*   ...*electromagnetic spectrum*   ...*frequency*   ...*ghosting*

Refraction of radio waves

All electromagnetic waves can be **refracted**. Radio waves are refracted in the upper layers of the atmosphere.

The amount of refraction depends on the **frequency** of a wave. Waves with a long **wavelength** and low frequency show most refraction.

Long-wave radio transmissions show so much refraction that the wave returns to the Earth's surface.

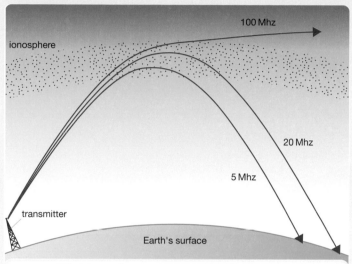

FIGURE 4: What type of wave shows most refraction?

Radio interference

Cirencester is about 100 miles north of Exeter. Radio Devon broadcasts from a transmitter in Exeter at a frequency of 95.8 MHz. Radio Gloucester broadcasts from Cirencester at the same frequency. It is common for a TV or radio frequency to be allocated to more than one station, but usually distance between these stations means that only one will be received.

Sometimes weather conditions mean that signals may travel further than normal and there is **interference** between the two stations. If you are listening to one station, you can hear the other one faintly in the background.

QUESTIONS

3   A local radio station broadcasts with a frequency of 103.4 MHz. Why will the signal not be refracted back to Earth from the upper atmosphere?

4   Suggest why people who live in the south of England sometimes hear foreign radio stations in the background when they are listening to their radios.

Diffraction

When water waves pass through a gap that is a similar size to the wavelength of the waves, the waves spread out on the other side of the gap. This is called **diffraction**.

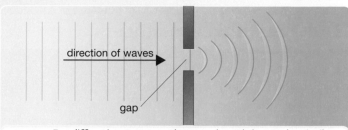

FIGURE 5: For diffraction to occur the wavelength has to be similar to the size of the gap.

If the gap is much larger than the wavelength of the waves, the diffraction effect is not so noticeable.

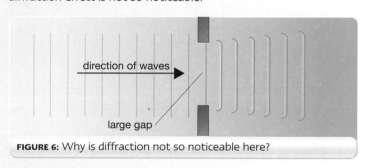

FIGURE 6: Why is diffraction not so noticeable here?

A similar spreading happens with radio waves when they meet an obstruction.

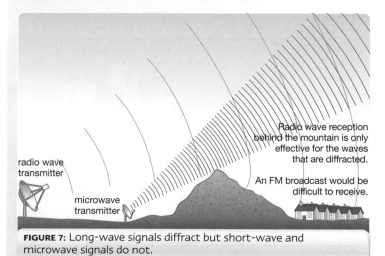

Radio wave reception behind the mountain is only effective for the waves that are diffracted.

An FM broadcast would be difficult to receive.

FIGURE 7: Long-wave signals diffract but short-wave and microwave signals do not.

QUESTIONS

5   Jamie lives in a house in a valley. He can listen to long-wave and medium-wave stations on his radio. He cannot get any signal on his mobile phone and VHF reception is very poor. Explain these differences.

Around the world in 0.134 seconds!

You will find out:

● how worldwide transmission of radio signals is achieved

One of the layers in the Earth's atmosphere is called the **ionosphere**. Radio waves are reflected from the ionosphere. Water is also able to reflect radio waves, but land masses are not good reflectors.

Radio signals can be received out of line of sight because of continuous reflection from the ionosphere and the oceans.

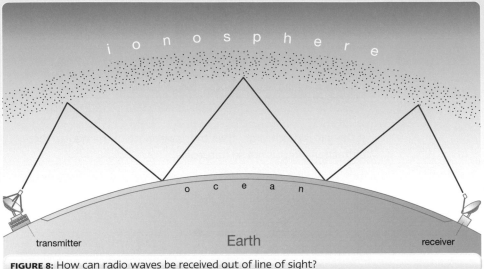

FIGURE 8: How can radio waves be received out of line of sight?

Microwaves are not reflected back to the surface of the Earth. They pass through the ionosphere and are received by **satellites orbiting** the Earth. The satellite amplifies the signal and then re-transmits the signal back to Earth.

Communications satellites orbit the Earth every 24 hours at a height of 36 000 km above the equator.

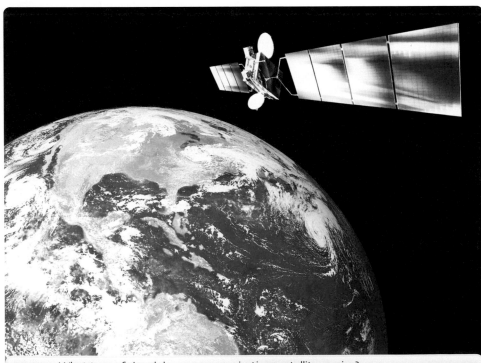

FIGURE 9: What type of signal does a communications satellite receive?

...ionosphere   ...orbit

Communication problems

The refraction of radio waves in the atmosphere needs to be taken into account, particularly when transmitting a signal to a communications satellite. The size of the aerial dish on the satellite is not very large and a focused beam of energy needs to be transmitted.

The shape of the transmitting aerial is designed to transmit a slightly divergent beam.

There is, however, some diffraction at the edges of the dish and this means some energy loss.

Many radios now receive digital signals and this reduces the amount of interference. For an explanation see page 193.

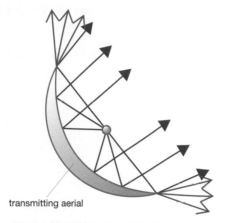

transmitting aerial

FIGURE 10: Why does a focused beam of energy need to be transmitted from a transmitting aerial?

QUESTIONS

6   Suggest why signals to satellites are transmitted as a slightly divergent beam and not as a parallel beam.

7   Why does the size and shape of a transmitting dish aerial dictate the use of microwaves instead of long-wave radio signals?

Light

You will find out:
- about the features of a transverse wave

007

Goldfinger: 'You are looking at an industrial laser, which emits a light not found in nature. It can project a spot on the Moon, or at closer range cut through solid metal – I will show you.'

Bond: 'I think you've made your point Goldfinger, thank you for the demonstration.'

Goldfinger: 'Choose your next witticism carefully Mr Bond, it may be your last!'

Bond: 'Do you expect me to talk?'

Goldfinger: 'No Mr Bond. I expect you to die.'

Transverse waves

A Mexican wave ripples round a stadium as people stand up and sit down.

Water particles move up and down as a wave spreads out from where a pebble is dropped into water.

A Mexican wave and a water wave are **transverse** waves.

A transverse wave travels in a direction at right angles to the wave vibration.

Light is another example of a transverse wave.

The speed of light, and all waves in the electromagnetic spectrum, is 300 000 km/s.

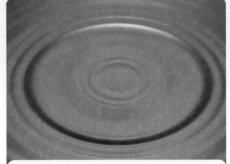

FIGURE 1: A transverse wave spreads out from where a pebble is dropped into water.

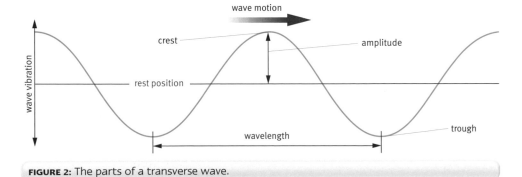

FIGURE 2: The parts of a transverse wave.

QUESTIONS

1 What is the speed of radio waves?
2 What is the speed of microwaves?
3 The speed of sound is 300 m/s. In a thunderstorm, why do we see lightning before we hear thunder?

...amplitude ...crest ...frequency ...hertz

Wave properties

- The **amplitude** of a wave is the maximum displacement of a particle from its rest position.
- The **wavelength** of a wave is the distance between two adjacent points on the wave of similar displacement. The unit of wavelength is the metre (m).
- The **frequency** of a wave is the number of complete waves passing a point in 1 second. The unit of frequency is the **hertz** (Hz).
- Surfers ride the **crest** of a wave. This is the point of maximum displacement above the rest position.
- The **trough** of a wave is the maximum displacement below the rest position.
- The speed of a wave is calculated using the equation:

  wave speed = frequency × wavelength

  the unit is metres per second (m/s).

FIGURE 3: What part of a wave does a surfer ride?

example

Eric throws a pebble into a pond. The distance between the ripples is 0.25 m and five waves reach the edge of the pond each second. Calculate the speed of the water wave.

wave speed = frequency × wavelength

wave speed = 5 × 0.25

wave speed = 1.25 m/s

Watch Out The abbreviation for a unit begins with a capital letter only if it is named after a person.

EXAM HINTS AND TIPS

Practise changing the subject of equations so you do not waste time working it out in the examination.

QUESTIONS

4   The distance between the crest of a wave and the next trough is 4 m. What is the wavelength of the wave?

5   The height of a wave from crest to trough is 30 cm. What is the amplitude of the wave?

6   A dolphin produces a sound with a frequency of 120 000 Hz. The wavelength is 1.25 cm (0.0125 m). Calculate the speed of sound in water.

QUESTIONS

7   Radio waves travel at 300 000 km/s. Radio 4 broadcasts at a frequency of 200 kHz. Calculate the wavelength of Radio 4.

8   Earthquake waves of wavelength 500 m travel through the Earth at 7 km/s. Calculate their frequency.

Early messages

Ancient Greek soldiers sent smoke signals; so did the American Indians.

The British still use chains of beacons to celebrate important events such as the Millennium.

Some messages are too difficult to send by smoke signal.

Sometimes a message has to be sent a great distance.

Runners, horses and motorbikes have been used to get messages from one place to another quickly.

FIGURE 4: Suggest what messages ancient Greek soldiers might have communicated in their smoke signals.

Messages can be sent very quickly by a flashing signal lamp. A code is used to represent the different letters.

FIGURE 6: Why are two people needed to communicate successfully with another ship in this picture?

Navies used signalling lamps until 1999.

Laser

Light Amplification by Stimulated Emission of Radiation

A **laser** produces a narrow intense beam of light. It is capable of cutting, burning or vaporising materials. Other uses of a laser are in communication and eye surgery.

WOW FACTOR!

The marathon is named after a Greek town. There is a legend that says about 2500 years ago a messenger ran 26 miles from Marathon to Athens. He had to tell the people how the Greek army had defeated the Persians.

FIGURE 5: This mounted messenger is riding in wartime and carrying an important message. He is wearing a gas mask to protect him from a gas attack. What else may he need for himself and his horse on his journey?

QUESTIONS

9 Why is it dangerous to look at a laser beam?

10 Science fiction films often show a coloured laser beam coming from a laser gun as a special effect.

Suggest reasons why we would not see a beam coming from the laser gun.

...compact disc ...laser

Morse code

Mirrors and signalling lamps have been used to send messages using the **Morse code**.

The code is a series of dots and dashes that represent individual letters of the alphabet.

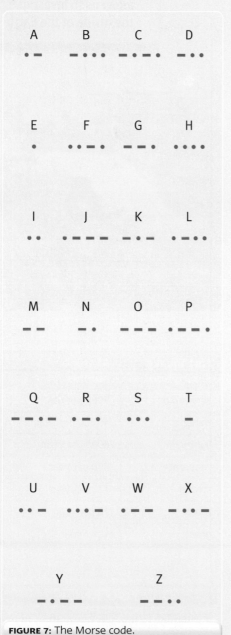

FIGURE 7: The Morse code.

████ QUESTIONS ████

11 Translate this code:

•——• •••• —•—— ••• ••

—•—• •••

•• ••• ••—• ••— —•

Sending signals

Signals can be sent by light, electricity, radio waves or microwaves. Each type of signal has advantages and disadvantages.

- They are all almost instantaneous.

- Light signals can be easily sent with nothing more sophisticated than a torch, but the signal needs to be coded and is not secure. Anyone can see what is being sent.

- Electrical signals need equipment and wires linking the sender and receiver of the signal. Wires can be cut or damaged. The signal needs to be amplified at regular intervals because of energy loss in the form of heat due to the electric current.

- Radio waves and microwaves can travel large distances and through the atmosphere. They can even travel across Space!

Laser light

White light, from a bulb, is made up of many different colours, each of a different frequency and out of **phase**.

The light from a laser is at one frequency and in phase.

Compact disc

The plastic **compact disc** (CD) is pressed with a series of fine pits. The pits represent a digital musical signal. The signal is read by a laser.

- The music layer is coated with a fine film of metal that follows the pits exactly.

- The shiny metal film reflects the laser light.

- The metal layer is covered by another layer of transparent plastic.

- The music is sandwiched between two layers of plastic. This stops dust and scratches from affecting the sound.

FIGURE 8: How can you tell that these two waves in white light are out of phase?

FIGURE 9: The crests and troughs occur at the same time in these two laser light waves. What term describes this?

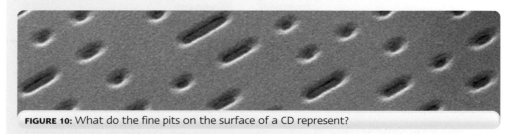

FIGURE 10: What do the fine pits on the surface of a CD represent?

████ QUESTIONS ████

12 Suggest why:

   a telephone signals between a house and a local exchange are sent by an electric current.

   b telephone signals between England and America are sent by microwaves.

Stable Earth

You will find out:

- how earthquakes are detected
- about the types of waves that earthquakes produce
- how the properties of earthquake waves allow us to investigate the inside of the Earth

Devastating wave

On Sunday December 26 2004 an undersea earthquake in the Indian Ocean was the cause of the Asian tsunami that claimed many lives. A tsunami is a gigantic wave.

With a distance of 500 km between crests and a wave height of 10 m, the wave travelled at a speed of 800 km/h towards islands such as Sri Lanka and The Maldives and also touched the mainland coastline. No one was prepared for the devastating results.

Earthquakes

An earthquake happens when rocks break suddenly at a **fault**.

Shock waves pass through the Earth and travel around its surface. It is the surface waves that cause damage to houses and other structures.

We detect earthquakes using a **seismometer**.

- A heavy weight with a pen attached is suspended above a rotating drum. There is paper on the drum. The base is bolted to solid rock.
- During an earthquake, the base moves but the pen stays still.
- A trace is drawn on the paper.

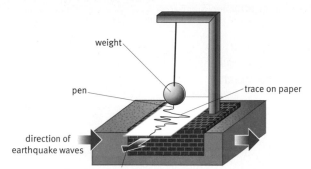

weight
pen
trace on paper
direction of earthquake waves
direction of movement of paper

FIGURE 1: A seismometer is used to detect and measure the size of an earthquake.

Earthquake description	Average number
very minor	9000 per day
minor	49 000 per year
light	6000 per year
moderate	800 per year
strong	120 per year
major	18 per year
great	1 per year

DID YOU KNOW?

Earthquakes happen more often than you think.

Thankfully, only a few lead to the sort of disaster seen in the Indian Ocean in 2004.

⊞ QUESTIONS ⊞

1. What force attracts the pen of a seismometer towards the centre of the Earth?
2. Why is the base of the seismometer bolted to solid rock?

...epicentre ...fault ...focus ...L wave ...longitudinal ...P wave ...S wave

Earthquake waves

An earthquake happens below the Earth's surface at the **focus**. The **epicentre** is the point on the Earth's surface above the focus.

Surface waves travel out from the epicentre relatively slowly. They are called **L waves.**

An earthquake produces two other types of **seismic wave** (in Greek 'seismos' means 'a shaking').

- A **P wave** is a primary (pressure) wave. It is a **longitudinal** wave and is similar to a sound wave. It travels through the Earth at a speed of between 5 and 8 km/s.

- An **S wave** is a secondary (shear) wave. It is a **transverse** wave and travels through the Earth at a speed of between 3 and 5.5 km/s. It is slightly slower than a P wave.

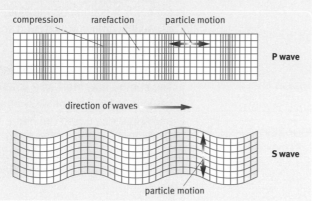

FIGURE 2: Seismic waves. What type of wave is a P wave? What type of wave is an S wave?

The **seismograph** trace from a seismometer shows the three types of wave.

These waves are important because they help to tell us about the structure of the Earth.

- P waves pass through solids and liquids.
- S waves pass only through solids.

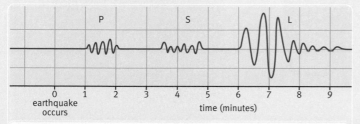

FIGURE 3: Look at this seismograph. Which type of wave travelled fastest during the earthquake?

QUESTIONS

3   Which type of earthquake wave is similar to a wave in the electromagnetic spectrum?

4   Why does the trace from a seismometer have three separate wave patterns?

Inside the Earth

Scientists use the properties of seismic waves to find out more about the Earth's structure.

P waves pass through the Earth and are refracted by the core. The paths taken by P waves help scientists to calculate the size of the Earth's core.

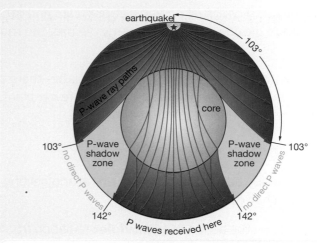

FIGURE 4: What do P waves help scientists find out?

S waves cannot be detected on the opposite side of the Earth to an earthquake. This tells scientists that there is some liquid in their path. S waves are detected over the same area as P waves, which indicates that the liquid is found in the Earth's core.

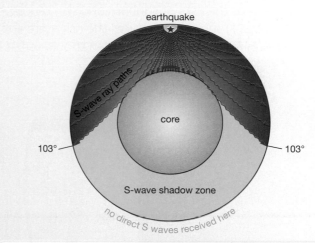

FIGURE 5: What do S waves help scientists find out?

QUESTIONS

5   a   Draw a trace from a seismometer to show the pattern when all three types of seismic wave are received.

b   Draw a second trace to show the pattern from the same earthquake received by a seismometer on the opposite side of the Earth to the earthquake.

...seismic wave   ...seismograph   ...seismometer   ...shock wave   ...transverse

Global warming

The planet is getting warmer. This is because there are more polluting gases in the atmosphere. (See page 81 for more on global warming.) These gases are sometimes called **greenhouse gases**.

The main greenhouse gas is carbon dioxide. Whenever a fuel burns, carbon dioxide is formed. Fossil fuel power stations, cars and other vehicles all produce carbon dioxide. The more energy we use, the more carbon dioxide is produced.

The more rainforests we destroy the fewer plants there are. Plants use carbon dioxide in photosynthesis. If there are fewer plants, less carbon dioxide is taken out of the atmosphere.

Suntan or skin cancer?

Many people enjoy being out in the sunshine and getting a 'healthy suntan', but what causes a suntan?

A tan is caused by the action of **ultraviolet** radiation from the Sun on the skin.

If you spend too much time in the Sun you can get sunburnt. Your skin becomes red and starts to peel.

Even more exposure to the Sun can cause skin cancer.

Sunscreen can reduce the risks of sunburn and skin cancer. A high Sun Protection Factor (SPF) sunscreen reduces the risk more and means you can stay out in the Sun for longer. Young children should use at least SPF 30.

DID YOU KNOW?

The most common sign of skin cancer is a change on the skin, especially a new growth or a sore that does not heal.

Not all skin cancers look the same. The cancer may start as a small, smooth, shiny, pale or waxy lump. It can appear as a firm red lump. Sometimes, the lump bleeds or develops a crust. It can also start as a flat, red spot that is rough, dry or scaly.

Skin cancers are found mainly on areas of the skin that are exposed to the Sun but they can occur anywhere on the body.

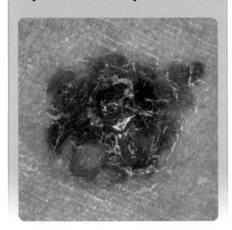

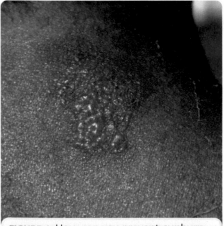

FIGURE 6: How can you prevent sunburn when you are spending time outside on a sunny day?

FIGURE 7: You should always use sunscreen with a high SPF when spending time in the Sun.

■ QUESTIONS ■

6 Suggest why young children should use sunscreen with a high SPF.

7 Cricketers often spend a long time in the Sun during a game. Which part of their body is most likely to develop skin cancer if they do not apply enough sunscreen?

...greenhouse gas   ...melanin   ...ozone

Module quiz

1 Why does a cup of coffee cool down when left on the kitchen table?

2 What is a thermogram?

3 How can a homeowner reduce energy loss through their windows?

4 How can a homeowner reduce energy loss through their roof?

5 How can a homeowner reduce energy loss through their walls?

6 Why does fur keep a bear warm in winter?

7 What causes a hot air balloon to rise?

8 Which radiation transfers the most energy?

      microwaves   **infrared**

9 What chemical in food absorbs energy from microwaves?

10 Why do some people think mobile phones and phone masts are dangerous?

11 Write down **one** use of an infrared transmitter.

12 Draw diagrams to show the difference between an analogue signal and a digital signal.

13 What device combines digital signals to allow them to be transmitted simultaneously?

14 Write down **one** advantage of using a wireless laptop.

15 What causes ghosting on a television picture?

16 What is the speed of all waves in the electromagnetic spectrum?

17 What is meant by the amplitude of a wave?

18 Write down the equation that relates frequency, wavelength and wave speed.

19 What radiation causes suntan, sunburn and skin cancer?

20 Write down **two** causes of global warming.

Numeracy activity

This table shows the heat equivalents and costs for four fuels.

Quantity	Fuel	Heat equivalent (in kWh)	Cost (in £)
1 unit	electricity	1.0	0.11
50 kilograms	house coal	416.8	10.90
15 kilograms	bottled gas	205.0	18.50
1 litre	heating oil	10.5	0.38

QUESTIONS

1 John wants to heat his home as cheaply as he can. Which fuel should he use?

2 Suggest reasons why John might choose each of the other fuels, instead of the cheapest.

Exam practice

Exam practice questions

1 **a** When ice at 0 °C is heated, its temperature does not rise until it has all melted. Explain why. [2]

b Explain what is meant by specific latent heat of vaporisation. [2]

c When the same amount of heat energy is supplied to a pan containing 2 kg of water and a pan containing 2 kg of oil, the oil heats up more quickly. Explain why. [2]

d Higher tier: The water has a specific heat capacity of 4200 J/kg °C. How much energy is required to heat it by 80 °C? [4]

[Total 10 marks]

2 The following table details information about three methods of insulating the home.

Method	Installation cost	Expected annual saving
draught excluders	£8	£15
double glazing	£2000	£60
loft insulation	£240	£80

a Calculate the payback period for loft insulation. [2]

b Explain two ways in which double glazing can prevent heat loss. [4]

c Energy efficient bulbs are used to reduce electricity bills. If a bulb transfers 25% of the electricity supplied into light, what is its efficiency? [3]

[Total 9 marks]

3 **a** Explain what is meant by:
  i the amplitude of a wave. [1]
  ii the wavelength of a wave. [1]

b Sound waves travel at 330 m/s. If the wavelength of a sound wave is 15 m, calculate its frequency. [4]

[Total 6 marks]

4 Seismic waves are shock waves created during an earthquake.

a When there was a minor earthquake in Dudley, two sets of waves could be detected 50 miles from the epicentre. Explain why. [2]

b Which type of wave was detected first? [1]

[Total 3 marks]

5 **a** Explain why a person with a darker skin is at less risk of skin cancer than a fair skinned person. [2]

b Microwaves can be used to cook food. Explain why food to be cooked in this way should be cut thinly and placed in a glass or plastic dish, but not a metal one. [3]

[Total 5 marks]

6 Optical fibres act as narrow light guides that allow light to travel from one end to the other without leaving through the sides.

a Name the effect that occurs inside optical fibres. [1]

b Copy and complete the following diagram showing the path a beam of light will travel through the optical fibre.

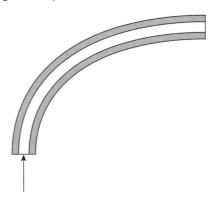

[3]

[Total 4 marks]

a Volcanoes can throw up a vast amount of dust when they erupt. Explain how the dust from a volcano may affect the local weather pattern. [2]

b Explain why a city near the volcano may find that the cloud causes local warming. [2]

c Satellites communicate with Earth using different types of electromagnetic radiation. State whether visible or microwave radiation would be best able to communicate with satellites after a volcano erupts. Give reasons for your answer. [3]

This answer is not detailed enough for two marks. The dust reflects the Sun's radiation so some radiation cannot reach the Earth's surface, causing cooling.

a   The dust causes cooling.

b   The cloud keeps the heat from the city in.

c   The light can't pass through the cloud.

Again, this answer is not quite detailed enough to earn both marks. The dust reflects the heat back to the city so it cannot spread away, which causes heating.

The student hasn't fully answered the question Microwave radiation is best because it can pass through the cloud, but the cloud absorbs visible light.

Overall Grade: C/D

How to get an A

Always remember to answer the question in full, and give reasons for your answer if you are asked for them.

P2 Living for the future

Comets are made from ice and dust. Most comets are too faint to be visible without a telescope, but a few each decade become bright enough to be seen with the naked eye.

If an asteroid collided with Earth, it would mean the end of life on the planet as we know it. Dust and water vapour would be thrown up by the collision and this would block out the Sun. Temperatures would fall and giant tsunamis would destroy vast areas.

One theory has it that 65 million years ago an asteroid hit the Yucatan Peninsula, creating a crater 170 km wide and causing the extinction of the dinosaurs.

Asteroids and comets on a possible collision course with Earth are called Near Earth objects.

Asteroids are rocks left over from the formation of the Solar System.

Collecting energy from the Sun

You will find out:
- how photocells work
- why photocells are used in particular situations

Total eclipse of the Sun

On August 11 1999 in Cornwall, the Moon passed over the face of the Sun. The temperature fell by several degrees. Dogs started to bark. Birds flew to their nests. Streetlights suddenly lit up. An eerie silence descended.

It was a total eclipse of the Sun.

Unlimited energy

The Sun is the source of energy for the Earth.

Without solar energy there would be no life on Earth.
- Light from the Sun allows plants to photosynthesise.
- Heat from the Sun provides the warmth for living things to survive.

Photocells and solar cells

A **photocell** changes light into electricity. A **solar cell** uses light from the Sun. The larger the area of a photocell, the more electricity is produced.

Photocells can be used in places where mains electricity is not easily available.

The large area of photocells on the International Space Station provides a **direct current** (dc) supply to run the spacecraft.

FIGURE 1: Would we survive without the Sun's energy?

WOW FACTOR!

The Sun loses 4 000 000 000 kg of its mass every second as energy.

It still has enough mass left to last for another 5 000 000 000 years!

FIGURE 2: How do photocells help to run the International Space Station?

▣▣ QUESTIONS ▣▣

1 What is the energy source for:
   a a photocell?
   b a solar cell?

...direct current ...n-type silicon ...photocell ...photon

Electricity from light

The direct current from a photocell is similar to the current from a battery. It is in one direction.

FIGURE 3: Why do you think there is a photocell on top of the parking meter?

Photocells have many advantages over other electrical systems.

- They are very robust and need little maintenance.
- No fuel or lengthy power cables are needed.
- They do not contribute any pollution to the atmosphere in the form of dust or greenhouse gases.
- They use a renewable energy source.

The only disadvantage is that they do not produce electricity when it is dark such as during the night or when it is cloudy.

How do photocells work?

It is not only tropical countries that benefit from using photocells. Even in the United Kingdom some houses have been built with photocells on their roofs, which produce enough electricity for the occupants.

FIGURE 4: What do these photocells produce?

A photocell consists of two special pieces of silicon joined together.

Pure silicon is neutrally charged but if a small amount of an impurity such as phosphorus is added, there are more free electrons which make this a better conductor than pure silicon. This is known as **n-type** (negative) **silicon**.

If a different impurity, such as boron, is added there is an absence of free electrons. The absence of an electron is known as a hole and the silicon is known as **p-type silicon**.

When these two types of silicon are placed together it is called a **p-n junction**. An electric field is created between the two layers.

Sunlight is made up of tiny packets of energy called **photons**. When photons are absorbed the energy causes electrons to become free. They move to the negative layer and leave the junction to flow in an external circuit.

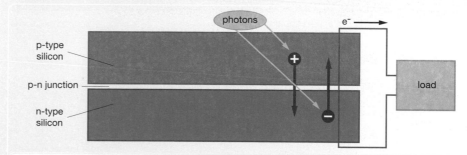

FIGURE 5: How is an electric field set up in a photocell?

QUESTIONS

2 The current from a photocell is sometimes used to charge a battery. When would the battery be used?

3 Why are photocells placed on south-facing roofs in England but on north-facing roofs in Australia?

4 a In a photocell, what is the charge of a hole?
  b Suggest what the 'p' in p-type silicon stands for.

You will find out:

- how passive solar heating can reduce demand on other energy resources
- about the advantages and disadvantages of wind technology

Renewable energy

The Sun is a **renewable** source of energy.

As well as being used to produce electricity from a photocell, the energy from the Sun can be used for heating.

A solar water heater on the roof of a building is made from rectangular collectors. Inside each collector is a series of small tubes. These tubes pass over a black plate.

The black plate absorbs sunlight and warms the water passing through the tubes.

Warmed water rises to the storage tanks as it is heated. Colder water sinks down into the collector.

Wind

The temperature difference between land surfaces causes a **convection current**.

FIGURE 6: What is the large shiny cylinder above the solar panels?

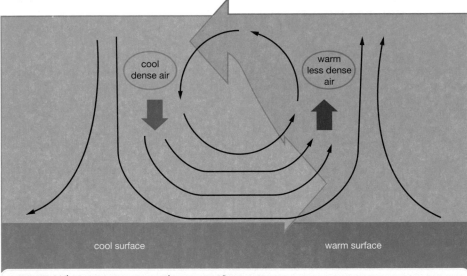

cool dense air

warm less dense air

cool surface

warm surface

FIGURE 7: What causes a convection current?

This movement of air is usually called **wind**.

Wind is used to turn a wind turbine and produce electricity.

WOW FACTOR!

A typical wind turbine provides enough electricity for 1500 homes.

QUESTIONS

5 What is the best colour for absorbing radiation?

6 Which process (conduction, convection or radiation) describes the transfer of energy by the water in a solar water heater?

FIGURE 8: A wind farm. Why do you think the turbines are placed high up on hills?

...convection current   ...focus   ...global warming   ...kinetic energy   ...passive solar heating

Passive solar heating

A home that uses **passive solar heating** makes full use of direct sunlight for heating purposes.

The home has large windows in its south-facing walls and small windows in its north-facing walls. This allows natural light and heat from the Sun to be used and reduces the need for electricity.

During the day, energy from the Sun warms the walls and floor of a room.

At night the energy is **radiated** back into the room from the warm walls and floor.

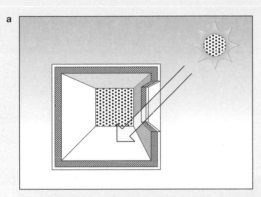

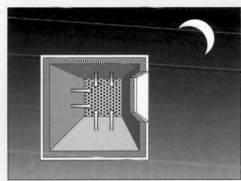

FIGURE 9: Passive solar heating in a home **a** during the day and **b** at night.

Curved solar reflectors **focus** energy from the Sun.

Kinetic energy transfer

Moving air has **kinetic energy** which is transferred by a wind turbine into electricity.

QUESTIONS

7 Why should south-facing windows in homes in the UK be large?

8 Why are the reflecting surfaces of solar collectors curved?

More on passive solar heating

The temperature inside a greenhouse is higher than the temperature on the outside.

This is why plants that normally only grow in tropical climates can grow at the Eden Project in Cornwall.

FIGURE 10: Why is it cooler outside a greenhouse?

The Sun is very hot and produces radiation with a very short **wavelength**. Glass is transparent to this short wavelength radiation. The ground and plants inside the greenhouse absorb this radiation, warm up and re-radiate infrared radiation. The plants are not as hot as the Sun and the wavelength radiated is therefore longer. This radiation will not pass through glass but is reflected back inside.

It is not just greenhouses that are warmed in this way. The temperature inside your home rises for the same reason.

To make sure that a solar reflector works as efficiently as possible, a computer moves the dish to face the Sun throughout the day.

FIGURE 11: Why are these solar reflectors all pointing the same way?

Wind farm – friend or foe?

There is a lot of controversy surrounding wind farms.

Few people dispute the fact that they are a renewable energy resource that do not discharge polluting gases into the atmosphere and do not contribute to **global warming**.

There are, however, major concerns about their visual impact on the countryside and their noise. They do not work if there is little wind and must be shut down if wind speeds are greater than 88 km/h.

QUESTIONS

9 Wind farms take up a lot of space if they are to generate large amounts of electricity. Some farmers do not mind their fields being used for wind turbines. Suggest why.

...radiate ...renewable ...wavelength ...wind

Generating electricity

You will find out:

- how a dynamo generates electricity
- how electricity is moved around the country

Lighting up

Rajab goes for a bicycle ride at dusk.

His bicycle is fitted with a dynamo. When Rajab pushes the pedals round, the movement energy is changed to electrical energy and is used to light up his bicycle light.

This means he does not need a direct current battery for his light.

Mini generator

A bicycle **dynamo** is a small electrical **generator**.

A magnet rotates inside a coil of wire and an **alternating current** is produced.

If a magnet is moved near to a coil of wire a current is produced in the wire.

If a wire is moved near to a magnet a current is produced in the wire.

Alternating-current voltage changer

A **transformer** increases or decreases the size of an alternating current.

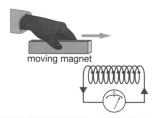

FIGURE 1: How does this dynamo produce an alternating current?

moving magnet

FIGURE 2: What happens when the magnet is moved closer to the coil of wire?

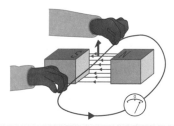

FIGURE 3: What happens when the wire is placed in the magnetic field between the two magnets?

FIGURE 4: Suggest why there are a lot of transformers in this electricity substation.

RED LANE
H/V SUBSTATION
0700198

DANGER OF DEATH
KEEP OUT

IN CASE OF EMERGENCY
Phone 0800 626 441
Midlands Electricity plc.

QUESTIONS

1   What is the difference between a current from a battery and a current from a dynamo?

...alternating current   ...cycle   ...dynamo   ...frequency   ...generator

Larger currents and voltages

There are three ways to increase the current from a dynamo:

- use a stronger magnet
- increase the number of turns of wire on the coil
- rotate the magnet faster – on a bicycle this means pedalling faster.

The dynamo produces a changing voltage and current. An **oscilloscope** shows how the alternating voltage changes with time. The maximum voltage and the **frequency** can be found from the trace.

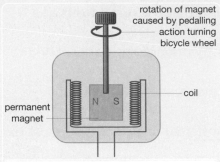

rotation of magnet caused by pedalling action turning bicycle wheel

coil

permanent magnet

FIGURE 5: What changes could you make to this dynamo to increase the current output?

FIGURE 7: Birds on an overhead power line.

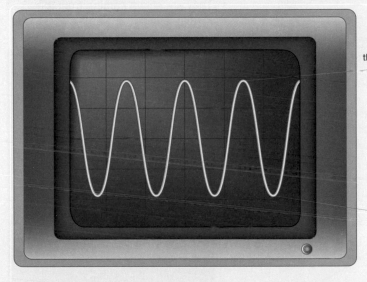

the height of the wave is the maximum (peak) voltage

the length of the wave shows the time for one **cycle**, called the period

FIGURE 6: The maximum voltage and frequency are measured from an oscilloscope trace.

To calculate the frequency, the following equation is used.

frequency = 1 ÷ period

The unit is hertz, Hz

The **National Grid** distributes electricity around the United Kingdom at voltages as high as 400 000 V. The high voltage leads to:

- reduced energy loss
- reduced distribution costs
- cheaper electricity for consumers.

Transformers in the National Grid step down (reduce) or step up (increase) the voltage.

Transmission loss

Electricity in the United Kingdom is generated at a frequency of 50 Hz.

This means 50 **cycles** of output each second.

When a current passes through a wire the wire gets hot. The greater the current, the hotter the wire.

When a transformer increases the voltage the current is reduced. This means there is less heating effect and therefore less energy lost to the environment.

QUESTIONS

4 Suggest why birds like to sit on overhead power lines.

5 Calculate the period of **one** cycle of electrical output generated in the United Kingdom.

QUESTIONS

2 Describe the brightness of the bulb in Rajab's bicycle light connected to his dynamo when he has stopped at traffic lights.

3 What happens to the brightness of the bulb in Rajab's bicycle light connected to his dynamo when he pedals very fast downhill?

Carrying electricity

Most electricity is produced in power stations that use **fossil fuels** as a source of energy.

- Electricity is transmitted round the country through the National Grid to **consumers**.
- Consumers are homes, farms, offices, schools, shops, factories and hospitals.
- Some of the energy from coal is not transferred to electricity. It is lost to the environment, usually as heat.

You will find out:

- how electricity is carried
- how electricity is produced
- about energy efficiency

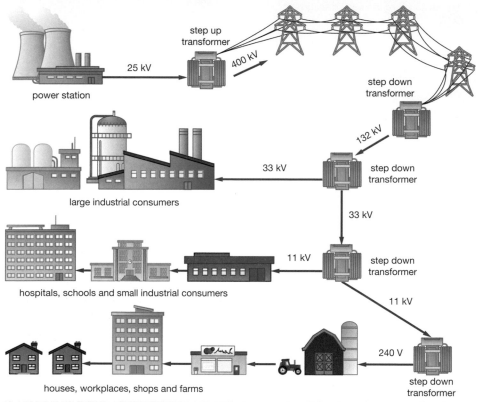

FIGURE 8: Suggest why there are step up and step down transformers in the National Grid.

Watch Out The dense white clouds you see coming from a power station are not smoke.

They are steam coming from the cooling towers.

DID YOU KNOW?

In power stations almost half the energy stored in coal is lost as heat from cooling towers.

QUESTIONS

6 What chemical is cooled in cooling towers in a power station?

7 Explain what is meant by a consumer of electricity.

...consumer ...efficiency

Simple alternating current generator

Like a dynamo, a generator in a power station works on the principle that a magnetic field rotating inside a coil generates a voltage in the coil.

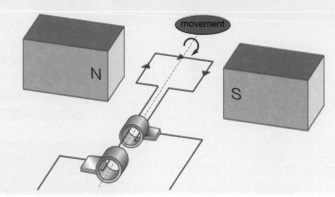

movement

N

S

FIGURE 9: A simple alternating current (ac) generator. What causes a current to pass through the coil?

In a simple alternating current generator:

- a coil of wire is free to rotate between the poles of a magnet
- as the coil rotates it cuts the magnetic field and a current passes through the coil.

The same thing would happen if the coil was stationary and the magnet rotated around the coil. It is the relative movement between the two that is important.

Generators in power stations

- A generator in a power station is coupled to a **turbine**.
- The turbine is turned by steam under high pressure.
- A fuel such as coal is burned in a boiler room to heat water and produce steam.
- A lot of energy from the fuel is wasted and not transferred to electricity.

turbine

boiler room

generator

coal pile

FIGURE 10: What is the role of a boiler room in a power station?

QUESTIONS

8 Other than from the cooling towers, where is energy lost in a coal-fired power station?

9 What happens to the steam after it has turned a turbine in a power station?

Energy efficiency

Energy **efficiency** is a measure of how well a device transfers energy.

$$\text{efficiency} = \frac{\text{electrical energy output}}{\text{fuel energy input}}$$

A power station is not very efficient:

- For every 100 J of energy stored in coal, 15 J is wasted in the boiler.
- A further 45 J is wasted in the cooling towers and 5 J in the generator.

The remaining energy is converted to electricity.

fuel energy input	=	waste energy output	+	electrical energy output

QUESTIONS

10 Calculate the energy efficiency of a power station where 67 per cent of available energy is lost to the environment.

11 A power station is 35 per cent efficient. It produces 2 million joules of energy each second. How many joules of energy are lost to the environment each second?

...fossil fuel ...turbine

Fuels for power

You will find out:
- about the types of fuels used in power stations
- about power
- about the disadvantages and advantages of different types of power stations

'Chill out, dad'

The electricity bill has arrived and Holly's dad is asking her not to leave the television and light on in her room.

But compared to the energy used in other parts of the house such as the kitchen, the amount Holly's things use in her room is very small.

Most televisions and lights have a power rating of less than 100 watts.

A typical toaster or kettle has a power rating of at least 2000 watts (2 kilowatts).

Appliance	Power in W
	60
	180
	750
	1000
	2250

Power station fuels

Fossil fuels are the most common energy source for power stations.

Fossil fuels are:
- coal
- natural gas
- oil.

Fossil fuels are **non-renewable** energy resources. This means that eventually they will all run out.

Some power stations are using **biomass** as a fuel.

Biomass is a **renewable** energy resource.

Biomass fuels are:
- wood
- straw
- manure.

Renewable energy resources will not run out. For every tree that is cut down a new one can be planted.

A different type of fuel that is used as the energy resource in **nuclear** power stations is **uranium**.

FIGURE 1: When a new fossil fuel power station is to be built what do you think it should be near to?

QUESTIONS

1. Why are coal, oil and natural gas called fossil fuels?
2. What is the advantage of using a renewable energy resource?

...biomass ...ferment ...fossil fuel ...kilowatt-hour

What is a fuel?

A fuel burns in air to release energy in the form of heat. Coal, oil and natural gas all burn.

Biomass can be burned but more often it is allowed to **ferment**. Fermentation generates **methane** which is burned.

Uranium fuel rods are used in a nuclear power station. The fuel rods do not actually burn. The uranium becomes unstable and the atoms split. Atoms of new elements are formed that have a smaller mass than uranium. A lot of energy is released as heat when the atoms split. The reaction in a nuclear power station has to be carefully controlled. If it is not there could be a nuclear explosion.

Measuring power

Power is a measure of the rate at which energy is used.

power = voltage x current

The unit is watt (W).

Most electrical appliances show their power rating.

Electrical consumption is the amount of energy that has been used.

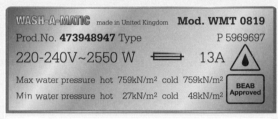

WASH-A-MATIC made in United Kingdom **Mod. WMT 0819**
Prod.No. **473948947** Type   P 5969697
220-240V~2550 W   13A
Max water pressure hot 759kN/m² cold 759kN/m²
Min water pressure hot 27kN/m² cold 48kN/m²
BEAB Approved

FIGURE 2: Most electrical appliances show their power rating. What is the power of this electrical appliance?

The amount of energy used is measured on a **kilowatt-hour** meter. If you look carefully at an electricity meter you will see a rotating disc. The faster the disc rotates the more electrical energy is being used. When a shower or cooker is being used the disc goes round very quickly. If only a light is switched on the disc hardly moves.

energy used = power x time

The unit is kilowatt hour (kWh).

The cost of using an electrical appliance depends on the energy used.

cost = energy x cost per kilowatt hour

The unit is pence (p).

Single Phase Credit Meter
1 9 9 1 9
kWh
rotating disc
N. 836082020   Hz 50
V 209   1kWh

FIGURE 3: Read this electricity meter. What is the value of the electrical consumption?

Choosing a fuel

There are advantages and disadvantages in using each type of fuel.

When fossil fuels such as coal are burned carbon dioxide is formed. This is a greenhouse gas that contributes to global warming. Sulfur dioxide is also produced which dissolves in rainwater to form acid rain.

Biomass energy sources are renewable but carbon dioxide is still a product of their combustion.

Nuclear power stations do not have tall chimneys billowing smoke. No fuel is burned in a nuclear power station so there is no greenhouse gas produced. There is no smoke or other pollution.

FIGURE 4: A nuclear power station. What are the advantages and disadvantages of nuclear fuel?

Cheaper electricity

If electricity is used at night it is cheaper. This is because electricity still has to be produced but most consumers do not need to use it. For example, you can programme a washing machine to wash clothes overnight.

QUESTIONS

3 A 7000 W shower is used for 3 hours a week.

   a How much energy is used?

   b Electricity costs 9 p per kWh. How much does it cost to use the shower each week?

4 A microwave oven is designed to operate at 250 V. A current of 3 A passes.

   a Calculate the power rating of the microwave.

   b It takes 12 minutes to cook a meal. Electricity costs 9 p per kWh. How much does it cost to cook the meal?

QUESTIONS

5 A toaster has a power rating of 2.3 kW. Mains voltage is 230 V. Calculate the current in the toaster.

...methane ...non-renewable ...nuclear ...renewable ...uranium

Nuclear waste

Nuclear power stations do not produce smoke or carbon dioxide.

Carbon dioxide is a greenhouse gas that causes global warming.

Nuclear power stations do produce some waste.

The waste is **radioactive**.

- Low-level radioactive waste is diluted in water as it goes into the sea.

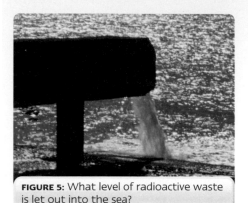

FIGURE 5: What level of radioactive waste is let out into the sea?

FIGURE 6: Why should high-level radioactive waste not be dumped at sea?

FIGURE 7: All radioactive substances are labelled with this special symbol.

- High-level radioactive waste is harmful to living things. It should never be dumped at sea.

Radioactive waste is stored in steel drums buried underground. Some sites are nearly 1 kilometre deep!

FIGURE 8: An underground burial site for nuclear waste. Suggest why these sites should not be built near to earthquake zones.

You will find out:

- about waste from nuclear power stations
- about the effects of radioactivity
- about the advantages and disadvantages of nuclear power

DID YOU KNOW?

The map shows the positions of nuclear power stations in the UK. What do you notice about where they are? Can you suggest a reason why?

QUESTIONS

6   Suggest why radioactive waste must be stored in steel drums deep in the ground.

7   Suggest **two** ways that radioactive waste can be taken in by fish.

...atomic bomb   ...ionisation   ...mutation

Effects of radioactive waste

Radiation from radioactive waste causes **ionisation**. In ionisation the radiation changes the structure of any atom exposed to the radiation.

The cells in our bodies are made up of many atoms, so body cells can be changed by radiation. One important chemical in a cell is DNA. If DNA changes due to ionisation the cell behaves differently. This is called **mutation**.

Sometimes when a cell mutates it divides in an uncontrolled way. This can lead to cancer.

The fuel used in a nuclear reactor is uranium. Once the uranium has been used the waste remains radioactive for thousands of years. Uranium is a non-renewable energy resource.

One of the waste products from a nuclear power station is **plutonium**. Plutonium can be used to make nuclear weapons.

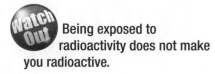
Watch Out Being exposed to radioactivity does not make you radioactive.

DID YOU KNOW?

Nuclear power provides 20 per cent of the UK's energy needs.

In France it provides nearly 70 per cent.

FIGURE 9: An atomic explosion. Why is the damage caused by this type of explosion so devastating?

An **atomic bomb** causes death and destruction over a very large area. The affected area remains radioactive and is unusable for many years.

Why choose nuclear power?

Despite the possible dangers from nuclear power and nuclear waste there are advantages in using nuclear power stations:

- Fossil fuel reserves are not used.
- No greenhouse gases are discharged into the atmosphere.

The disadvantages are:

- very high maintenance and decommissioning costs
- the risk of accidents similar to the one at Chernobyl.

QUESTIONS

9 Most nuclear power stations in the United Kingdom are to be closed down by 2020. Suggest how the energy needs of this country could be met in the future.

QUESTIONS

8 Describe what can happen to a body cell if it is exposed to radiation.

...plutonium ...radioactive

Nuclear radiations

You will find out:
- how to measure background radiation
- about the effects of different types of ionising radiation
- about the safe disposal of nuclear waste
- about the properties of ionising radiation

Resort near nuclear plant is worst cancer cluster

In July 2002 the following report appeared in one of the national newspapers.

'Cancer rates in a Somerset town close to a nuclear power station are up to six times higher than average.

'Burnham-on-Sea will be named this week as the most significant "cancer cluster" so far discovered near a British nuclear plant. The revelation will provide fuel for anti-nuclear campaigners who say the industry pollutes the environment and is potentially lethal for people living nearby.

'The residents of Burnham, which lies five miles downwind of the Hinkley Point plant, have demanded an official inquiry into the figures.'

Mark Townsend, Sunday July 14 2002, The Observer (Copyright Guardian Newspapers Limited 2002.)

FIGURE 1: Do you think Hinkley Point nuclear power plant should have been built near to people's homes?

Radiation all around us

Background radiation is always around us. It comes from many sources, most of which are naturally occurring.

Measuring radioactivity

Scientists measure **radioactivity** using a Geiger-Müller (GM) tube connected to a **ratemeter** or a counter. Sometimes the ratemeter has a loudspeaker attached so that the radioactivity being detected can be heard.

The common name for the apparatus is a **Geiger counter**.

There are three main types of ionising radiation, **alpha** (α), **beta** (β) and **gamma** (γ).

FIGURE 2: Even the granite rocks on Dartmoor contribute to background radiation.

FIGURE 3: What does this Geiger counter measure?

⸽ QUESTIONS ⸽

1. Suggest why Hinkley Point power plant is on the coast.
2. Hussein measures background radiation in Devon. The Geiger counter reads 60 counts per minute.

   Emily measures background radiation in London. The Geiger counter reads only 35 counts per minute.

   Suggest why there is such a large difference.

...alpha ...background radiation ...beta ...electron ...gamma ...Geiger counter

Background sources

It is not just atomic bombs and nuclear power stations that contribute to background radiation.

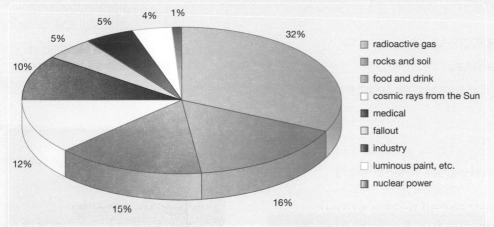

FIGURE 4: Sources of background radiation. Which source contributes most to the background radiation?

Properties of ionising radiation

Alpha, beta and gamma radiation come from the **nucleus** of a radioactive atom.

Nuclear radiation causes **ionisation** of materials that it passes through. Alpha radiation causes most ionisation and gamma radiation causes the least.

Ionisation produces charged particles.

The three radiations have different ranges in air and can penetrate different materials.

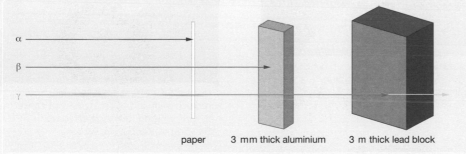

FIGURE 5: Different penetrations of the three main types of radiation. Which two radiations are absorbed by the material shown and which type of radiation penetrates the material shown?

Disposal of radioactive waste

- Low-level radioactive waste is discharged out to sea and buried in landfill sites.
- High-level radioactive waste is encased in glass and buried deep underground.
- Some radioactive waste can be reprocessed into new and useful radioactive material.

QUESTIONS

3   Which source of background radiation contributes 10 per cent of the total background radiation?

4   What percentage of background radiation comes from natural sources?

Ionisation

Atoms contain the same number of positively charged **protons** as negatively charged **electrons**. This means that overall the charge of an atom is neutral.

When an atom is ionised it either gains or loses electrons. If it gains electrons then it becomes negatively charged because there are more electrons than protons. If it loses electrons then it becomes positively charged because there are more protons than electrons.

Identifying radiation

Alpha radiation only travels a few centimetres in air. It is not very penetrating and is absorbed by a sheet of paper or skin.

Beta radiation has a range of about 1 metre in air. It will pass through paper but is absorbed by a few millimetres of aluminium.

The range of gamma radiation is, in theory, infinite. In practice the amount of radiation decreases until it cannot be distinguished from background radiation. Gamma radiation is very penetrating and can pass through several metres of lead or concrete.

QUESTIONS

5   A radioactive source emits alpha and gamma radiation. How can you show this using a Geiger counter and different materials?

Safe handling of radioactive material

Radiation from radioactive materials damages living cells.

The amount of damage depends on the type of radiation and how much radiation the cells have been exposed to.

To reduce exposure people who handle radioactive material:

- sometimes wear special protective clothing
- make sure that the distance between the radioactive substance and themselves is as large as possible
- use shielding to absorb radiation
- use the material for the shortest amount of time possible
- always use tongs or remote handling techniques when moving radioactive substances.

In school your teacher uses much lower levels of radioactive material than those used in industry.

Your teacher takes similar precautions when handling radioactive material.

Uses of ionising radiation

The fact that ionising radiation damages living cells means that exposure to radiation can be a cause of cancer.

It also means that the radiation can be used to kill cells and living organisms.

Cancer cells within the body can be destroyed by **radiotherapy**. **Cobalt-60** is a radioactive material used to treat cancers.

The instruments that doctors use are **sterilised** by gamma radiation. The radiation kills microbes and bacteria that could lead to infections in patients.

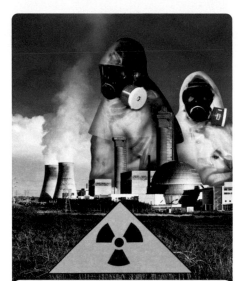

FIGURE 6: What precautions have these workers taken before handling radioactive material?

You will find out:

- how radioactive material is handled safely
- how radioactivity is used in the home, industry and medicine
- about the risks of radioactive material

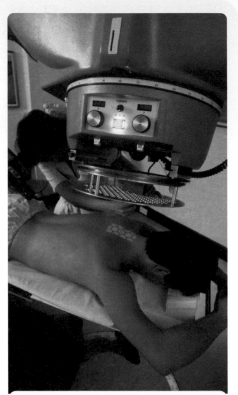

FIGURE 7: A patient undergoing radiotherapy in the treatment of cancer. Why is ionising radiation effective in treating cancer?

QUESTIONS

6 In schools only teachers are allowed to use radioactive sources. Why is it too dangerous to let students use them?

...cobalt-60 ...radiotherapy

Life-saving fire alarms in homes

Smoke alarms contain a radioactive source that emits alpha radiation. The radiation ionises the oxygen and nitrogen atoms in air. This causes a very small electric current that is detected.

When smoke fills the detector in the alarm during a fire, the air is not so ionised. The current is less and the alarm sounds.

FIGURE 8: How does a smoke detector work?

Measuring thicknesses in industry

Radioactive substances are used to measure and control the thickness of metals and paper as they are manufactured.

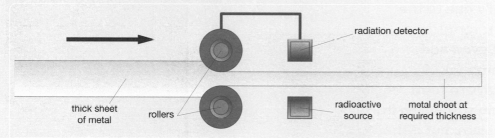

thick sheet of metal · rollers · radioactive source · metal sheet at required thickness · radiation detector

FIGURE 9: Using a radiation detector to keep the thickness of metal constant. What happens if the pressure on the rollers decreases?

As the sheet passes between the rollers it is pressed into the required thickness. If the pressure on the rollers is reduced the sheet becomes thicker. The amount of radiation passing through the sheet decreases. The radiation detector senses this and transmits a signal back to the rollers to increase the pressure.

Screening in medicine

Gamma radiation is also used in medicine to trace the passage of blood and other substances around the body. A radioactive liquid called a **tracer** is injected into the patient and after a time a special picture is taken.

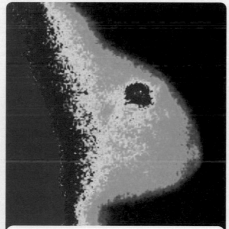

FIGURE 10: Picture of a patient's breast after a tracer has been given. The red part of the breast shows a high concentration of tracer due to an increased blood supply which indicates a cancer.

Problems of dealing with radioactive waste

Radioactive waste can remain radioactive for thousands of years so it has to be stored safely.

The waste must be stored so that it cannot get into the natural underground water systems and hence into lakes and rivers.

Although the waste is generally not suitable for making nuclear weapons there is a risk that terrorists could use waste to contaminate water supplies or areas of land both in towns and countryside.

QUESTIONS

7 Suggest **two** reasons why an alpha radiation source is suitable for use in a smoke detector.

8 What type of radiation is used to check the thickness of paper in a paper mill?

9 What type of radiation is used to check the thickness of aluminium in a rolling mill?

QUESTIONS

10 Suggest areas in the world where it is not safe to store radioactive waste. Explain your reasons.

The risks from radon

SELF-CHECK ACTIVITY

CONTEXT

Ellie lives in a house in Cornwall, in the south-west of England, with her parents and brothers. The house is quite a new one, but it is built in an area where there is a lot of granite. In Science lessons at Ellie's school her teacher had explained about a gas called radon.

Radon is a gas that forms naturally due to the decay of uranium in the ground. It forms in larger amounts in areas such as Devon and Cornwall where there is a large amount of granite in the ground. Radon decays to form radioactive particles, which remain suspended in the air. Normally this is not a problem, but if the particles are in air that is inside a building, the levels can rise further.

People inhaling air that contains these radioactive particles are exposed to alpha-radiation and are at a greater risk of developing lung cancer. This is a particular problem in houses with well-fitting doors and windows, as the air does not circulate as easily.

Ellie told her parents about what she had learnt and her mother said, 'I've been meaning to get something done about this. Diane, over the road, got some detector device to put in the house to see if the radon was a problem. We should do that as well.'

Her dad said that he would find out where they could get the detectors from. 'I don't know if we have to pay for them,' he said, but we should get them anyway. I just don't like the idea of there being any of that radiation here in our house.'

Ellie laughed. 'Don't be daft,' she said, 'There's radiation around wherever you are. It's the amount that matters.'

STEP 1

Think about Ellie's reaction to her dad, when he said that he did not want any radiation in their house. What might she have said to him to explain her ideas?

STEP 2

If they lived somewhere far away from granite rocks and radon, where might the radiation around them have come from?

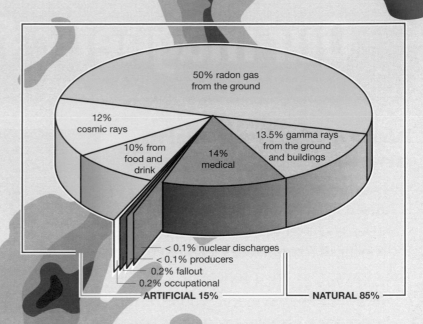

50% radon gas from the ground

12% cosmic rays

10% from food and drink

14% medical

13.5% gamma rays from the ground and buildings

< 0.1% nuclear discharges
< 0.1% producers
0.2% fallout
0.2% occupational

ARTIFICIAL 15%   NATURAL 85%

STEP 3

In fact, Ellie's Science teacher had been explaining to them about ionising radiation. Explain, using diagrams if it helps, what the word 'ionising' means.

STEP 4

Ellie has to do Science homework. She has to explain how the ionisation effects of radiation involve electrons being transferred. Using words or diagrams, suggest what she might write.

Maximise your grade

These sentences show what you need to be including in your work. Use these to improve your work and to be successful.

Grade	Answer includes...
F	Suggest a source of background radiation.
	State and recognise that there is background radiation in the environment that is always present.
	Describe background radiation.
	Describe background radiation and state one thing it is caused by.
C	Explain the meaning of ionisation. Describe background radiation and state that it is caused by radioactive substances, rocks, soil, living things and cosmic rays.
	Explain ionisation in terms of electron transfer.
A	Explain ionisation in terms of: ■ removal of electrons from particles ■ gain of electrons by particles.
	As above, but with particular clarity and detail.

Our magnetic field

Nature's free light show

The Aurora Borealis (northern lights) is caused by an interaction between cosmic rays from the Sun and molecules in the upper atmosphere.

The cosmic rays are a source of ionising radiation.

Magnetic fields

Earth behaves as if it contains a large **magnet** at its centre.

There is a **magnetic field** around Earth which is the same shape as a magnetic field from a bar magnet. The magnetic field is more concentrated at the North and South **poles**.

A compass points towards magnetic North. It shows the direction of a magnetic field.

FIGURE 1: In which direction is this compass pointing?

An electric current in a wire has a magnetic field around it. If a compass is placed near to a wire carrying a current the compass needle moves.

A coil of wire has a magnetic field around it as well. A current is caused by electric charges moving in the wire.

Earth's inner core contains a solid mass of iron.

The outer core is mainly **molten** iron. The temperature in the core is too hot for the iron to be magnetic.

FIGURE 3: Why is the iron in the Earth's core not magnetic?

a

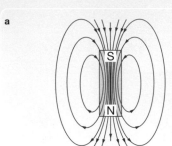

b

South magnetic pole   North geographic pole

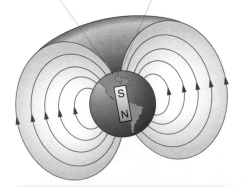

FIGURE 2: Compare the shape of the magnetic fields around **a** a bar magnet and **b** the Earth.

▣ QUESTIONS ▣

1 Why is the North pole of a compass called North?
2 What metallic element is found in the Earth's core?

...aurora   ...cosmic ray   ...dynamo   ...fluoresce

Magnetic field due to a coil

The shape of the magnetic field around a coil of wire carrying a current is similar to the fields around a bar magnet and the Earth.

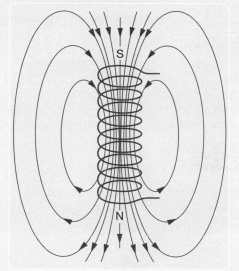

FIGURE 4: The magnetic field around a coil of wire carrying a current.

Magnetic effects

A magnet should not be brought close to a television screen or a computer monitor. The screens are covered with red, green and blue dots. The dots **fluoresce** when they are hit by a beam of electrons. Bringing a magnetic field close causes the electron beam to change direction and hit the wrong dots.

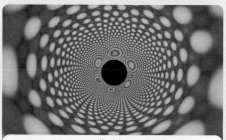

FIGURE 5: A normally blue monitor screen takes on a very different appearance when a magnet is brought close to it. Can you explain why?

QUESTIONS

3 What causes the dots on a television screen to fluoresce?

The Earth's dynamo

When a coil moves in a magnetic field, a current is produced in the coil. This is the principle of the **dynamo**. There is also a magnetic field around a coil carrying an electric current.

Deep inside the Earth, the solid inner core and liquid outer core move relative to one another. Electric currents are produced as a result of this movement within the magnetic field. These electric currents produce Earth's magnetic field.

An electric current is a flow of electric charge. Moving electric charges can be thought of as electric currents. Since an electric current has a magnetic field associated with it, so moving electric charges have magnetic fields associated with them.

Cosmic rays

Cosmic rays are not really rays at all; instead they are a stream of particles. The particles are ionised atoms ranging from a single proton up to an iron nucleus and larger. The most common cosmic ray is an alpha particle consisting of two protons and two neutrons.

Cosmic rays originate in space and are produced from sources such as:

- the Sun
- other stars
- supernova and their remnants
- neutron stars and black holes
- distant galaxies.

Cosmic ray particles are travelling very close to the speed of light and have a lot of energy.

The rays interact with Earth's magnetic field by spiralling around the field lines. As a result there is a concentration of cosmic rays at the North and South poles.

On certain nights at high latitudes on Earth, shifting patterns of light may be seen in the sky. These are the **auroras**. The bright lights are caused by cosmic rays streaming out from the Sun and striking Earth's upper atmosphere. Energy from these electrically charged particles is converted into light and forms visible glows, rays, arcs, bands and veils, which move around the sky. This light is usually greenish, but is sometimes red and purple as well.

Watch Out The model of the Earth's magnetic field pattern has a magnetic South pole at geographic North.

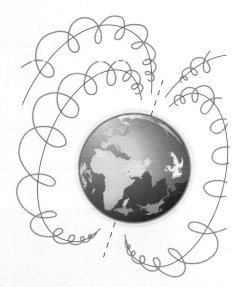

FIGURE 6: What causes cosmic rays to spiral?

DID YOU KNOW?

We live in the lowest layer of the atmosphere. Aeroplanes cruise in the layer of the atmosphere called the stratosphere. The Aurora Borealis (Northern Hemisphere) and the Aurora Australis (Southern Hemisphere) happen in the thermosphere. Above this is space.

QUESTIONS

4 Why is it fairly common to see auroras at the North and South poles, but rare to see them at latitudes of less than 80°?

...magnet ...magnetic field ...molten ...pole

Earth's remnant

Both the Moon and Earth are estimated to be 4.6 billion years old. There is evidence to suggest that the Moon was formed after two planets collided. Earth was formed as a result of the collision and the remaining debris collapsed together to form the Moon.

The Moon is a natural **satellite** that **orbits** Earth.

FIGURE 7: 'Earthrise.' How are Earth and the Moon thought to have formed?

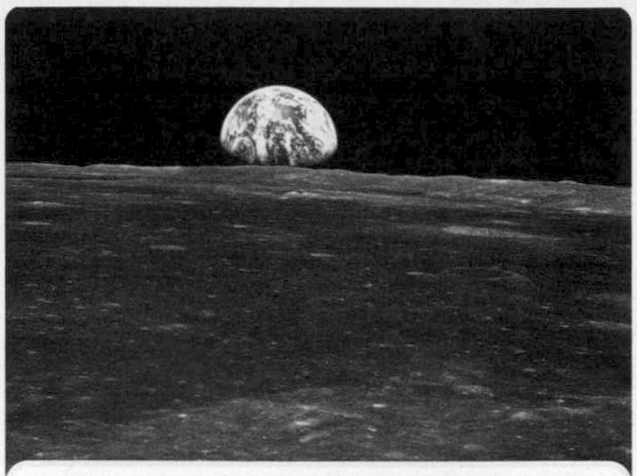

Artificial satellites

Weather satellites give information to scientists about the weather.

The information is used by the scientists to make forecasts.

GPS is a network of 24 satellites orbiting Earth that is used for navigation purposes. Communication satellites and spy satellites also orbit Earth.

Sun's effects

The Sun affects all forms of signals that are around the Earth. As well as being a source of ionising radiation, the Sun is also responsible for **solar flares**. A solar flare is an explosive eruption at an active region of the Sun. The flares result in disruptions to communications and spectacular auroras when they hit Earth a few days later.

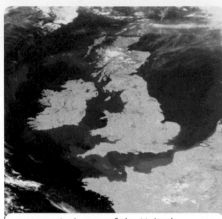

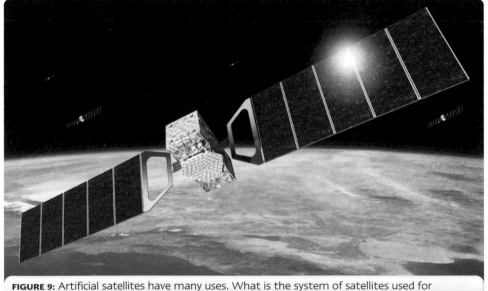

FIGURE 9: Artificial satellites have many uses. What is the system of satellites used for navigation called?

QUESTIONS

5 How old is Earth?

6 What is the common name for Global Positioning Systems?

You will find out:

- how the Moon was formed
- about the uses of satellites
- about the effects of the Sun on global communication

FIGURE 8: An image of the United Kingdom and Ireland taken by a weather satellite orbiting Earth. What do you notice about the pattern of cloud cover?

WOW FACTOR!

There are about 25 000 artificial satellites in orbit around Earth. Only 10 000 of them are still in use.

DID YOU KNOW?

Using GPS data, the latitude and longitude of any point on land can be located to within about 30 cm.

Some cars have GPS fitted to help drivers plan their routes.

...GPS ...mantle ...orbit

The origin of the Moon

When the Solar System formed there were probably more planets orbiting the Sun than the ones known today. During the first million years after its formation, there was a major disturbance of the Solar System. There was a collision between Earth and another planet the size of Mars. This planet had probably formed in the same orbit as Earth.

The force of the collision was sufficient to almost destroy both planets.

The dense molten iron became concentrated into Earth's core and the less dense rocks started to orbit the new Earth in a ring. These rocks clumped together to form the Moon.

The Moon was much nearer to Earth than today and both bodies were rotating much faster. The effect of the Moon was to slow down their rotation and now the same side of the Moon always faces Earth. Over the years, the radius of the orbit of the Moon has increased as the Moon has moved away from Earth.

Solar flares

A solar flare is a violent explosion above the Sun's surface. A large amount of energy is released. Solar flares may only last up to 10 minutes but they give out energy equivalent to a million hydrogen bombs!

There is a peak in such activity from the Sun every 10 to 11 years. During this maximum, large numbers of charged particles are emitted at very high speeds. This results in magnetic fields being produced that interact with Earth's magnetic field.

FIGURE 10: Earth collided with a smaller planet that broke up. The pieces joined together. What did they form?

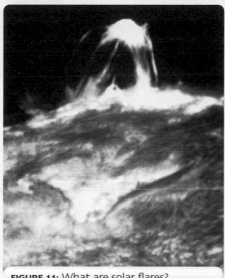

FIGURE 11: What are solar flares?

WOW FACTOR!

The temperature at the surface of the Sun is about 5500 °C (The Sun's core temperature is much hotter – about 15 million °C.)

Solar flares coil out a distance of 100 000 km into space.

Solar flares may only last up to 10 minutes but they give out energy equivalent to a million hydrogen bombs!

Evidence for the origin of the Moon

Earth has a large iron core but the Moon does not. This is because the iron in the Earth had already drained into the core by the time the collision happened. The debris blown out of both Earth and the other planet came from their iron-depleted **mantles**. The iron core of the other planet melted on collision and merged with Earth's iron core.

The evidence supports the model.

■ The average density of Earth is 5500 kg/m^3 while that of the Moon is only 3300 kg/m^3.

■ There is no iron in the Moon.

■ The Moon has exactly the same oxygen composition as the Earth, but rocks on Mars and meteorites from other parts of the Solar System have different oxygen compositions. This shows that the Moon formed in the same vicinity as Earth.

Solar flare effects

Only a small fraction of the energy from solar flares reaches Earth but it is enough to interfere with radio and microwave transmissions.

Solar flares can also affect electrical power distribution through the National Grid.

QUESTIONS

9 One earlier theory was that the Moon was formed at the same time as Earth as a 'double planet'. How would the Moon be different if this theory was correct?

QUESTIONS

7 There was a peak of solar activity in 2000. When is it likely there will be another high level of solar activity?

8 Describe how the motion of the Moon has changed since it was formed.

Exploring our Solar System

You will find out:

- about the bodies in space that make up the Universe
- about the planets in our Solar System
- why planets and moons stay in orbits

'Okay, Houston, we've had a problem here'

Imagine being a long way from home when your car breaks down and there is no one nearby to help.

Now imagine being over 300 000 km from home when there is an explosion in your spacecraft!

You have no light, electricity or water and your oxygen supply is running out.

You have to rely totally on scientists at Mission Control Centre in Houston, in the United States of America, to get you home.

Thankfully, the spacecraft was guided home successfully and the crew of Apollo 13 landed safely.

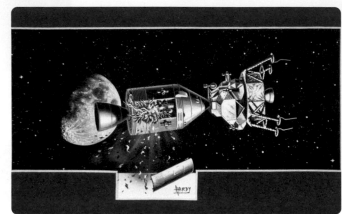

What's out there?

Scientists have studied the **Universe** for a very long time.

Stonehenge is an ancient monument. It was built over 4000 years ago. The people who built it knew where to place the massive stones.

Earth is just one of the planets that orbit the Sun in our **Solar System**.

It is easier to see objects in our Solar System in the night sky than it is during the day. You can see **stars** that are far away. They are very hot and produce their own light. Some stars are in our **galaxy**, which is called the **Milky Way**. Other groups of stars are in more distant galaxies.

The Moon can be seen as it orbits Earth.

Sometimes other planets, orbiting satellites, **meteors** and **comets** can be seen in the night sky.

Meteorites are large rocks that do not burn up as they fall to Earth.

Some things, such as a **black hole**, can never be seen.

FIGURE 1: On midsummer's day you can see the Sun rise between two special stones at Stonehenge.

EXAM HINTS AND TIPS

To help you remember the order of the planets you can use the mnemonic:

Many Vets Earn Money Just Sitting Under Nut Plants

QUESTIONS

1. Arrange the following in order of size, starting with the smallest.

   comet   galaxy   moon   planet   solar system   star   Universe

2. Which of the following produces its own light?

   comet   moon   planet   star

...*astronomer*   ...*black hole*   ...*centripetal*   ...*comet*   ...*elliptical orbit*   ...*galaxy*

Our Solar System

It is generally accepted that there are nine planets in our Solar System, orbiting the Sun.

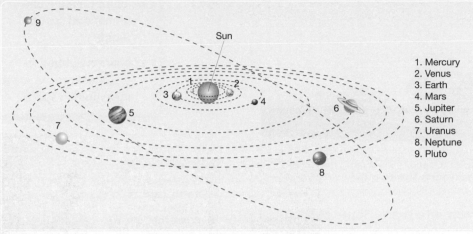

1. Mercury
2. Venus
3. Earth
4. Mars
5. Jupiter
6. Saturn
7. Uranus
8. Neptune
9. Pluto

FIGURE 2: Which of the planets shown here has an elliptical orbit?

Planet	Diameter in km	Average distance from Sun in millions km	Time to orbit Sun in Earth units
Mercury	4800	57	88 days
Venus	12 200	108	225 days
Earth	12 800	150	1 year
Mars	6800	228	1.9 years
Jupiter	143 000	778	11.9 years
Saturn	120 000	1429	29.5 years
Uranus	51 000	2870	84 years
Neptune	50 000	4500	165 years
Pluto	4000	5900	248 years

In 1999, some **astronomers** suggested that Pluto was too small to be a planet, but they were overruled.

Recently there have been two claims that astronomers have discovered a tenth planet. The first discovery is smaller than Pluto and three times further away. Astronomers decided it does not qualify as a planet. The second discovery was announced as a tenth planet in July 2005. It is also three times further away than Pluto, but it is larger than Pluto. The planet has not been named and is known as 2003 UB313.

▦ QUESTIONS ▦

3 Pluto was only discovered in 1930. Suggest why it took so long to discover Pluto.

4 Suggest why Mars is more likely to have a surface capable of supporting life than any other planet.

More on the Solar System

- Comets have very **elliptical orbits**. They pass inside the orbit of Mercury and then reach way past Pluto.

- Each star you see in the night sky is one of millions of stars that form a galaxy. Planets orbit stars and, with the help of space telescopes, planets that orbit other stars are being discovered.

- A meteor is made from grains of dust that get very hot as they come into contact with Earth's atmosphere. They burn up and heat the air around them. The air glows and a streak of light, called a 'shooting star', is seen. A meteorite is a larger rock that does not burn up when it falls to Earth.

- A black hole occurs where a large star used to be. It cannot be seen because light cannot escape from it.

Around and around

Everything moves in a straight line unless a force acts on it.

A force that acts towards the centre of a circle is called a **centripetal** force.

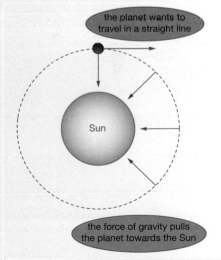

the planet wants to travel in a straight line

Sun

the force of gravity pulls the planet towards the Sun

FIGURE 3: Gravity pulls this planet towards the Sun. What is the force that acts towards the centre of a circle called?

▦ QUESTIONS ▦

5 What provides the centripetal force to keep the Moon in orbit around Earth?

Is anybody out there?

On December 12 1901 Marconi sent the first radio message from England to the United States.

On November 16 1974, scientists sent a coded message towards a star system near the edge of our galaxy. The message gave information about life on Earth.

Because of the large distances involved the scientists do not expect a reply for at least 40 000 years!

FIGURE 4: The Marconi radio transmitter used to send the first radio message across the Atlantic ocean.

Scientists have also sent unmanned spacecraft into space. Some of them carry pictures showing a man and woman and details of our Solar System.

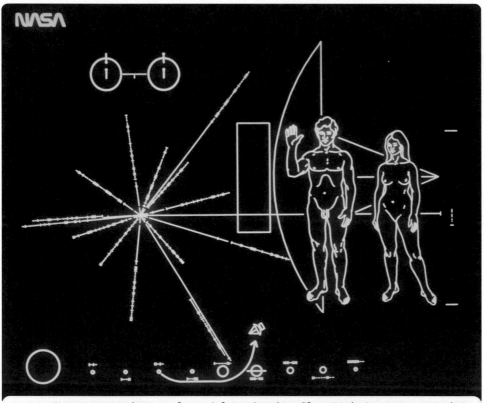

FIGURE 5: Some unmanned spacecraft carry information about life on Earth. Can you suggest why?

Other spacecraft contain long-playing records with sounds from Earth and greetings in many languages.

You will find out:

- about the distances involved in space travel
- about manned and unmanned space flights
- how very large distances are measured in space

Greetings from Earth. Earth is a planet that orbits the Sun. Blah... blah... blah...

Sorry, I missed that. Can you say it again?

WANT TO KNOW MORE?

You can find out where and when to see the Space Station in orbit from:

http://spaceflight.nasa.gov/station/

QUESTIONS

6 When did scientists first send a radio message into space?

7 Suggest **three** advantages of sending an unmanned rather than a manned spacecraft into space.

...light–year ...NASA ...probe

Exploring the planets

Unmanned spacecraft

For the past 50 years, unmanned spacecraft (**probes**) have been collecting information from outer-space. Some have landed on the Moon and some have landed on Mars. Probes have passed by or orbited the other planets, or have been sent to investigate comets.

A probe measures:

- temperature
- gravitational forces
- radiation
- magnetic fields.

Remote vehicles have driven over the surface of Mars. These robots take photographs, collect samples to bring back to Earth and analyse rocks and the atmosphere.

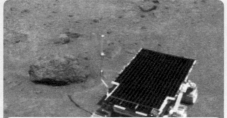

FIGURE 6: What measurements does this remote vehicle take on the surface of Mars?

The Hubble Space Telescope orbits Earth collecting information from the furthest galaxies.

Unmanned space probes can go where conditions are deadly for humans.

Manned spacecraft

Although astronauts wear normal clothing inside their spacecraft, when they go outside for a spacewalk, or for a walk on the Moon, they need to wear a special **spacesuit**.

- Without an atmosphere to filter the sunlight the surface of the suit facing the Sun might reach a temperature of 120 °C. The other side of the suit may be as cold as −160 °C. The spacesuit keeps the astronauts' bodies at a normal Earth temperature.

- A dark visor stops the astronaut being blinded.

- The suit is pressurised and has an oxygen supply for breathing.

FIGURE 7: Astronauts on a spacewalk. What do you think has to be taken into account when planning how many supplies to load on to a spacecraft?

If astronauts do visit other planets they will be away from home for a very long time. The spacecraft carries large amounts of fuel as well as food, water and oxygen for the astronauts. The environment in the spacecraft needs to be kept as similar as possible to that on Earth.

Throughout their mission the astronauts will be subject to lower gravitational forces than they are used to.

QUESTIONS

8   Why can an astronaut wear normal clothes inside a spacecraft?

9   The gravitational pull of the Moon is only one-sixth of the gravitational pull of Earth. How does this affect the ability of an astronaut to move around on the Moon?

A long way to go!

Earth is 150 000 000 km away from the Sun. That might seem a long way, but compared to some of the distances measured in the Universe it is not.

Light travels 300 000 km each second. So light from the Sun takes about 8 minutes to reach Earth.

Very large distances in Space are measured in **light-years**. This is the distance light travels in one year.

Is it all worth it?

In 2004 President Bush announced that **NASA** was working towards a permanent Moon base within 20 years and sending astronauts to Mars sometime after 2030. Experts have put the cost at as much as £400 billion.

Unmanned spacecrafts cost less and do not put lives at risk, but they have to be very reliable because there is usually no way of repairing them when they break down.

QUESTIONS

10   How long does sunlight take to reach Pluto? Give your answer in hours.

...remote vehicle   ...spacesuit

Threats to Earth

You will find out:
- about the properties of asteroids
- how asteroids have affected Earth in the past

Fatal collision

About 65 million years ago Velociraptors watched as a giant asteroid approached Earth.

The rock was between 10 and 20 km across and struck Earth in Mexico.

What happens when an asteroid hits Earth?

When an **asteroid** hits Earth it leaves a large **crater**.

The Barringer Crater in Arizona was formed over 50 000 years ago by the impact of an iron-containing meteorite colliding with Earth. The meteorite is thought to have had a mass of more than 10 000 tonnes. The crater is 183 m deep and has a diameter of 1200 m.

FIGURE 1: What caused this crater in Arizona?

The damage caused by the giant asteroid that hit Earth 65 million years ago was much worse.

- An enormous crater was made.
- Hot rocks rained down.
- Fires were widespread.
- **Tsunamis** flooded large areas.
- A cloud of dust and water vapour was thrown up into the upper atmosphere and spread around the globe.
- Sunlight could not penetrate the dust cloud and temperatures on Earth fell.

It is estimated that 70 per cent of all species on Earth, including the dinosaurs, became extinct as the Earth's climate changed.

FIGURE 2: What caused the climate changes that made life for the dinosaurs impossible?

QUESTIONS

1 Why did most plants become extinct 65 million years ago?

2 There is not a large lump of iron in the centre of the Barringer crater. Suggest what happened to the iron in the asteroid as it hit Earth.

...asteroid ...crater

Earth was struck 65 million years ago by a large asteroid 10 km in diameter.

What is an asteroid?

An asteroid is a mini-planet or 'planetoid' that orbits the Sun in a 'belt' between Mars and Jupiter. It looks like a lump of rock and is left over from when the Solar System was formed.

WOW FACTOR!

The largest asteroid is called Ceres and is about 1000 km across.

There may be 500 000 asteroids that are 0.5 km or more across and even more that are smaller than this. They are well spread out in a vast area with millions of kilometres between them.

Ida is another well-known asteroid. Although it is only 56 km in length, it has its own moon called Dactyl.

Dactyl is only 1.5 km across.

Why do asteroids not form planets?

All bodies in space, including planets, were formed when clouds of gas and dust collapsed together as a result of gravitational forces.

The size of gravitational forces depends on the mass of the object.

Jupiter has a very large mass compared to the mass of an asteroid, so its gravitational force prevents an asteroid joining with other asteroids to form a planet. The asteroids remain in a 'belt' and orbit around the Sun.

What evidence is there for asteroids?

Scientists know that asteroids have collided with Earth in the past because of the evidence they have found.

As well as large craters, geological evidence supports collisions from asteroids in the past.

In 1980 geologists were analysing rock samples near to where an asteroid was thought to have struck. They found low levels of the metal iridium. Iridium is not normally found in the rocks of Earth's crust but is quite common in meteorites. Asteroids contain many of the elements found in the interior of planets.

From this, they suggested the **impact hypothesis**.

Impact hypothesis

Earth was struck 65 million years ago by a large asteroid 10 km in diameter. The impact pulverised the asteroid and a large area of Earth's crust. The pulverised debris passed into the atmosphere, where it blocked sunlight and very quickly cooled the climate. The darkness meant that photosynthesis could not take place. This killed the short-lived oceanic phytoplankton, cutting off the food supply of herbivorous dinosaurs. That, and the cooling, was enough to cause the extinctions.

Fossil evidence

Fossil evidence also supports asteroids having collided with Earth. Many fossils are found below the iridium layer but few are found above it.

The 150 m high tsunami that followed the impact also disrupted the fossil layers. It carried debris that contained a variety of fossil fragments as far as 300 km inland.

QUESTIONS

4 Why does Jupiter have a larger effect on asteroids than any other planet?

5 Geologists have recently found fossil remains of animals that did not live in the same environment close together. They have also found 70 million-year-old fossils above those that are 65 million years old.

Explain these observations.

QUESTIONS

3 Most asteroids are in orbit between Mars and Jupiter. Eros has an orbit time of 1.76 years. Where does this asteroid orbit?

A comet's tail

A comet is a chunk of ice filled with dust and rock.

When a comet comes near to the Sun's heat, its ice core warms up and a glowing tail is thrown out.

The tail is formed from very small pieces of **debris**.

Near-Earth objects

Some asteroids and comets have orbit paths that pass close to the orbit of Earth. They are called near-Earth objects or **NEOs**.

A slight movement from their orbit may mean that they collide with Earth.

Scientists look for near-Earth asteroids and comets using a **telescope**.

FIGURE 3: A comet's tail can be seen from Earth. What is a comet's tail made from?

DID YOU KNOW?

In 1682 British astronomer Edmund Halley saw a comet and worked out it would next be seen in 76 to 77 years.

In 1759, right on time, the comet was seen again.

The next time Halley's comet is due to pass close to Earth is in 2062.

DID YOU KNOW?

New NEOs are being discovered almost every day.

About 100 NEOs pass close enough to Earth to be classed as a threat each year!

WANT TO KNOW MORE?

Most people find astronomy a fascinating subject.

Many areas of the country have a local astronomical society, or you can find out more from: www.ras.org.uk

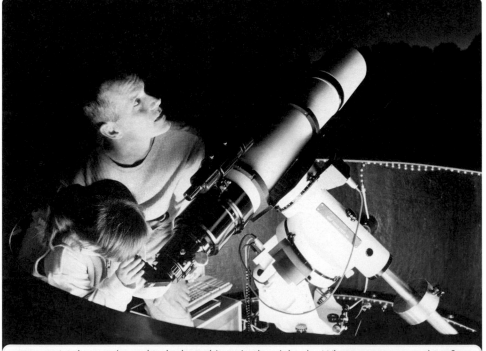

FIGURE 4: A telescope is used to look at objects in the night sky. What are two examples of NEOs that can be seen through a telescope?

QUESTIONS

6 You can only see a comet's tail when it is near the Sun. Suggest why.
7 Why can you not see asteroids in the night sky with the naked eye?

...debris ...elliptical

A comet's orbit

Most planets have circular shaped orbits.

The orbit of a comet is very **elliptical**. Most comets pass close to the Sun, inside the orbit of Mercury. They then pass well outside the orbit of Pluto.

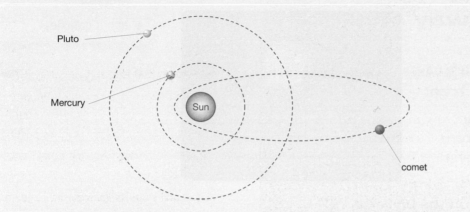

FIGURE 5: A comet has an elliptical orbit. Why does the shape of its orbit cause a comet to have a tail?

A comet is made of dust and ice, just like a dirty snowball. As a comet passes near to the Sun, the ice melts. A glowing cloud of gas and dust forms around the comet. Solar wind from the Sun blows the gas and dust into the comet's tail. This always points away from the Sun, so a comet travels tail first as it goes away from the Sun. The tail may be hundreds of millions of kilometres in length!

Predicting a collision

Imagine you saw an object at point **A** yesterday.

Today it is at point **B**.

If it carries on moving as it is, tomorrow it will be at point **C**.

But, if it speeds up, it may be at point **D**.

Or if it changes direction, **E** may be a likely place, then it may be at **F** the next day.

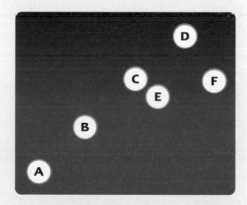

The longer we study the path of an asteroid or comet, the more information we have to predict its path. The orbit pattern of Earth is well known. The orbit of the asteroid or comet is plotted and continually updated to see if there is any risk of a collision.

WANT TO KNOW MORE?

You can find out more about the predicted paths of asteroids from:
www.nearearthobjects.co.uk

QUESTIONS

8 Astronomers have not been studying near-Earth objects for very long.
   Suggest why they sometimes change their minds about whether a particular asteroid is likely to collide with Earth in the future.

A comet's speed

The gravitational attraction from the Sun causes a comet's speed to increase as it approaches the Sun.

The further away from the Sun a comet is the slower it travels.

What do we do if a NEO approaches?

The positions of NEOs are constantly monitored by telescopes and satellites.

If an object was found to be on a collision course with Earth, there are several options.

One option would be to launch a rocket containing a very large explosive. This would be detonated a long way from Earth, near to the object.

The force of the explosion may be enough to change the path of the object so that it misses Earth.

If that did not work and the object did collide with Earth, it could be the end of life on Earth as we know it, just like it was for the dinosaurs 65 million years ago.

...it could be the end of life on Earth as we know it, just like it was for the dinosaurs 65 million years ago.

QUESTIONS

9 Why would an explosion to change the course of an asteroid on a collision course with Earth have to be a long way away?

The Big Bang

You will find out:

- about how the Universe started
- about the Big Bang theory and how it explains what is in the Universe
- about galaxies

What is furthest away from Earth?

It might just look like a bright spot, but it is very special. It is a quasar, which is incredibly bright.

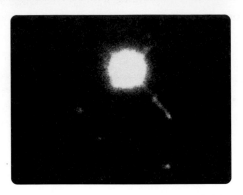

Light from this quasar has taken over 2 billion years to reach Earth. Light from some of the furthest quasars takes over 12 billion years to get here!

Quasars are the most distant objects in the Universe.

Studying quasars helps scientists find out more about the early Universe as the light from a quasar left it so long ago.

The first few seconds

About 15 billion years ago all of the matter in the **Universe** was in a single point.

The temperature was 1000 million million million million °C.

Scientists do not know what caused the Universe to explode but in the smallest fraction of a second it did. There was a massive fireball of particles and radiation.

The Universe expanded rapidly and cooled down. Scientists call this the **Big Bang**. After one-ten-millionth of a second the Universe had cooled to below 1 million million °C. After 1 second, there were electrons, protons and neutrons. Hydrogen and helium were formed after 3 seconds.

DID YOU KNOW?

What happens in the future depends on how much mass there is in the Universe.

Scientists have estimated that the mass of the Universe is about
30 000 000 000 000 000 000 000 000 000 000 000 000 000 000 000 000 000 kg!

If scientists are correct about the mass of the Universe then it will continue to expand.

If there is more mass than scientists estimate, then the Universe will reach a steady finite size.

If the Universe is a lot more massive it could reach a maximum size and then start to collapse. It would then return to the point it started from. Scientists call this the Big Crunch.

QUESTIONS

1 What were the first particles in the Universe to be formed?
2 What were the first elements in the Universe to be formed?

The expanding Universe

Scientists have found that, with only a few exceptions, all of the **galaxies** are moving away from Earth and apart from each other.

The furthest galaxies are moving fastest.

The Universe is expanding.

This behaviour of the Universe can be modelled very simply using a balloon.

Dots are drawn onto the balloon. These represent the galaxies.

As the balloon is blown up, the dots move apart from each other. The bigger the balloon gets, the faster the dots move apart.

FIGURE 1: How does this model show that the Universe is expanding?

Microwave signals are constantly reaching Earth from all parts of the Universe.

Red shift

If you listen to a Formula One racing car or the siren of an ambulance as it approaches, the **pitch** of the sound increases. As the vehicle moves away, the pitch decreases.

A stationary sound sends out circular sound waves. A moving sound also sends out circular waves, but the centre of the wave moves with the sound.

This means that a person listening to an approaching sound appears to hear a sound with a shorter **wavelength** (higher pitch). Someone listening to a sound going away appears to hear a sound with a longer wavelength (lower pitch).

FIGURE 2: When a racing car is stationary on the grid it sends out circular sound waves.

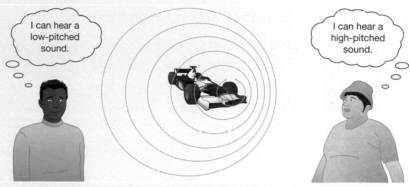

The same thing happens with light. When a source of light is moving away, the wavelength appears to increase. This shifts the light towards the red end of the **visible spectrum**.

When scientists look at the spectrum of light from the Sun it has lines on it.

When scientists look at light from a distant star, there is the same pattern of lines in the spectrum but the lines have moved closer together and towards the red end of the spectrum.

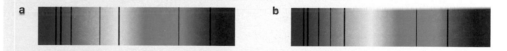

FIGURE 3: a The spectrum of white light from the Sun (the black lines show that helium is present) and **b** the spectrum of light from a distant star showing red shift.

This is known as **red shift** and it shows that the star is moving away from Earth. The faster the star is travelling, the more the amount of red shift is observed.

Scientists use this information to calculate the age and starting point of the Universe.

QUESTIONS

3 The Andromeda galaxy is moving much more slowly than the Centaurus galaxy.

Explain how you know which one is furthest away from Earth.

QUESTIONS

4 Blue shift occurs when a galaxy is moving towards Earth.

a Describe what a scientist sees when she looks at light from a galaxy moving slowly towards Earth.

b What will she see if she looks at light from a galaxy moving very quickly towards Earth?

...*red shift* ...*Universe* ...*visible spectrum* ...*wavelength*

A star is born

The stars in the sky have not always been there. New stars are forming all the time.

A star starts its life as a swirling mass of gas in a cloud.

FIGURE 4: The birth of a star. Why do stars look so small in the night sky?

It is easy to believe that a star will stay forever.

Man has been studying the stars for a very long time. Star maps are not new.

The **constellations** have been drawn for centuries.

All stars, including the Sun, will one day die.

Some stars become **black holes**. Not even light can escape from a black hole.

FIGURE 5: This picture of Leo is based on a map published in 1690.

QUESTIONS

5   How does a star start its life?
6   Constellations have names such as Pisces, Capricorn, Scorpio and Libra. What is a constellation?

...*black dwarf* ...*black hole* ...*constellation* ...*fusion* ...*nebula* ...*neutron star*

A star's life history

A star starts its life as clouds of gas and dust. These **nebula** clouds start to come together. Gravity pulls them closer together as a spinning ball of gas. The gas ball is so tightly packed that it gets hot and starts to glow.

This **protostar** is shining, but it cannot be seen because of the gas and dust surrounding it. As gravity causes the protostar to become even smaller, it gets hotter and shines brighter.

After millions of years, the temperature in the core of the protostar is high enough for nuclear **fusion** to take place. This is the joining together of hydrogen nuclei to form helium nuclei. Energy is released.

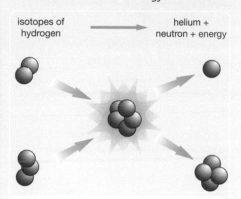

isotopes of hydrogen → helium + neutron + energy

FIGURE 6: What has to happen to a protostar before nuclear fusion can take place?

The star is now visible and remains visible while there is enough hydrogen. The life of a star depends on its size. Small stars live longer than large stars. Although large stars have more hydrogen, they use it at a faster rate. A medium-sized star, like the Sun, may shine for 10 billion years. A large star may only shine for a few million years.

What happens to a star at the end of its life depends on its size.

QUESTIONS

7   What causes dust and gas to collect together to form a star?

8   What happens during nuclear fusion?

Gone – but not forgotten

What happens to a star at the end of its life depends on its size. When a star has used up all of the hydrogen in its core, the core contracts and no more energy is produced.

The Sun

As the core of a medium-sized star such as the Sun contracts, the outer part expands. It cools and changes colour from yellow to red. The star becomes a **red giant**.

The Sun will become so big that it will swallow up Mercury and Venus and reach Earth. While the star is in its red giant phase, shells of gas are thrown out. These are called **planetary nebula**. The nebula from the Sun will stretch to the edge of our Solar System.

The core of the original star shrinks until it is about the same size as Earth. It is very hot and shines brightly as a **white dwarf**. It is not making energy so eventually cools, changing colour from white, through yellow to red and becomes a **black dwarf**.

FIGURE 7: Planetary nebula. What causes these?

More massive stars

A massive star only shines for a few million years before it too uses up all its hydrogen. The core starts to contract and the outer part expands as a red **supergiant**. Suddenly, in less than a second, the core collapses and the whole star explodes and is thrown outwards. This explosion is called a **supernova** and the small remaining core is a **neutron star**. Neutron stars are very dense. A neutron star contains mainly neutrons and just one teaspoonful has a mass of 100 000 000 tonnes!

The material thrown out as the core explodes, collides with gas and dust in space and forms a glowing cloud of gas called a supernova remnant. The Crab Nebula is an example of a supernova remnant.

Over a period of time, the supernova remnant merges with other dust and gas in space. As gravitational forces act, so a new star is formed.

The core of a neutron star could continue to collapse even more. It becomes so dense and gravitational forces are so large that not even light can escape. This is a black hole.

FIGURE 8: Crab Nebula is a supernova remnant formed in 1054 that is still visible today.

QUESTIONS

9   Our Sun is sometimes referred to as a 'second generation star'. Suggest why.

10   Atoms have a nucleus that contains protons and neutrons. The nucleus is surrounded by a cloud of electrons.

Use your knowledge of the structure of an atom to explain why a neutron star is so dense.

Module summary

Concept map

Energy sources

Kinetic energy from moving air turns the blades on a wind turbine to produce electricity.

The Sun is a stable energy source. It transfers energy to Earth as light and heat.

Photocells use the Sun's light to produce electricity.

Electricity generation

A dynamo produces electricity when coils of wire rotate inside a magnetic field.

Transformers change the voltage and current of electricity.

Fossil fuels and biomass are burned to produce heat. Nuclear fuels release energy as heat.

Nuclear fuels are radioactive. The radiation produced can cause cancer.

The main forms of ionising radiation are alpha, beta and gamma.

The Earth's field

The Earth is surrounded by a magnetic field, similar in shape to that of a bar magnet.

When two planets collide, a new planet and a moon may be formed.

The Earth and Universe

Planets, asteroids and comets orbit the Sun in our Solar System.

Most asteroids are between Mars and Jupiter, but some pass closer to Earth. An asteroid strike could cause climate change and species extinction on Earth.

The Universe is explored by telescopes located on Earth and in space.

Scientists believe that the Universe started with a Big Bang.

The Universe consists of many galaxies.

Module quiz

1 What device uses light from the Sun to produce electricity?

2 What causes wind?

3 What does a transformer do?

4 How is an alternating current different from a direct current?

5 Write down **three** examples of a fossil fuel.

6 What is biomass?

7 What is the unit of electrical power?

8 Coal and wind are both energy resources but only coal is a fuel. Why is coal a fuel?

9 How is high level radioactive waste disposed of?

10 Which type of ionising radiation can penetrate several metres of lead?

11 Write down **three** sources of background radiation.

12 Which type of ionising radiation is used in a smoke detector?

13 Which metal is present in the Earth's core in large amounts?

14 What are solar flares?

15 What is the common name for the *Aurora Borealis*?

16 Which planet is closest to the Sun?

17 Which force keeps the Earth in orbit around the Sun?

18 Why do astronauts wear spacesuits when they go outside their spacecraft?

19 What body in space is made from ice and dust?

20 What do scientists believe happened 15 billion years ago to form the Universe?

Literacy activity

The Daily Telegraph

Devon wins fight against wind farm

By Richard Savill

The Government's alternative energy strategy has suffered a setback after local campaigners successfully fought plans for the first wind farms in Devon. In the past two months, Torridge district council has turned down applications to build turbines at three separate sites near the villages of Ashwater, and Bradworthy, and the town of Great Torrington. Council planners, who received scores of letters of objection, backed the scheme at Great Torrington because they considered the site to be sufficiently remote. But councillors bowed to local opposition and rejected the plans.

QUESTIONS   1   List the advantages and disadvantages of generating electricity using wind turbines.

Exam practice

 1 **a** Photocells are used on satellites to provide electricity. List four advantages of using this type of cell. [4]

b Higher tier: Explain how light produces electricity in a photocell. [3]

[Total 7 marks]

 2 **a** A dynamo is attached to a bicycle and used to generate electricity for the light. State three things that could be changed to make the light brighter. [3]

b Explain how coal is used to generate electricity in a power station. [4]

c The following table provides information about a lamp.

Appliance	Voltage	Current
lamp	230 V	0.5 A

i State the equation used to calculate the power of an appliance. [1]
ii Calculate the power of the lamp. [2]
iii If 1 kWh costs 10p, calculate the cost of having the lamp on for 3 hours. [4]

[Total 14 marks]

 3 **a** Copy and complete the following table which compares the different types of ionising radiation. [4]

Type of radiation	Alpha	Beta	Gamma
Charge		−1	
Mass		negligible	

b State one reason why:
   i gamma rays can be used to treat cancer. [1]
   ii beta rays can be used to control the thickness of paper. [1]

c Explain what is meant by background radiation. [2]

[Total 8 marks]

 4 **a** Describe the shape of the Earth's magnetic field. [2]

b Higher tier: Explain how cosmic rays cause the Aurora Borealis. [3]

c Manned space travel between planets is unlikely in the near future. Give three reasons why this is the case. [3]

d State two advantages and one disadvantage of using unmanned spacecraft for space exploration. [3]

[Total 11 marks]

The diagram below shows part of an AC generator.

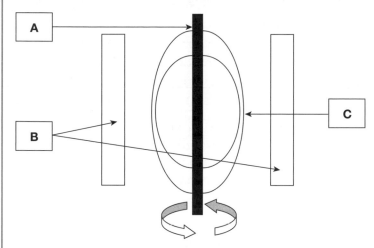

a   Name parts A, B and C on the diagram.   [3]

b   What is the job of part A in the generator?   [2]

c   State two ways to change the generator so the voltage
generated is larger.   [2]

This answer achieves full marks.

a   A = spindle, B = magnet, C = coil of wire.

b   It lets the coil move.

c   The coil can have more turns and the
magnet can be bigger.

The student loses one mark here – the spindle lets the coil *spin*.

The student also loses one mark here – the magnet must be *stronger*.

Overall Grade: B

How to get an A

Try to make your answers as clear as possible. If the examiner is unsure what you mean, they may not be able to give you the mark.

Introduction

A third of the marks towards your GCSE Science examination come from work that is marked by your teachers. This allows you to build up your marks whilst you are still following the course. The work is designed to motivate you and give you a sense of achievement.

There are two types of work:

- Can-Do Tasks
- Report on Science in the News

Can-Do Tasks

These are a series of short activities. Some of them are practically based. You do an experiment, record the results and discuss your findings. Some activities are research based. This may involve using books, the Internet or other secondary material.

There are three levels of difficulty for Can-Do Tasks. Each task is valued at one, two or three points. Your best eight tasks are used to produce your final mark.

ONE POINT TASKS

These are simple, practical tasks such as:

- I can use Ishihara colour charts to identify colour vision deficiency.

- I can measure the temperature of a liquid.

- I can read a domestic electricity meter.

When your teacher has seen you do any of these tasks, you will be given one point towards your GCSE.

TWO POINT TASKS

These are more complicated tasks that require more than one skill. Examples of two point tasks are:

- I can collect data from various sources for a named disease and identify danger sites on a world map.
- I can extract a sample of copper from a copper ore such as malachite.
- I can send and receive a message in Morse code.

For these tasks, you need to do more than one thing. If we look at the first task above, you have to research a disease and transfer the information onto a map to show where the disease is most common. If you write a long report about the disease, but do not transfer the information onto a map, you will not score any points.

If, in the third task above, you send a message in Morse code, but do not receive a message, you will not score any points.

Can-Do Tasks are all or nothing.

THREE POINT TASKS

These are extended activities; you will have to perform a series of tasks. Examples of three point tasks are:

- I can do an experiment on enzyme action and record the results and conclusion.
- I can do an experiment to find the energy output per gram of a liquid fuel.
- I can do an experiment to find out how the voltage produced by a photocell changes with distance from the light source.

Practical hints

Results tables:

- Do not forget to head table columns with quantity and unit.
- Make sure that your readings are reliable and recorded to the same degree of accuracy.

Calculations:

- Always show how you work out an answer – it is easier to see where you go wrong if you make a mistake.

Graphs:

- Make sure graphs are as large as possible, but choose sensible scales for both axes.
- The quantity you change is plotted on the x-axis; the quantity you measure as a result is plotted on the y-axis.
- Draw a line of best fit, this may be a straight line or smooth curve – look for the overall pattern.
- Never draw a graph as a series of straight lines from one point to the next.

Conclusion:

- If you have been asked to find a value, remember to include the unit.
- If you have plotted a graph, comment on the shape of the graph.
- Two quantities are proportional if the graph is a straight line passing through the origin.
- Remember to identify a trend using an '–er statement', which is when you compare results by saying something like:

  The warmer the water, the quicker the ice melted.

Introduction

You will be given some stimulus material. It may be an article from a magazine or newspaper, or it may be some scientific data. You will also be given your task. It is most likely to be in the form of a question.

You will then have about a week to find out more about the subject. You will be allowed to look at books and other sources of information.

At the end of the week, you must write an answer to the question using the stimulus material and the other information you have gathered. You will need to explain the reasons behind your answer.

Here are a few examples of the type of task you may be set:

- Should wind farms be built in the UK?
- Should Heathrow have an extra runway?
- Should the maximum speed on motorways be reduced to 60 mph?
- Should all cyclists be made to wear protective headgear?
- Should factory farming be allowed in the UK?
- Does selling bottled mineral water make economic sense?
- Would greatly increasing the tax on alcohol make the nation healthier?
- Should children be encouraged to walk to school?

SCIENCE IN THE NEWS

Whenever you look at a newspaper, read a magazine or watch television, it isn't long before you are faced with some new scientific idea. News items may be about a drug to cure cervical cancer, concern about global warming or the discovery of a new planet beyond Pluto. Magazine articles may refer to the dangers of passive smoking, the use of laboratory animals or the problems caused by eating certain foods.

It is important that you are able to examine these ideas and decide how they may affect you. After you have studied a particular topic, you will be given a question and some stimulus material. This may contain some written articles, photographs or data in the form of graphs, charts or other diagrams. Sometimes the articles may contradict one another and one article may be from a more reliable source than another.

Over the next week, you will have to find out as much as you can to answer the question. This will mean reading books, looking at CD-ROMs and searching the Internet. You may need to photocopy pictures or articles to help you answer the question.

When the week is up, you will have time during lessons to write your answer. Often there will not be a right answer. What is important is how you have looked at more than one side of an argument and made a decision based on the evidence. Your answer must be between 400 and 800 words. Anything longer means you have not been selective. Try to include pictures, graphs or diagrams to support your answer. Remember to list all sources of information you have used. If you quote from an article, book or website you must include that information. Your work can be handwritten or word processed, but the quality of your spelling, punctuation and grammar will be looked at as well.

HOW ARE MARKS AWARDED?

The question Should laboratory animals be used for testing cosmetics and drugs?

The stimulus material
- Articles from an animal welfare group and a research laboratory.
- Data on how the numbers of animals used has changed over the past 25 years.
- Publicity material from a cosmetics company that does not test its products on animals.
- Information from a chemical company listing the chemicals used in making cosmetics that have been tested on animals.

Six areas of report writing will be marked. Each area can score up to six marks.

You will not be allowed to redraft your report. During the course, you may be given two or three opportunities to write a report like this. The idea is that you learn from the feedback you are given each time. Your best report, the one that scores the most marks out of 36, will be the one that counts towards your GCSE.

What do you need to do? How are you going to do it?

Look at the stimulus material you have been given.

Are there any gaps in the information? Are there any conflicts that need to be examined further? For example, the cosmetics company does not test its products on animals, but have the chemicals used to make the cosmetics been tested on animals?

Look at different sources of information and make a list of the ones you use. Sort the information into a logical sequence.

What does the evidence you collect really mean?

Is there a trend in what you have found? Are the numbers of animals being used for cosmetics testing going down, but those used for drugs testing going up?

Are there any pieces of information that don't fit the pattern?

Can you support your conclusion?

It is no good to say that animal testing is bad and should be stopped unless you can give reasons why. You need to explain the reasons using the evidence you have collected.

It is a good idea to present both sides of an argument and then support one side. You can take the middle ground and say that it is alright to use animals for drugs testing but not cosmetics, but you must still give reasons for saying this.

How good is your evidence?

Which pieces of evidence are the most reliable? Is an independent scientific enquiry more reliable than an animal welfare group or a drugs company?

How is what you have found out important in everyday life?

You need to think about social, moral and financial considerations, as well as the emotional aspects. If you include a picture of an animal suffering, remember to also include one of a patient whose life has been saved because the drugs they were given had been tested.

How well have you presented your report?

Can someone reading your report understand what you have written and follow your argument?

Will they find it interesting? Is the text broken up with pictures or graphs? Have you used scientific words correctly?

Other things may need to include in your report

- An appendix – make a list of all of the sources of material you have used in writing your report.
- Raw data – if you have summarised data or identified a trend, you need to include the original data you used.

Physical quantities and units

Fundamental physical quantities	
physical quantity	unit(s)
length	metre (m); kilometre (km); centimetre (cm); millimetre (mm)
mass	kilogram (kg); gram (g); milligram (mg)
time	second (s); millisecond (ms); hour (h)
temperature	degree Celsius (°C); kelvin (K)
current	ampere (A); milliampere (mA)
voltage	volt (V); millivolt (mV)

Derived physical quantities	
physical quantity	unit(s)
area	m^2; cm^2; mm^2
volume	m^3; cm^3; mm^3; litre (l); millilitre (ml)
density	kg/m^3; g/cm^3
force	newton (N)
speed	m/s; cm/s; km/h
acceleration	m/s^2; cm/s^2
energy	joule (J); kilojoule (kJ); megajoule (MJ); kilowatt-hour (kWh)
power	watt (W); kilowatt (kW); megawatt (MW)
frequency	hertz (Hz); kilohertz (kHz); megahertz (MHz)
gravitational field strength	N/kg
radioactivity	becquerel (Bq)
specific heat capacity	J/kg°C; J/kgK
specific latent heat	J/kg

Equations used in Science

energy transferred = mass × specific heat capacity × temperature change

energy transferred = mass × specific latent heat

$$\text{efficiency} = \frac{\text{useful energy output}}{\text{total energy input}}$$

wave speed = frequency × wavelength

power = voltage × current

energy transferred = power × time

The maths you need

While studying this course, you will find lots of opportunities to use Mathematics. The maths skills you need are listed below.

Items in the left hand list may be examined in written exam papers covering both Foundation and Higher Tiers. Items in the right hand list may be examined in written exam papers covering the Higher Tier only. You may want to copy the lists and tick off each item when you are satisfied that you can do it.

Both Tiers

I can...

- add, subtract, multiply and divide whole numbers
- recognise and use expressions in decimal form
- make approximations and estimates to obtain reasonable answers
- use simple formulae expressed in words
- understand and use averages
- read, interpret and draw simple inferences from tables and statistical diagrams
- find fractions or percentages of quantities
- construct and interpret pie charts
- calculate with fractions, decimals, percentage or ratio
- solve simple equations
- substitute numbers in simple equations
- interpret and use graphs
- plot graphs from data provided, given the axes and scales
- choose, by simple inspection, and then draw the best smooth curve through a set of points on a graph

Higher Tier only

I can...

- recognise and use expressions in standard form
- manipulate equations
- select appropriate axes and scales for graph plotting
- determine the intercept of a linear graph
- understand and use inverse proportion
- calculate the gradient of a graph
- use statistical methods, for example cumulative frequency, box plots and histograms

Periodic table

Key

| relative atomic mass |
| atomic symbol |
| name |
| atomic (proton) number |

Example:
| 1 |
| H |
| hydrogen |
| 1 |

1	2												3	4	5	6	7	8
																		4 He helium 2
7 Li lithium 3	9 Be beryllium 4												11 B boron 5	12 C carbon 6	14 N nitrogen 7	16 O oxygen 8	19 F fluorine 9	20 Ne neon 10
23 Na sodium 11	24 Mg magnesium 12												27 Al aluminium 13	28 Si silicon 14	31 P phosphorus 15	32 S sulfur 16	35.5 Cl chlorine 17	40 Ar argon 18
39 K potassium 19	40 Ca calcium 20	45 Sc scandium 21	48 Ti titanium 22	51 V vanadium 23	52 Cr chromium 24	55 Mn manganese 25	56 Fe iron 26	59 Co cobalt 27	59 Ni nickel 28	63.5 Cu copper 29	65 Zn zinc 30		70 Ga gallium 31	73 Ge germanium 32	75 As arsenic 33	79 Se selenium 34	80 Br bromine 35	84 Kr krypton 36
85 Rb rubidium 37	88 Sr strontium 38	89 Y yttrium 39	91 Zr zirconium 40	93 Nb niobium 41	96 Mo molybdenum 42	[98] Tc technetium 43	101 Ru ruthenium 44	103 Rh rhodium 45	106 Pd palladium 46	108 Ag silver 47	112 Cd cadmium 48		115 In indium 49	119 Sn tin 50	122 Sb antimony 51	128 Te tellurium 52	127 I iodine 53	131 Xe xenon 54
133 Cs caesium 55	137 Ba barium 56	139 La* lanthanum 57	178 Hf hafnium 72	181 Ta tantalum 73	184 W tungsten 74	186 Re rhenium 75	190 Os osmium 76	192 Ir iridium 77	195 Pt platinum 78	197 Au gold 79	201 Hg mercury 80		204 Tl thallium 81	207 Pb lead 82	209 Bi bismuth 83	[209] Po polonium 84	[210] At astatine 85	[222] Rn radon 86
[223] Fr francium 87	[226] Ra radium 88	[227] Ac* actinium 89	[261] Rf rutherfordium 104	[262] Db dubnium 105	[266] Sg seaborgium 106	[264] Bh bohrium 107	[277] Hs hassium 108	[268] Mt meitnerium 109	[271] Ds darmstadtium 110	[272] Rg roentgenium 111								

Elements with atomic numbers 112–116 have been reported but not fully authenticated.

* The Lanthanides (atomic numbers 58–71) and the Actinides (atomic numbers 90–103) have been omitted.
Cu and Cl have not been rounded to the nearest whole number.

A,T,C,G	The four bases found in DNA, Adenine, Thymine, Cytosine and Guanine.	40, 41
Absolute scale	A scale linked to an external value, for example the absolute scale of temperature uses the value of −273 °C as zero.	174,175
Acetylcholine	A chemical that carries signals across the tiny gaps between nerve cells.	28, 29, 33
Aerobic respiration	Aerobic respiration breaks down glucose using oxygen to make energy available for chemical reactions in cells.	14, 15
Alkane	Chemicals containing only hydrogen and carbon with the general formula C_nH_{2n+2}, for example methane.	108, 109, 114
Alkene	Chemicals containing only hydrogen and carbon with the general formula C_nH_{2n}, for example ethene.	108, 114
Allele	Inherited characteristics are carried as pairs of alleles on pairs of chromosomes. A characteristic may be the result of a single gene acting or may involve several genes working together. Different forms of a gene are different alleles.	46, 47
Alloy	A mixture of a metal element with one or more other elements.	148, 149, 152, 155
Alternating current	Current that rapidly reverses in direction. Mains electricity is supplied as alternating current, or ac.	218
Amino acid	The sub-units making up protein molecules. There are over 20 different amino acids used by living things.	18, 19
Amphibian	An animal that spends some of its life cycle in water and some on land.	58, 59
Anaerobic respiration	A series of chemical reactions that transfer energy from glucose into life processes without using oxygen. Carbon dioxide and lactic acid are the end-products.	14, 15
Analogue	A signal that shows a complete range of frequencies. Sound is analogue.	192, 193
Anode	The positive electrode in a circuit or battery.	146, 147
Antibody	Chemicals, produced by white blood cells, which attack invading microorganisms.	24, 25
Antigen	Chemicals found in cell membranes and cell walls which trigger a reaction by the immune system.	24, 25
Antioxidant	Chemicals which delay the oxidation of other chemicals. They are important in paints, plastics and rubbers, where they slow down degradation of the material. Vitamin C is an antioxidant in the body.	98
Arbitrary scale	A scale that only works within a given situation, for example to say a value is twice a lower value without connecting either value to an external fixed point.	174, 175
Artery	A blood vessel carrying blood away from the heart under high pressure.	16
Artificial ecosystem	An ecosystem that is maintained by human intervention, for example a field of crops or the ecosystems in the large domes at the Eden Project in Cornwall.	84, 85
Ascorbic acid	The chemical name for Vitamin C.	98
Benign	A tumour is benign if the cells are contained and have not invaded other tissues. Benign tumours do not stimulate the growth of tumours in other parts of the body.	22, 23
Big Bang	The event believed by many scientists to have been the start of the Universe.	244
Binding medium	The substance, usually a thin glue, used to stick pigment in paints to the wall.	134
Binocular	Something with two eyepieces or two eyes, for example binocular vision uses two eyes to judge distances.	26, 27
Biodegradable	A substance that can be broken down by biological action in the environment.	118, 119
Biodiversity	A term used to describe the range of different organisms in an area.	54, 55
Blood pressure	The pressure of blood in your arteries and veins.	16, 17
Breed	To produce young.	60, 61
Carbohydrase	An enzyme that can digest carbohydrates.	20, 21
Carbohydrate	Carbohydrates are chemicals found in all living things. They contain the elements carbon, hydrogen and oxygen. Sugars and starches are carbohydrates.	96, 97
Carbon dioxide	A gas containing only carbon and oxygen. Its chemical formula is CO_2.	62

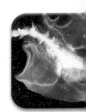

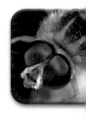

Glossary

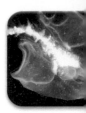
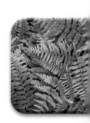

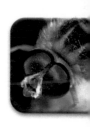

Glossary

Fibreglass	A material containing extremely fine glass fibres embedded in a type of solid glue. It is used in making various products, such as yarns, fabrics, insulators, and structural objects or parts.	178
Finite resource	Resources that will run out because they are not being produced at the same rate as they are being used up.	106, 107, 154
Fossil	Preserved evidence of a dead animal or plant. Fossils can be body parts or evidence of activity like tracks, burrows, nests or teeth marks.	76, 77
Fossil fuel	Coal, oil and natural gas formed by the decay of dead organisms over millions of years.	106, 107, 220, 222
Frequency	The number of vibrations per second. Frequency is measured in Hertz.	200, 201
Galaxy	A large, self-contained collection of stars and planets. Our galaxy is called the Milky Way.	236, 244, 245
Gamete	Special cells that join to form a new individual during sexual reproduction.	43
Gene	The length of DNA that codes for a particular characteristic.	40, 41, 44, 45
Generator	A device for converting energy of movement (kinetic energy) into electrical energy (current flow).	218, 221
Genetic code	The sequence of bases in DNA that carries the information needed to create an organism.	40, 41
Gland	An organ in the body that produces a secretion, for example the sweat gland. Endocrine glands pass their secretions, called hormones, directly into the bloodstream.	38
Glucose	A type of sugar. Glucose is sometimes called dextrose.	14, 15, 62, 63, 65
Gradient	A slope or difference in measurements between two areas, for example there is a concentration gradient between water molecules inside and outside a cell.	162
Greenhouse gas	A gas, for example carbon dioxide, that increases the greenhouse effect.	159, 206
Hallucinogen	A drug, like LSD, that gives the user hallucinations.	32, 33
Herbicide	A chemical that can kill plants, usually used to mean a chemical that kills weeds.	55
Heterozygous	An individual who has two different alleles for an inherited characteristic. For example, someone with blond hair may also carry an allele for red hair.	47
Homeostasis	All living organisms attempt to maintain the conditions in their cells within certain limits. This is known as homeostasis.	36, 37
Homozygous	An individual who has two alleles that are the same for an inherited feature. For example, a blue-eyed person will have two blue alleles for eye colour.	47
Host	An organism that is carrying another one inside its body.	22, 23
Hybrid	An organism made when two different species breed together.	60, 61
Hydrocarbon	Hydrocarbon molecules are molecules that contain only carbon and hydrogen atoms.	107, 114, 115
Hydrophilic	A molecule or part of a molecule that dissolves easily in water. Hydrophilic means, literally, 'water loving'.	101
Hydrophobic	A molecule or part of a molecule that does not dissolve easily in water. Hydrophobic means, literally, 'water hating'.	101, 116, 117
Hypothermia	A condition caused by the body getting too cold. Hypothermia can lead to death if untreated.	36, 37
Igneous	Rocks formed from solidified molten magma.	138, 139, 144, 145
Immune system	The parts of the body that protect against illnesses. The lymph glands are particularly important in the immune system.	24
Indicator species	A species that is particularly sensitive to environmental pollution. The presence or absence of an indicator species is often used to assess the degree of pollution in an environment.	82, 83

Infrared	Radiation beyond the red end of the visible spectrum. Infrared radiation is efficient at transferring heat.	184–187
Inherit	To receive something from your parents, usually used to describe characteristics that can be passed down through sperm and eggs.	44
Insoluble	A substance that will not dissolve. Something that is insoluble in water may be soluble in other liquids.	102
Insulation	A substance that slows down the movement of energy. For example, heat insulation in the loft of a house slows down the movement of warmth to the cooler outside.	178
Interference	Waves interfere with each other when two waves of different frequencies occupy the same space. Interference occurs in light and sound and can produce changes in intensity of the waves.	188, 189, 193, 197
Invertebrate	An animal without a backbone.	58, 59
Ionisation	The formation of ions (charged particles).	224, 225, 227
Joule	A unit of energy. It takes 4.2 J to raise the temperature of 1 g of water by 1 °C.	174, 175
Kilojoule	1000 joules.	18, 19
Kinetic energy	Energy due to movement.	160, 161, 183, 187, 216, 217
Kwashiorkor	An illness caused by protein deficiency due to lack of food. Sufferers of kwashiorkor often have swollen bellies caused by retention of fluid in the abdomen.	19
Lactic acid	A toxic chemical produced by anaerobic respiration in animals.	15
Laser	A special kind of light beam that can carry a lot of energy and can be focussed very accurately. Lasers are often used to judge the speed of moving objects or the distance to them.	202
Latent heat	The energy needed to change the state of a substance.	176
Lava	Molten rock thrown up by a volcano.	144, 145
Legume	A family of plants with root nodules that can fix nitrogen from the air. Beans and peas are legumes.	68, 69
Life cycle	The changes an organism goes through throughout its life.	22, 23
Limiting factor	A factor that prevents a reaction from speeding up. At low light levels the light keeps the rate of photosynthesis low – an increase in the light intensity will produce a rise in the rate of photosynthesis. At higher light levels another factor, for example carbon dioxide levels, may be limiting. At this stage a rise in light levels will have no effect on the rate of photosynthesis.	64, 65
Lipase	An enzyme that can digest fat.	20, 21
Lithosphere	The outer part of the Earth, consisting of the crust and upper mantle, approximately 100 km thick.	142, 143
Longitudinal	In longitudinal waves, the vibration is along the direction in which the wave travels.	204, 205
Lymphatic system	The interconnected system of spaces and vessels between body tissues and organs by which lymph circulates throughout the body.	21
Magma	Molten rock inside the Earth.	144, 145
Magnet	An object that is magnetic is attracted by a magnet.	232, 233
Magnetic field	An area where a magnetic force can be felt.	232, 233
Malignant	A malignant tumour is one whose cells can spread into other tissues and cause more tumours.	23
Malleable	Can be beaten into flat sheets. Metals are malleable.	154
Melanin	A naturally occurring dark pigment found in skin, hair, fur and feathers.	206, 207
Metamorphic	Metamorphic rock forms when heat and pressure change the characteristics of an existing rock.	138, 139
Methane	A colourless, odourless gas that burns easily to give water and carbon dioxide.	123, 138

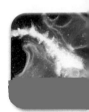

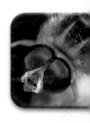

Glossary

Peripheral nervous system	The nerves leading from the brain and spinal cord.	28, 29
Pesticide	A chemical designed to kill a pest. Different types of pesticides kill rats, rabbits, worms or insects.	55
Phosphorescent	Phosphorescent materials glow gently even after the original light source has been removed.	136
Photocell	A device which converts light into electricity.	214, 215
Photon	A photon is a unit or particle of electromagnetic energy. Photons travel at the speed of light but have no mass.	214, 215
Photosynthesis	The production, in green plants, of sugar and oxygen from carbon dioxide and water using light as an external energy source.	63, 64, 65, 156, 157
Pigment	Chemicals which absorb certain wavelengths of light and so look coloured.	134, 135, 136
Pitfall trap	A beaker or pot buried in the ground, with the rim level with the ground. Ground-dwelling insects fall into the pot and can be identified later.	56
Placebo	A treatment with no active ingredient used in drug trials.	25
Pollination	The transfer of pollen (male gametes) from one flower to another.	75
Polymer	A molecule made of many repeating subunits, for example polythene or starch.	99, 109, 112, 116, 117, 118
Polymerisation	The process of forming large polymers from smaller monomer molecules.	112, 113
Pooter	A device used to transfer small insects safely between containers in a laboratory.	56
Predator	Animals that hunt and kill other animals.	68, 69
Prey	Animals that are hunted by other animals.	68, 69
Product	Something made by a chemical reaction.	124, 125, 160, 161
Progesterone	A female hormone produced by the ovary.	38, 39
Protease	An enzyme that can digest protein.	21
Protein	A group of complex molecules that contain carbon, hydrogen, oxygen, nitrogen and usually sulfur. They are made of one or more chains of amino acids. Proteins are important parts of all living cells and include enzymes, hormones, and antibodies. They are essential in the diet of animals for the growth and repair of tissue and can be obtained from foods such as meat, fish, eggs, milk, and legumes.	95
Proton	A positively-charged particle with a mass of one atomic mass unit. It is found in the nucleus of an atom.	227
Protozoan	A microorganism belonging to the group Protozoa. They are simple organisms but do have a nucleus, unlike bacteria and viruses.	23
Quadrat	Frames or pointers used to mark out a sample of an area for more intensive study.	56
Radiation	Energy that travels as light or electromagnetic waves. Some sorts of nuclear radiation contain particles, for example beta radiation consists of a stream of high speed electrons.	181, 184, 185, 225, 226, 227, 228, 229
Radio wave	A form of electromagnetic radiation used to carry radio signals.	187, 196, 197
Radioactive	Material which gives out radiation.	224, 225, 226, 227, 228, 229
Radiotherapy	Using radiation to treat certain types of disease, for example cancer.	228
RDA	The Recommended Daily Allowance of a foodstuff, perhaps a vitamin, is the amount dieticians recommend for a healthy diet.	19
Reactant	A chemical taking part in a chemical reaction.	160, 161
Reaction time	In biology – the time taken to respond to a stimulus. In chemistry – the time taken for a reaction to finish.	162, 163
Recessive	The characteristic that does not appear when a gene contains two different alleles.	17
Refract	To bend – light is refracted, or bent, as it passes through a glass block.	27

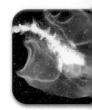

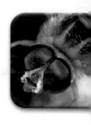

Turbine	A device that converts movement in a fluid into circular movement, usually to drive a generator. Turbines are essential parts of a windmill and a hydroelectric power plant.	221
Ultraviolet	Radiation just beyond the blue end of the spectrum of visible light. UV light is important in tanning and some sorts of skin cancer.	206, 207
Universe	Everything, everywhere.	236, 237, 244, 245
Unsaturated	An unsaturated hydrocarbon contains one or more double bonds between carbon atoms.	113
Uranium	A radioactive metal used in nuclear power stations and bombs.	222, 223
Vasoconstriction	The small blood vessels in the skin get narrower making the skin look white. Vasoconstriction reduces heat loss from the body.	37
Vasodilation	The small blood vessels in the skin get wider making the skin look pink or flushed. Vasodilation increases heat loss from the body.	37
Vertebrate	An animal with a bony backbone or spine.	58, 59
Withdrawal symptoms	The combination of physical and psychological symptoms produced when an addictive drug is withheld for a period of time.	32, 33
XX chromosomes	The sex chromosomes present in a human female.	45
XY chromosomes	The sex chromosomes present in a human male.	45
Yeast	A unicellular fungus used extensively in the brewing and baking industries.	96, 97

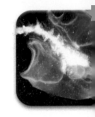

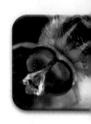